D1616033

FROM ONE LANGUAGE TO ANOTHER

Functional Equivalence in Bible Translating

FROM ONE LANGUAGE TO ANOTHER

Functional Equivalence in Bible Translating

Jan de Waard
Eugene A. Nida

THOMAS NELSON PUBLISHERS
Nashville • Camden • New York

Published in Nashville, Tennessee, by Thomas Nelson, Inc., Publishers and distributed in
Canada by Lawson Falle, Ltd., Cambridge, Ontario.

Printed in the United States of America.

Library of Congress Cataloging-in-Publication Data

Waard, Jan de.
  From one language to another.

  Bibliography: p.
  Includes index.
  1. Bible—Translating.   I. Nida, Eugene Albert, 1914–   II. Title.
BS449.W32 1986   220.5   86-16328
ISBN 0-8407-5437-X

Contents

Preface

This treatment of *Functional Equivalence In Bible Translating* has been in preparation for several years. Some seven years ago the two authors discussed various new developments in translating, particularly in view of some important insights from sociosemiotics, which has provided a new approach to the issue of meaning, not merely for words but also for syntax and rhetoric.

A few years later the two authors collaborated in Freudenstadt, Germany, on the Hebrew Old Testament Text Project and at that time had an opportunity to discuss various aspects of the proposed book and to work out a tentative outline in which the basic approach to meaning began with the larger units and successively treated the smaller units. Later, during a translator's institute in South Africa, the two authors again discussed various aspects of this volume and finally, in discussions both in the United States and in Europe, the authors put final touches to this volume.

The first author has been responsible for the Old Testament materials and has made major contributions to both the order of presentation and the theological implications of a functional approach to Bible translating. The second author has been responsible for a draft of the theoretical material and of New Testament illustrative data. All of the material has been reviewed several times in attempts to formulate a sound theoretical basis for functional equivalence and to highlight the practical implications for a translator's work.

One conspicuous difference in terminology in this volume in contrast with *Theory and Practice of Translation* and *Toward a Science of Translating* is the use of the expression "functional equivalence" rather than "dynamic equivalence." The substitution of "functional equivalence" is not designed to suggest anything essentially different from what was earlier designated by the phrase "dynamic equivalence." Unfortunately, the expression "dynamic equivalence" has often been misunderstood as referring to anything which might have special impact and appeal for receptors. Some Bible translators have seriously violated the principle of dynamic equivalence as described in *Theory and Practice of Translating* and *Toward a Science of Translating*. It is hoped, therefore, that the use of the expression "functional equivalence" may serve to highlight the communicative functions of translating and to avoid misunderstanding.

In this volume both Greek and Hebrew occur in transliterated form. For Greek the only unusual signs are possibly *kh* for the letter *chi* and the superscript macron to mark *eta* and *omega*. For Hebrew no attempt has been made to mark certain distinctive vowel qualities and length, nor has the doubling of consonants been indicated. The consonant *heth* has been indicated by a subscript dot. In a few instances only the Hebrew consonants are transliterated, since this facilitates the recognition of certain similarities and contrasts.

1

Translating Is Communicating

"It would be easy enough to translate if I only could really know the meaning." This is the way one Bible translator expressed both his frustration and his insight into the essential problems of producing functional equivalents in translating. Functional equivalence, however, means thoroughly understanding not only the meaning of the source text but also the manner in which the intended receptors of a text are likely to understand it in the receptor language. Unfortunately, some translators, even when they do know the meaning of the source text, are reluctant to make the text meaningful in the language into which they are translating.

Some Bible translators cling to old-fashioned language even when the meanings of the words have radically changed. The Revised Standard Version, for example, retains in Psalm 23:1, "The Lord is my shepherd, I shall not want," even though *want* no longer means "to lack" but rather "to desire." Thus, many persons understand this traditional rendering to mean: "The Lord is my shepherd whom I shall not want." Even the New English Bible, which claims the use of "timeless English," preserves *want* in the clause, "I shall want nothing," but such an expression can be too readily understood as a total lack of desire (excellent Buddhist doctrine!) rather than an assurance that a person will lack nothing.

For some persons, old-fashioned language seems to carry connotations of authority and lasting tradition. But for many people, old-fashioned language only makes the Bible a kind of museum relic, hardly relevant for the demands of the present day.

Some readers seem to prefer the Scriptures in a language that is beautifully obscure. In fact, when one person was questioned as to why he preferred such a translation, he frankly confessed, "The words are so beautiful, but I don't have to do a thing about it."

Still other persons prefer an obscure Bible translation if such a translation reflects more "faithfully" (or literally) all kinds of peculiarities in the biblical languages. At the beginning of the sixth century A.D., a revision

9

of the rather idiomatic Syriac New Testament (the Peshitta Version) was initiated by Philoxenus of Mabbug. This revision copied as closely as possible the Greek text considered as the only inspired one (Metzger, 1977, 65, and Barbara Aland, 1982, 165). The presence of a theological motive is fully apparent. The same kind of motivation can be found in some modern Bible translations; for example, those of Buber-Rosenzweig and Chouraqui, in which the "God of mercy" strangely becomes the "God of the womb." But Bible translators are not unique in seeming to favor obscure literalisms; some preachers apparently take delight in highlighting minor exotic details of the biblical texts.

The assumption that Bible translations should be in an obscure and strange form of language is not, however, based merely upon the nature of traditional versions of the Scriptures or upon theological presuppositions. In many cases people assume that any translation of a text should be somewhat strange and awkward, for this is what they have learned about translating when studying foreign languages in school. In foreign language courses teachers have too often insisted that students produce literal translations, presumably so the teacher can be sure that the student recognizes the grammar and the literal meanings of the words. As a result, students have assumed that translating should mean a literal reproduction of the syntactic and lexical features of the source text, even though such renderings may make little or no sense and even though they are crude distortions of one's own mother tongue.

If a message is unimportant, there is no point in translating it. But if a message is important (and this certainly is the claim for the Scriptures), there is certainly nothing to be gained by making the message obscure, unless one is certain that the original author was also purposely obscure. When, for example, the author of Revelation 13:18 stated that the number 666 stands for a person's name, he was probably using a cryptogram in which the number 666 represents the sum of the numerical values of letters either from the Hebrew or the Greek alphabet. According to this principle, and in terms of the Hebrew alphabet, he may have meant to refer to "Nero Caesar," having been purposely obscure for political reasons (Charles, 1971, 365). Given no further clues, there is uncertainty as to which person was identified, but at least some of the original receptors must have understood the reference. Purposeful obscurity, however, is not a general characteristic of the biblical writers. Most of what is obscure in the Scriptures is due to our own ignorance of the historical and cultural backgrounds of the messages and not to the author's intent to convey a difficult message.

All translating, whether in the foreign language classroom or in the rendering of the Scriptures, should aim at the closest natural equivalent of the message in the source language. In other words, a translation should communicate. This means not only the equivalent content of the message but, in so far as possible, an equivalence of the form. To ascertain equivalence, either of content or form, one must focus upon the functions involved. In other words, what functions does a text perform? And how are these functions communicated by the lexical, grammatical, and rhetorical structures?

The Nature of Communication

In order to understand the nature of translating, it is essential to recognize what is involved in communication, both within a single language (intralingual communication) and between languages (interlingual communication). By appreciating some of the important similarities and contrasts between these two forms of communication, one can more readily understand the basic elements of translating.

For any communication there are eight principal elements: source, message, receptors, setting, code, sense channel, instrument channel, and noise. In this present discussion of communication we are, however, limiting the meaning of communication to events in which a person purposely produces signs which communicate something to receptors. We are thus eliminating from consideration natural events which may be interpreted by people as having meaning; for example, the coming of a comet as a sign of doom or the flight of a wood dove over a hut in Central Africa as a sign of death. In this treatment of communication we are restricting the discussion to language and to language-related codes.

Source. The source of any message is usually one person, but written documents may result from collaboration of a number of different persons—for example, committee activity, though often with lamentable results, since in order to please everyone, little or nothing is said.

In speaking of the Scriptures, however, there is a tendency to use the term *source* in an ambiguous way. For example, sometimes a writer uses *source* in speaking of (1) the original author of the book in question or (2) the redactor of a particular biblical document. In other instances *source* refers to (3) the activity of God or the Holy Spirit as the source of the inspiration. In still other instances *source* is essentially equivalent to (4) documentary evidence in the Greek, Hebrew, or Aramaic texts. Finally, *source* may designate (5) certain hypothetical documents, such as the *Logia* or the *Testimonia* collection.

In some instances there is general agreement as to the person or persons who were involved in the production of particular biblical texts. But in most instances no one is certain as to who wrote any one text. The evidence suggests that the Psalms were produced by a number of different persons over a rather long period of time, and the same must surely be true of the book of Proverbs. If, however, one regards the source as being simply the existing text of the Scriptures, then the problems are by no means eliminated, for textual evidence points to numerous differences of wording.

The Hebrew Old Testament Text Project has involved an analysis of some five thousand different textual problems in the Old Testament in which there are significant differences of meaning. For the Greek New Testament there are more than 1400 instances of manuscript evidence in which there are significant differences that are meaningful. For example, in Romans 5:1 one letter makes the difference between "we have peace with God" or "let us have peace with God." In the case of Ecclesiastes 2:25 the difference of one letter, combined with the possibility of two different interpretations of one and the same word, leads to four diverse renderings (de Waard, 1979, 511):

(1) For who can eat, who can enjoy himself, except me?
(2) For who can eat, who can enjoy himself, without me?
(3) For who can eat, who can enjoy himself, except him?
(4) For who can eat, who can enjoy himself, without him?

The problems of Old Testament textual analysis involve a very complex history of oral tradition, commitment to writing, compilation of material, and later redactions, especially in the so-called deuteronomic period. What can be recovered of the text by means of text-critical techniques is likely to be the text of the second century B.C. This was essentially the text of New Testament times, despite the fact that there are certain basic diversities, as reflected in various readings of the Septuagint Greek translation.

For the New Testament text the United Bible Societies sponsored the work of an international and interconfessional committee, which studied all of the relevant manuscript evidence in order to produce the earliest recoverable text. This text, published as The Greek New Testament (at present in the corrected third edition) and the Nestle-Aland twenty-sixth edition, has been particularly appreciated by those who hold most firmly to the view of inspiration, since they naturally are anxious to have a form of the text which is as close as possible to the original autographs. This is to be determined by weighing the evidence of the earliest and most reliable manuscripts.

Unfortunately, some translations of the Bible continue to contain expressions which have practically no textual justification. For example, Acts 8:37 is omitted by all of the principal uncial manuscripts, the best papyri, and even the so-called Byzantine tradition. It is included in some relatively poor manuscripts and in various forms, all of which suggest its lack of authenticity. Similarly, some translations of the Bible still contain 1 John 5:7–8, which speaks of the three heavenly witnesses, but this passage occurs in no early Greek manuscript and is not to be found even in Latin until the fourth century. The late Greek manuscripts in which this passage occurs give every evidence of being forgeries.

A failure to follow the evidence of the earliest and best manuscripts often results in renderings which are less theologically significant than they should be. For example, in John 1:18 many translations read, "The only begotten Son who is in the bosom of the Father has revealed him," but the best Greek evidence points to the fact that instead of the Greek term *huios*, "son," one should read *theos*, "God." Accordingly, John 1:18 may be rendered as "no one has seen God at any time; he who is uniquely God and is one with the Father has revealed him."

Message. The message consists of both the linguistic form and the ideational content, but it would be a serious mistake to distinguish categorically between external form and internal meaning, for the form itself so frequently carries significant meaning, especially in terms of emphasis, focus, impact, and appeal. If, for example, in a concentric (or chiastic) form of discourse (A B C—C′ B′ A′) there happens to be a central part which is not matched in the global structure (A B C —X—C′ B′ A′), this structure frequently serves to highlight the information contained in the central X. Such an organization of the discourse is very often found both in the Old Testament and in the New Testament, as will be illustrated later.

The verbal form of any message consists of words, phrases, clauses, sentences, paragraphs, and even larger sections. In normal interpersonal communication in an oral context, there are added elements of voice quality, loudness, speed of utterance, and pitch (often spoken of as paralinguistic features of communication). Written communication lacks most of these paralinguistic features, although punctuation marks and format (for example, poetic lines) may signal something about certain paralinguistic features. A written text, however, is a highly truncated image of the oral communication. This reduction in paralinguistic features is even more apparent when one realizes that Hebrew verse was most probably sung. The syntax of a verse is largely predictable from its structural framework, but the intonation patterns of speech can be completely wiped out by the melodic patterns of song renditions (O'Connor, 1980, 162).

The impoverished nature of a written text can perhaps be better appreciated when one realizes how much can actually be communicated by various features of the voice. For example, speakers may increase emphasis by loudness or by drawing out the length of some expression. On the other hand, it is also possible to attract special attention by reversing the process and reducing the volume to a whisper. The quality of voice may in fact completely reverse the meaning of a linguistic message, as when one growls out the sentence *I love you* with the clear indication of communicating hatred, not love. Voice quality may be soothing or frightening; different levels of pitch may communicate various degrees of excitement, anger, or frustration. In handwritten documents one can often detect nervousness, anxiety, or strong determination, and incorrect spelling often signals a good deal about a source's personality; for example, laziness and inadequate concern for detail.

Receptors. The greatest potential for miscommunication probably results from the diversities in the backgrounds of receptors. They often differ greatly in terms of education: primary, secondary, university, with either general training in such subjects as literature and history or with highly specialized training in some field of science or technology. Differences of age are also important, for they often indicate differences of interest, extent of exposure to the receptor language, and degree of understanding of the culture. Communications designed for children, teenagers, and adults must be quite distinct. In addition, the length of time during which a minority group has been exposed to a dominant language and/or culture is also crucial.

The task of a Bible translator as a secondary source is always a difficult one, since he is called upon to faithfully reproduce the meaning of the text in a form that will effectively meet the needs and expectations of receptors whose background and experience are very different from those who were the original receptors of the biblical documents. The translator must strive to identify intellectually and emotionally with the intent and purpose of the original source, but he must also identify with the concerns of his potential receptors. He is drawn in two directions at the same time, for he realizes that the original writer was not addressing the same audience that the translator hopes to reach. The translator, however, wants the receptor-language audience to appreciate fully the relevance and significance of such a culturally and historically "displaced message."

If the Bible translator is to do his work well, he must become an intellectual bridge which permits receptors to pass over the chasms of language and culture to comprehend, in so far as possible, the full implications of the original communication. Stated in a different manner, the translator must be a person who can draw aside the curtains of linguistic and cultural differences so that people may see clearly the relevance of the original message.

Translations prepared primarily for minority groups must generally involve highly restrictive forms of language, but they must not involve substandard grammar or vulgar wording. Translations prepared for deaf persons, who use a form of language which does not reflect standard usage (for example, American Sign Language in contrast with Signed English), must also be specially designed in both vocabulary and grammar.

Receptors' motivations, in terms of their felt needs, also influence radically the way in which people receive and understand messages. Any speaker who is insensitive to how an audience feels or thinks will soon be speaking to a listless audience or to an empty room. Similarly, the translation of the Scriptures must also be guided by the motivations of potential receptors. What type of marginal helps are most needed? Which illustrations are likely to be most appealing, leading the reader to the text rather than being mere substitutes for the text? Which books or collections of books are likely to be most acceptable and most helpful? Rarely, for example, does one translate Leviticus as the first book to be published in a new language, but this was precisely the request of one mission society in Asia, which placed great emphasis on the taboos found in this book.

The expectations of receptors as to what a translation of the Scriptures should be like may also be an important factor in formulating the principles to guide a particular translation project. Some persons, for example, react very strongly against a translation of the Bible in plain, ordinary language, even though this is precisely the kind of language which occurs in so much of the New Testament and in many parts of the Old Testament. What people cherish, they almost inevitably want to embellish. They may insist upon a stylistically elaborated biblical text as a means of showing their devotion to the message.

Setting. In some discussions of communication, the factors of setting are rarely mentioned, but they are crucial to fully satisfactory understanding. A word such as *damn* has two quite different meanings, depending on whether it is uttered in church or on the golf course.

Many problems of interpreting the Scriptures derive specifically from our inability to reconstruct or appreciate the original setting. This is especially true for some of the passages in 2 Corinthians. If we only knew what had prompted certain statements by Paul, it would be so much easier to understand what he was trying to communicate.

Translating involves particularly complex problems since there are two quite different types of settings: (1) the original setting of the communication (who wrote to whom about what, in what way, at what time, under what circumstances, and for what evident purpose) and (2) the setting in which the translation is read to or by receptors. Even in the case of the original setting there is often a problem of determining what is the relevant interpretive perspective. For example, scholars have pointed out that some of the expressions of the Psalms bear striking similarities to cultic hymns in the Ugaritic language of the ancient Near East. What, then, is to be the translator's interpretive perspective as to the relevant setting of such expressions? Is he to adopt the Ugaritic setting and determine the meaning of the passage in terms of its earliest history? Or, is the proper interpretive perspective the manner in which such expressions were used in the Temple worship in Jerusalem? For example, it makes a difference whether Psalm 29 is connected with the beginnings of Israelite history in Canaan or with the invasion of Palestine by Alexander the Great. It also makes a difference whether this psalm is considered (1) an original Canaanite "hymn of praise," detached from its mythic context and thus "Yahwehized," and preserved as an independent liturgical composition, or (2) as an original Israelite composition showing certain Canaanite influences. Likewise, a difference of setting (a New Year Festival or an enthronement ritual) will change the interpretive perspective (Cunchillos, 1976, 177–184).

Literary pre-history can certainly shed important light upon the meaning of a text, but the proper meaning of a text must be determined by its use in those communication events in which it was recognized as Holy Scripture.

Some New Testament scholars insist, for example, that Jesus did not use the expression "Son of Man" in speaking of himself. Without entering into the details of the very complex debate about the "Son of Man", and without excluding the possibility of a Greek mistranslation of an original Aramaic expression in some contexts, it is, however, clear that the term "Son of Man" is often and clearly Jesus' designation of himself in the Gospels.

The interpretive perspective of a translator must rely on the document as produced by the author. Literary reconstructions based on various types of critical studies can shed considerable light on the biblical texts. But the results of such studies are too tenuous and debatable to constitute a basis for radical alteration in existing texts.

The secondary setting of a Bible translation involves circumstances in which the text is ultimately communicated to receptors. Such circumstances are primarily of four different types: (1) listening to the reading of the Scriptures, (2) the reading of the Scriptures aloud by a group of persons, (3) private devotional reading, and (4) detailed study of a text.

A text of Scripture which is to be used primarily for public reading to a congregation, either in church or over the radio or television, must avoid forms which are orally, though not graphically, ambiguous. For example, in the Revised Standard Version 1 Chronicles 25:1 has the phrase "prophesy with lyres," which most listeners would interpret as "prophesy with liars," since the use of lyres in prophesying is rare in present-day cultures, but liars who prophesy are in abundant supply. In another English translation, an early draft had a statement "lead us back to the land, Lord," which in graphic form is perfectly clear, but in oral form would certainly be understood to mean "lead us back to the landlord." Likewise, the French expression *opérer les signes* ("to do signs") in John 3:2 of the French Ecumenical Translation may, because of the strangeness of the expression, easily be understood by the hearer as *opérer les cygnes* ("to operate swans")!

In addition to avoiding aural ambiguity, translators must also use a level of language which can be readily grasped when it is heard. This is precisely the issue that distinguishes the translation of a play of Ibsen to be read in private from one to be used by actors on the stage. Unless the audience can immediately catch the meaning and the implications of a dialogue, the whole point may be lost.

Translations made for public reading by a number of persons must be especially constructed to facilitate group participation. For example, in English (and in many other languages which have a strong rhythmic accent) one must avoid a series of more than three potentially unaccented syllables involving clitic terms; for example, most prepositions, conjunctions, pronouns, and auxiliaries. Otherwise, the audience is likely to stumble in placing the primary stress.

Codes. Communication codes are of many different types. They consist essentially of signs and combinations of signs. They may be as minute and as intricate as the DNA in the nucleus of all living cells (equivalent in total information to one hundred encyclopedias), or they may be as obvious as traffic lights or as complex as any and all languages.

Together with the language code there are certain dependent codes, for example, the Morse Code and semaphore signaling, which are based upon the orthographic form of a language. In fact, the orthography of a language is itself a kind of language-dependent code.

In addition to language and its dependent codes, there are certain accompanying codes which are especially important in oral communication. These consist, for example, of such extralinguistic features as gestures (for example, movements and position of face, eyes, hands, and body), stance, and proximity. For example, people in the Mediterranean world normally stand much closer together when they are speaking with one another than do northern Europeans or Americans. In fact, the study of distance in communication has developed into a rather elaborate discipline of proxemics.

Written messages may also have very important extralinguistic features. The face and size of type, the format, the quality of paper, and the kind of binding all communicate a great deal. For example, an important leader of a number of churches in a rural section of Mexico always writes out with pencil on school notebook paper his petitions to government authorities. His spelling is sometimes incorrect, and the wording reflects the writer's own limited formal education. When asked why he did not obtain the help of a lawyer in preparing more formal documents, he replied, "When government officials see my petitions, they know they are reading the words of an honest man."

A Bible translator is often faced with problems involving such paralinguistic factors as (1) competing orthographies in a particular language, (2) the need for different type faces for the text, the section headings, and the marginal notes, and (3) the use of poetic lines for liturgical passages. Even the extralinguistic features of the color of binding may be important. While some people insist that a Bible should have a black binding, for other persons black is a very foreboding symbol. A binding in gold color seems to be attractive in many parts of the world, while yellow is far less appealing. The duplicated form of a translated text may also be extremely crucial in some circumstances. For example, in one Latin American country there was a request during a revolutionary crisis to publish the book of Amos, especially for distribution to university students, since the message of Amos about social justice was regarded as being so pertinent to the immediate situation. At first, plans were made to put out a translation of Amos on good paper and with attractive illustrations, but involved university students, who were to be responsible for the distribution of this material, insisted that if the translation was to attract the attention of students, it should be poorly mimeographed on cheap paper, like other typical clandestine publications. Only then would university students regard it as relevant to their situation.

For private devotional reading of the Scriptures people normally prefer a text which is not encumbered with numerous references and footnotes. Section headings, however, are usually appreciated as a help in identifying meaningful units of the text.

Those who wish to engage in a detailed study of the Scriptures are much more interested in marginal notes concerning such features as alternative texts and interpretations, cultural and historical data, and formal features of the original text; for example, the fact that some of the Psalms have an acrostic structure, with each successive line, strophe, or section beginning with a different letter in the order of the Hebrew alphabet (see Psalms 111, 112, 119, and 145). This last type of note is particularly important for anyone who is curious as to why in certain instances a series of themes seems to be arranged in an apparently arbitrary way.

Sense channel. The sense channel involves matters of sight, feeling, hearing, smell, and taste, though for verbal communication, hearing, sight, and feeling are dominant. In immediate interpersonal communication, hearing and sight combine in the interpretation of the language code as well as the accompanying codes, which are designed either to reinforce one another or to signal that there is some important contrast between the words that are spoken and the underlying intent. The sense of feeling becomes an important sense channel in Braille and in the touch communication of persons who are both deaf and blind.

Instrument channel. The instrument channel in normal oral communication involves (1) air to transmit sound and (2) light to transmit the extra-linguistic features, but one may also speak of the following examples as instrument channels: radio, television, newsprint, magazines, letters, telegrams, computer screens, and the printouts of word processors.

Noise. In electronic communication noise is a very serious factor. It may be defined as anything which distorts a message between the emission by the source and the reception by the addressee. Even in normal oral communication too much physical noise can result in serious distortion, but usually more important than physical noise is what may be called "psychological noise": preoccupation, worry, boredom, and emotive opposition to the content or to the source of a message.

In the case of Bible translating one may regard the difficulties which have arisen in the transmission of the text as constituting noise, in the sense that scribal errors and intentional alterations of the text all result in a distortion of the message.

Organization of This Book

Before launching into a discussion of the underlying theory of this presentation of functional equivalence in Bible translating (Chapter 4), it has seemed wise to consider first the functions and roles involved in translating (Chapter 2) and some basic issues which are fundamental to decision-making in translating (Chapter 3). Chapter 4, entitled "Translating Means Translating Meaning," explores the sociosemiotic factors which are crucial in determining functional equivalents. Particular attention is paid to the concept of isomorphisms, which seem to provide the most significant way of dealing with degrees of functional equivalence.

Chapter 5 deals with rhetorical functions and Chapter 6 discusses in detail a number of rhetorical processes which are crucial in creating impact and appeal. Chapter 7 is concerned with a number of grammatical problems in translating and treats these in terms of the meaningful relations between syntactic units. Finally, Chapter 8 considers a number of problems relating to the meanings of words and idioms.

There are two appendices: the first treats a number of theories of translation as they directly and indirectly relate to the history of Bible translating, and the second consists of a rather detailed description of various procedures which are applicable to the preparation of biblical texts.

A bibliography lists not only authors referred to in the text but provides a number of items which may prove to be useful to readers wishing to explore certain aspects of translation in greater depth.

2

Functions and Roles in Bible Translating

Any discussion of Bible translating must begin with a thorough explora-
tion of the theological basis for translating and some of the implications of
this specialized task.

Theological Basis and Implications

To appreciate some of the theological bases for and implications of Bible
translating, it is important to treat (1) the motives for translating the Scriptures, (2) the nature of the religious language of the Scriptures, and (3) the
interpretive principles that are applicable to the Scriptures, both from the
standpoint of biblical usage and contemporary views of valid exegesis.

Motives. In contrast with the largely centripetal view of the Old Testament, in which the nations were invited to come to Jerusalem to worship
the Lord, the New Testament is essentially centrifugal in its evangelistic
outreach. The disciples were commanded to "go and make disciples of all
nations" (Matt. 28:19). In Acts 1:8 the movement is from Jerusalem to all
of Judea and Samaria and finally to the ends of the earth. The symbolism
of this outward movement is well represented by the miracle of Pentecost,
when people from various nations exclaimed, "All of us hear them speaking in our own languages about the great things that God has done."

The Christian church had already experienced the significance of the
translation of the Old Testament into Greek in the Septuagint version,
accomplished largely during the second century B.C. It was not strange,
therefore, that Christians soon began to translate the Greek New Testament into Latin, Syriac, Coptic, Armenian, and later Gothic. But as the
ancient world became defensive and began to contract as well as splinter,
the church likewise became defensive and finally during the Middle Ages
became a bastion of learning but not a source of creative dialogue and
discovery. It was only the Renaissance which again opened the world to
new ideas and to new regions. Roman Catholic missionaries then became

20

involved in the translation of catechetical materials in various languages. Soon Protestant missionaries were engaged increasingly in the translation of the Scriptures.

When the printing press was invented in the middle of the fifteenth century, there were only thirty-three languages which had anything of the Scriptures. When the Bible Societies movement began at the beginning of the nineteenth century, only seventy-two languages possessed something of the Scriptures. By the end of 1984, however, 1808 languages had at least some portion of the Scriptures, with 286 languages having received the entire Bible and 594 more languages the New Testament. These languages represent approximately 97 percent of the world's population. But those who do not as yet have anything of the Scriptures represent at least another thousand languages which should have something.

Religious language. The content of the Scriptures is best described as "primary religious language." Since it deals with supernatural events for which there are no finite models and since it reflects transcendental experiences for which ordinary language seems to be so inadequate, it is not at all strange that this primary religious language is in certain respects rather different from ordinary discourse.

In one important respect primary religious language is often figurative. It employs many symbols, is filled with metaphors and metonymies, and makes extensive use of poetic forms. The language of the Scriptures may be regarded as "semantically open-ended" in its attempt to sense the transcendent quality of exalted and sublime religious experience. Note especially some of the rhetorically elaborate structures of Psalm 91:1–4, Isaiah 55:12–13, 1 Corinthians 13, Ephesians 1:3–14, and Romans 8:37–39.

Primary religious language is also timeless: It proclaims a truth which goes beyond time and history. Accordingly, it makes extensive use of mythic and parabolic language. Its treatment of history is primarily dramatic, but certainly the Scriptures take history seriously, since the God of the Bible enters uniquely into history.

In primary religious language, experience generally outweighs rationality. Accordingly there is no hesitation to speak of miracles. The writers seem not to worry about *apparent* inconsistencies, paradoxes, and contradictions, as in the Synoptic accounts or in quotations in the New Testament from the Old Testament.

It is almost inevitable that in primary religious language new and unusual expressions become hallmarks of the new community of faith, so that there is a good deal of in-group vocabulary; for example, *I am that I am, thus saith the Lord, the glory of the Lord, in the heavenlies, in Christ, emptied himself, became flesh,* and *saved by his blood.*

Primary religious language almost always involves a good deal of instruction, but it is normally not codified or systematized as it would be in catechetical material. The one exception to this is to be found primarily in the book of Leviticus.

One important feature of the primary religious language of the Scriptures is the appeal to commitment. Writers are not primarily concerned with defending the good news or trying to prove its validity. Explanations contained in primary religious language are designed mainly to communicate to others the unique character of the religious experience.

One cannot escape the impression that primary religious language generally recognizes the failure of words to communicate the truth. There is always something "unutterable" about religious experience. It is "the Spirit himself which intercedes for us with sighs too deep for words" (Rom. 8:26).

Though the truth is presented in propositions (that is to say, in sentences), the approach is not strictly logical and propositional but rather presentational (Langer, 1951), since the truth is proclaimed through events such as the death and resurrection of Jesus Christ and through ritual acts such as the communion and baptism.

The primary religious language of the Scriptures contains a great deal of ethical content. But for the most part the spiritual takes precedent over the ethical, and ethical behavior is regarded as resulting from a change in one's spiritual relationships. The ethical is therefore derivative of the spiritual.

In contrast with primary religious language, derivative or secondary religious language is often quite different. In the first place, it tends to be explanatory and exegetical rather than kerygmatic. Often the focus of secondary religious language is a logical, rational, and systematic presentation of truth—the type of language used in systematic theology or in books on biblical theology. In many instances secondary religious language attempts to reinterpret primary religious language by translating the symbolic into literal statements.

Secondary religious language is often "apologetic" in the technical sense of the term. It attempts to provide proof or a framework for the truth by showing its relationship to some existing philosophy. In general, secondary religious language focuses upon the ethical rather than the spiritual, and it frequently develops its own technical language, for example, *kerygma, Heilsgeschichte,* and *realized eschatology*.

As valuable as secondary religious language may be, it is not the language to be employed in the translation of the Scriptures. To do justice to primary religious language, one must persevere in translating something of the transcendent quality of the forms. It would be wrong to eliminate all of the "sublime obscurity" and try to rewrite primary religious language in the style of a textbook on biblical theology. Overzealous attempts to explain everything in the Scriptures may actually rob the primary religious language of its creative power to effect commitment and reorient human lives.

Contemporary exegetical principles. One of the serious problems involved in Bible translating concerns the interpretive orientation within the Scriptures themselves as well as that perceived in present-day attitudes toward valid exegetical principles.

In the New Testament itself there is no hesitation to interpret words out of context. This was in line with approved exegetical principles used by Jewish rabbis of that time. For example, in Matthew 2:15 the expression "out of Egypt have I called my Son" is applied to Jesus, although in Hosea 11:1 (the source of the quotation) the reference is certainly to Israel, not to the Messiah. Matthew renders either the Hebrew or a Greek text like that of Aquila, and not the Septuagint, which reads "his children" and which therefore cannot function as a messianic proof text (Stendahl, 1954, 101). In Galatians 3:16 Paul interprets the singular of "seed" as referring specifically to Christ, even though in Genesis 12:7 (the source of the quotation) the term "seed" refers to the lineage of Abraham and not to any one specific person.

Similarly, in Hebrews 1:5 the author employs a quotation from 2 Samuel 7:14 which refers to David, but he applies this to the relationship between God and Christ. Since the messianic use of 2 Samuel 7 was pre-Christian, the early church not only appropriated such a use but also established its interpretation by means of its own midrash (Ellis, 1978, 195).

Since New Testament writers regarded the New Testament as simply the fulfillment of the Old Testament, there was a converse tendency to interpret the Old Testament in light of the New Testament. In Isaiah 7:14 the Septuagint translation of the Hebrew *almah* as *parthenos* led New Testament writers to see the relationship between this passage and the New Testament miracle of the virgin birth, but reading a virgin birth back into Isaiah 7:14 would mean either that the text was completely irrelevant for Ahaz (even though the context indicates clearly its immediate significance) or it would be necessary to postulate two virgin births for the Scriptures. In fact, in the Isaiah text both the Hebrew and its Greek equivalent mean "young woman," whereas Matthew 1:23 uses *parthenos* in a restricted sense (Dodd, 1976, 301–05).

Since for New Testament writers the Septuagint translation of the Old Testament was regarded as valid as the Hebrew (in fact it is more frequently quoted in the New Testament than is the Hebrew text itself), it is not strange that in Hebrews 1:7 the Hebrew rendering of Psalm 104:4 is completely altered. The Hebrew simply means that God makes winds his messengers and fire and flame his ministers. In the New Testament the meaning is reversed in view of the Septuagint rendering, so that in Hebrews 1:7 the text reads, "Who makes his angels winds and his servants flames of fire."

These difficulties of interpretive orientation in the New Testament pose serious problems for many Bible translators who find it difficult to accept the total cultural context in which these principles were applicable. Some translators are so disturbed by these problems that they seek to harmonize the Old Testament and the New Testament in various ways. Rather, however, than attempting to harmonize the Old Testament and the New Testament, most translators feel that it is much better to let the Old Testament and the New Testament convey their own messages in the light of their respective contexts. Psalm 2, for example, is probably an enthronement psalm—a psalm used in the ritual of enthroning a king. But it is possible that this psalm also has messianic implications. This does not mean that one should take the liberties that the Living Bible does in rendering the last part of Psalm 2:2 as "the Lord and his Messiah, Christ the King."

In addition to letting the Scriptures speak for themselves, it is essential to accurately reflect the cultural contexts of biblical times, whether ideological, sociological, or ecological. In biblical times the earth was regarded as flat, and the sky was simply a dome for the sun, moon, planets, and stars. People took demons seriously, and God is described with many human characteristics. The biblical culture was also a male-oriented culture, and to try to rewrite the Scriptures in so-called "inclusive language" introduces cultural anachronisms and serious contextual distortions. To insist that God be spoken of as both "father and mother" is to create a bisexual God, not a sexually neutral God.

By shifting a form into the passive to avoid a pronominal reference to God in John 1:12, one seriously distorts the message about how people become God's children. In Matthew 3:9 the committee preparing liturgical materials in inclusive language for the National Council of Churches has produced an almost incredible distortion which would certainly never be uttered by Pharisees or Sadducees. In place of the Greek text which reads, "We have Abraham as our father," this rendering in "inclusive language" has, "We have Abraham as our father and Sarah and Hagar as our mothers."

In addition to avoiding harmonization of different passages of the Scriptures, it is also important to avoid harmonizing biblical statements to agree with contemporary historical or scientific perspectives. For example, in Matthew 2:9 the Greek text reads, "The star went before them until it came and stood over where the baby was." In the Living Bible, however, the text is translated as, "The star appeared to them again, standing over Bethlehem." When this translational discrepancy was brought to the translator's attention, he insisted that the astrologers who came to worship Jesus were fully acquainted with the stars and they would never have been deceived by a star seeming to move ahead of them and then stopping over the place where the baby was. Therefore, the event must have been as the Living Bible has described it, despite the fact that Matthew depicts the event in quite a different way. The translator of the Living Bible, in effect, claimed that Matthew could not have meant what he wrote.

Communicative Functions of Language

In order to understand the significance of a number of basic principles of translation, it is important to know something about the different communicative functions of language and how languages operate to perform such functions. Those communicative functions which are especially relevant for the understanding of principles of translation are: expressive, cognitive, interpersonal, informative, imperative, performative, emotive, and aesthetic.

In addition to these principal functions, there is one additional function which may be significant for certain types of communication, namely, the metalingual function. The metalingual function in communication involves the use of language to speak about itself. In fact, language is a unique code in the sense that it can be used to describe itself. For the metalingual function of language, the Bible has a rather limited vocabulary. In Hebrew there are such lexical units as *dabar*, "word;" *torah*, "law;" *mitsvah*, "commandment;" *besorah*, "message;" *nebu'ah*, "prophecy;" *hidah*, "riddle, ambiguous speech;" and *mashal*, "parable, proverb, dictum, satire."

For Greek the principal terms are *dialektos* and *glossa*, "language, dialect;" *rhēma*, "saying;" *periokhē* and *graphē*, "passage, part of a discourse;" *diēgesis*, "account, narration;" *parabolē* and *paroimia*, "parable, figure of speech;" *biblos*, "written record;" *gramma*, "account;" *epigraphē*, "inscription;" *epistolē*, "letter;" *logos*, "account, message;" and *nomos*, "law."

Expressive function. The expressive function in communication focuses upon the source, with little or no concern for possible receptors. The source, for example, may be simply pouring out deep feelings of sorrow, joy, or anxiety, often expressed in highly specialized forms, for example, lyric poetry, song, and chant. In the Scriptures expressions such as *hallelujah* and *hosanna* are essentially matters of expressive function. The psalms of personal confession involve this expressive function of language. These psalms later became liturgical expressions of Israel's joint confession. In this use they are understood as a kind of collective, expressive language used by people to identify themselves with the circumstances and emotions of the original author.

In dealing with expressive forms of language, it is important for the translator to identify with the creative expression of the source by creating a functionally equivalent form in his own receptor language. The form will almost never be identical with the form of the source text, but one can usually produce what is a functional equivalent, since language functions are universals. For example, the Hebrew text of Psalm 104:27-30 shows a complex poetic structure. Each verse consists of two lines, with the exception of verse 29, which has three. There is a significant chiastic relationship in the number of syllables of verses 27 and 28, namely, 9-7 and 7-9. Similar sounds can be noted in the case of the final verbs of the first line in verses 27, 29, and 30.

The latest Dutch translation has attempted to represent something of this complex structure but in a somewhat modified form. For example, a chiastic relationship exists between the number of lines of the four verses, with a pattern of 3-4-4-3. There are similarly parallel types of sounds in a highly rhythmical prose, but these do not occur at precisely the same positions as in the Hebrew text.

Cognitive function. The cognitive function in communication involves the use of language for either thinking out complex semantic relations or for anticipating the manner in which one will later either speak or write. In the cognitive use of language the source is also the receptor, so that one can describe this cognitive function as a matter of internal speech. In the Scriptures the cognitive function of language is illustrated by the many monologues contained in the book of Ecclesiastes.

Interpersonal function. The interpersonal function of language is extremely important, since it is crucial to three different interpersonal relationships: (1) identifying and establishing status, (2) negotiating, and (3) interpersonal contact. People identify status most obviously by titles or terms of address such as *sir, teacher, lord, friends,* and one may preserve self-identity as a member of an in-group by using typical in-group terminology, for example, *saved to serve* and *bound by the Spirit.*

A source may establish status in an oral context by tone of voice, type of pronunciation, or ways in which he may speak of himself. This function of language to establish status is apparent in the enumeration by Paul of his own merits in Philippians 3:4-6 and in the description which Paul gives of his mystical experiences in 2 Corinthians 12:2-5. The solemn and rhythmical language of this last text is particularly complex (Weiss, 1897, 191).

In many languages the interpersonal function in negotiation is very elaborate. This use of language is illustrated in Genesis 23:3-16, in which Abraham negotiates for the cave of Machpelah as a place to bury his wife Sarah. Even today, bargaining in the Near East follows very much the same pattern of discourse.

The contact, or phatic, function of communication involves the use of language as a means of maintaining interpersonal relations, but it is often highly formalized. Expressions such as *how do you do, hi, hello,* and *goodby* are typical of such contact uses. Chatting about the weather with a stranger or uttering the expected platitudes at receptions are all part of contact language. Polite interruptions during conversations with expressions such as *yes, uh,* and *uhhuh* do not necessarily indicate assent but simply the fact that a person is listening. In the Scriptures the use of *amen* falls into this category, and the salutation *grace and peace be to you* can likewise be regarded as primarily a part of the contact function of language.

The two major factors in interpersonal relations are power and solidarity—one's position in the hierarchy of relational dependency and the extent to which people identify with one another more or less on the same level of social standing. It is not strange, therefore, that in the use of language various terms, syntactic constructions, and rhetorical devices serve to mark the varying degrees and relationships of power and solidarity. In the Scriptures terms such as *lord, king, governor, emperor, centurion,* and *chief priest* all mark varying degrees of power, while the terms *brothers, beloved, friends,* and *daughter* (Mark 5:34) point to different degrees of solidarity. An expression such as "my children" (1 John 2:1, 18 and elsewhere) indicates not only solidarity but also authority. A similar double role is indicated by the use of *son* (Prov. 1:10, 15, and elsewhere).

The lexical, syntactic, and rhetorical devices which are employed for various types of interpersonal functions include a wide variety of verbal forms. Titles such as *master, lord, tetrarch, governor,* and *sir* are perhaps the most obvious, but expressions of direct address—for example, *friends, brethren,* and *fathers*—are similarly important.

The avoidance of names may also mark a very high degree of deference in status, as in the case of substitutes for the name of God in expressions such as *the Almighty, heaven,* and *the Majesty on high.* The avoidance of naming deity by means of passive constructions, as in Matthew 5:3–10, is another example of indirect marking of status.

In many languages there are distinct forms of the second person pronouns to indicate difference of status. In Spanish, for example, one uses *usted* in speaking to persons of higher rank or to persons whose rank one does not know, while *tu* is used in speaking to persons with whom one is on friendly, familiar terms, to servants and to subordinates, but also in addressing God. Similar distinctions exist in German and French. In Japanese there are not only distinctions for second person pronouns but also a series of important differences in the way in which one refers to oneself.

Even the order of pronouns may signal something about relative status. In Greek and Latin the normal order of pronouns in any discourse would be first, second, and third (the basis for the grammatical terminology), but in English the order is generally reversed, or, at least in combination with the first person singular pronoun, other pronouns precede.

Grammatical forms may also mark important interpersonal relations. In Classical Greek and in the Atticized Greek of New Testament times, one would normally speak to a pagan deity using optative forms, but in the New Testament imperatives are employed, as in the Lord's Prayer. Such imperatives might seem out of place in speaking to God, but in view of the fact that God is addressed as "Father," it is only natural that imperatives be employed, since these are the forms which would be used in Koiné Greek in addressing one's own biological father.

In a number of languages (for example, Javanese, Balinese, Thai, Burmese, Japanese, and Korean) there are important obligatory lexical and grammatical distinctions which mark relative status. In the Thai language, for example, one would expect a religious leader such as Jesus to be addressed with so-called honorific expressions, while in reality the Pharisees and Sadducees would scarcely have wanted to use honorific terminology in speaking to or about Jesus. In some languages it seems appropriate at first to make distinctions in referring to Isaiah and to Jeremiah, for Isaiah probably came from a distinctly higher social class. According to Jewish tradition, Isaiah's father would have been the brother of King Amaziah, father and predecessor of King Uzziah, so that Isaiah would have been of Davidic descent. This is not totally to be excluded in view of the special connections between Isaiah and the circles of the court, as noted in Isaiah 7:3ff (Wildberger, 1965, 5). Jeremiah, on the other hand, came out of a priestly family. However, no certainty as to Isaiah's social status can be ascertained. For Isaiah a cultic setting has also been proposed as a pure hypothesis (Clements, 1980, 13-14).

In some languages the use of direct or indirect discourse also marks the relationship between a speaker and hearers. For example, commands expressed as direct discourse may suggest haughtiness and a superiority complex on the part of a speaker. Indirect discourse, therefore, marks a more congenial interpersonal atmosphere.

The level of language—whether ritual, formal, informal, casual, or intimate—is clearly diagnostic of interpersonal relations. To use so-called "highbrow language" when persons are on good, friendly terms certainly distorts the interpersonal relations.

In some languages there are very distinct forms, both grammatical and lexical, between men's and women's speech. Such distinctions occur frequently in several indigenous languages in Latin America and to some extent in many standard world languages. To violate the patterns of a receptor-language usage certainly leads to misunderstanding various conversations recorded in the Scriptures.

Not only words and grammar but elaborate rhetorical forms may also mark important interpersonal relations. Note, for example, the inspired

words of Amasai in 1 Chronicles 12:18, as rendered in the German text of
Die Gute Nachricht:

> Dir, David, gehören wir!
> Zu dir stehen wir, du Sohn Isais!
> Sieg und Erfolg sei dir gegeben,
> dir und allen, die bei dir sind;
> denn deine Hilfe kommt von Gott!

This German rendering of 1 Chronicles 12:18 may be translated into English as follows:

> David, we are yours!
> We stand by you, Son of Jesse!
> Success and victory be yours,
> and for all who are with you,
> for your help comes from God!

Questions about the level of language apply not only to the context of
the Scriptures itself but also to the relationship between a translator and
receptors. If the language is too high and erudite, receptors are likely to
react against a translator and accuse him of trying to "show off" his learning. On the other hand, if the language is too low and substandard, it is
generally interpreted as paternalizing.

Informative function. The informative function in communication focuses
upon the content of the message. The evident purpose of the source is to
influence the thinking of receptors. Indirectly, the informative function
also serves to influence behavior. It would be a mistake, however, to think
that the informative function in communication is the dominant one. In
ordinary communication between two persons, the informative function
is probably no more than twenty percent. Though it is true that most communications have some informative function, the imperative, emotive,
performative, and interpersonal functions are often far more important
than the informative one.

Imperative function. The imperative function focuses upon a change in
the behavior of receptors who respond to the content of the message and
the impact of its form. The imperative function, however, is not restricted
to expressions using imperative forms of verbs. Proverbs, for example,
contains a great deal of urgent counsel, and the Pauline Epistles certainly
involve strong exhortations for radical changes in behavior.

The imperative function, which some speak of as the operative or cona-
tive function of language, can also be detected in texts such as Isaiah
40:21. The appealing force of the Hebrew rhetorical form has been very

effectively rendered in a functionally equivalent form in the latest Dutch Version (Reiss, 1976):

> Weten jullie het niet,
> hebben jullie het niet gehoord,
> is het je nooit verteld?
> Hebben jullie dan geen vermoeden
> wie de aarde heeft vastgezet?

This Dutch Version of Isaiah 40:21 may be rendered in English as:

> Don't you know,
> didn't you hear,
> has it never been told to you?
> Don't you have any idea of
> who has established the earth?

Performative function. The performative function in communication involves the use of language to change the state or status of an object. When a pastor or priest declares two persons to be "man and wife," this is clearly a performative function. Similarly, when a jury or judge declares an individual guilty, this is performative. In the Scriptures blessing and cursing are performative functions of language. In fact, such utterances could not be retracted. In Genesis 27:27-29, Isaac's blessing of Jacob becomes irreversible even though it was obtained by deceit. The fact that such performative language could not be retracted, despite its basis in deception, produces serious problems of misunderstanding in some cultures. In many societies a blessing obtained by guile automatically turns into a curse. Similarly, the performative function in Jephthah's promise (Judg. 11:30-31) is difficult to reconcile with most views of social responsibility, especially when it leads to human sacrifice. This act of Jephthah, however, may not be so different from the ways in which some people in our own day sacrifice family and friends for the sake of personal success.

Emotive function. The emotive function focuses on the emotional responses of receptors. The purpose of such language is to influence the emotive state of those who hear or read the message. Political orators are especially skilled in appealing to the emotions, usually with a minimum of solid information. Some preachers also create far more emotion than understanding in their audiences. The emotive function of communication, however, is almost always combined with other functions.

In the poetry of the Old Testament the emotive response is one of the principal purposes. Emotive factors in communication are almost always heightened by highly figurative language and elaborate rhetorical devices. Note, for example, the emotive language in Isaiah 40:12-15, as given in the New English Bible:

> Who has gauged the waters in the palm of his hand,
>   or with its span set limits to the heavens?
> Who has held all the soil of earth in a bushel,
>   or weighed the mountains on a balance
>   and the hills on a pair of scales?
> Who has set limits to the spirit of the LORD?
> What counsellor stood at his side to instruct him?
> With whom did he confer to gain discernment?
> Who taught him how to do justice
>   or gave him lessons in wisdom?
> Why, to him nations are but drops from a bucket,
>   no more than moisture on the scales;
> Coasts and islands weigh as light as specks of dust.

Aesthetic function. The aesthetic function of language (often called the poetic function) involves the use of language to heighten impact and appeal, both on the level of thematic organization as well as on the level of those rhetorical devices which contribute greatly to the effectiveness of any communication; for example, repetition, condensation, shifts in order, figurative language, reversals of meaning (irony), and rhythm. Because the rhetorical features are so significant in communication, these will be discussed in Chapters 5 and 6 before taking up grammatical and lexical meaning.

Some languages mark the function of a message in rather explicit ways. For example, in Lisu (a language of southeast Asia) the sentence *Asa la-a ni* means "Asa is coming," but the function is purely expressive in the sense that one can determine from the final word *ni* that the hearer is to understand this as a case of a speaker talking to himself. On the other hand, the sentence *Asa la-a lu* is again best translated into English as "Asa is coming," but the function is informative. In contrast with this, *Asa la-a na* (likewise translatable as "Asa is coming") has an imperative function, and the speaker expects some action or change of opinion on the part of receptors. The sentence *Asa la-a xu* has primarily an emotive function and indicates by the final word that the speaker is complaining and expects sympathy. This type of marking obviously becomes crucial in cases in which narratives are presented as proofs of certain attitudes.

Sometimes it is difficult to determine which communicative function is predominant. In the famous lament over Jerusalem (Matt. 23:37-39 and Luke 13:34-35), one may at first be tempted to stress the emotive function when reading, "How often would I have gathered your children together as a hen gathers her chicks under her wings, but you would not!" But when it is seen that this is a wisdom saying quoted by Jesus, and that the thrust of the entire saying is to castigate Jews who do not recognize Jesus as the one sent by Yahweh, it becomes clear that the informative function is dominant (Edwards, 1976, 132).

The rhetorical features of language are those which are most important in marking the various communicative functions. These rhetorical features are also the most crucial in providing an acceptable and appropriate style, which is so relevant for both the impact and appeal of any message. It is, however, precisely in this particular area of communication that Bible translations are usually deficient. All too frequently attempts at formal correspondence of words and grammar violate rhetorical patterns, and the result is an awkward and unbecoming style. In view of the fact that stylistic quality seems to be the most determining factor in the acceptability of Bible translations, it is essential to pay increasing attention to those features which carry so much meaning.

Role of the Translator

The role of a translator as a secondary or intermediate source involves primarily communicating the intentions of the original author. With this principle most translators would fully agree, but many do not understand the numerous subtle and pervasive influences which can undermine some of the most conscientious resolves to be unbiased in one's work. For example, a translator's ideas about how the author thought of his own message can be very significant. Did the original author, for example, want everyone to understand the message or was he only trying to communicate with a well-instructed group of believers? Was the original author fully conscious of all the possible nuances in the message? That is, was he trying to say several things at the same time or was he directly concerned with only a single issue or aspect of the problem? Was the original author basing the message upon what he knew personally or was he somehow taking dictation by God's Spirit? Satisfactory answers to these interpretive questions are crucial to the manner in which a translator approaches the task of translating the Scriptures.

If a translator believes that whenever the original author used a term or phrase, he must have had in mind all that present-day scholars have regarded as possible meanings, then the translation will be more like a commentary than a translation. Or if a translator believes that there must not be any apparent differences of perspective among various biblical authors, then he will be inclined to harmonize diverse accounts in much the same way as some ancient scribes did. For example, early scribes evidently believed that they needed to change the form of the Lord's Prayer as recorded in the gospel of Luke in order to make it more like the fuller form of the prayer as found in the gospel of Matthew.

The ancient prophets and the New Testament evangelists undoubtedly felt a sense of divine constraint in what they proclaimed and wrote, but there is no clear evidence that they thought they were actually writing part of "The Bible," at least not in a sense in which many people today view the Holy Scriptures.

Perhaps even more important than a translator's view of the original author's concern for communication are the translator's attitudes toward himself. One of the greatest protections against exegetical errors is a profound respect for one's personal ignorance, expressed in a firm determination not to introduce idiosyncratic interpretations. Genuine humility is an essential ingredient in being a true "proxy source" and thus an important protection against the tendency to try to improve on the original, as when some translators try to harmonize the accounts of the descent of the Holy Spirit upon Jesus by changing the account in Mark 1:10 to agree with John 1:32. Some translators do this because they regard the gospel of John as "more spiritual" and hence more true.

Some translators have even refused to render the statement "God repented himself," since they insist that God cannot change his mind, for he knows the end from the beginning. Apparently, it takes a special brand of intellectual honesty to let the Bible say things which seemingly contradict one's own theology.

Intellectual humility can also be a protection against "showing off" one's knowledge by introducing highly technical vocabulary or by insisting on literal translations as a means of revealing one's competence in Greek and Hebrew. Most of all, a spirit of humility combined with intellectual honesty can be the best insurance against the tendency to promote by means of Bible translating the cause of a particular theological viewpoint, whether deistic, rationalistic, immersionist, millenarian, or charismatic.

Role of the Receptors

For a functionally equivalent translation the role of the receptors is an integral factor. They are not just the passive "target" of communication, as some terminology would suggest, but active participants in the process. In fact, the question as to the correctness of any translation can only be answered by asking another question: "For whom?" Can those for whom a translation has been prepared really understand what is meant or is the text both obscure and misleading? If the text is understandable, a still further question must be asked: "Do the receptors understand the message in the correct manner?" For example, the traditional rendering of Psalm 1:1c, "Nor stands in the way of sinners," is understandable but often in quite a wrong sense, since "to stand in someone's way" normally means to prevent a person from going some place, and only in Psalm 1 is the phrase supposed to mean "to associate with."

When receptors attempt to understand any text, especially one involving figurative meanings, they almost inevitably draw upon knowledge based on the usage of their own language and the customs of their own culture. Actually, proper understanding of a text is more likely to be a problem of cultural diversity than of linguistic differences. For example, Greek and Hungarian belong to different families of languages, but the problems of translating the New Testament from Greek into Hungarian are by no means as complex as translating from Greek into Hindi, which belongs to the same language family as Greek, namely, Indo-European. But the cultural differences between the Greek-speaking world of the New Testament and the Hindi-speaking society of present-day India are enormous, especially in the area of religious concepts.

Some church leaders, however, have felt that translations should not attempt to bridge any language-culture gaps but should stick to more or less literal renderings of the biblical text. Any needed explanations would then be taken care of by an informed clergy, who could instruct people as to the correct interpretation. In general, however, such an approach has been woefully inadequate. In Romans 1:17 practically all laymen and many of the clergy understand the phrase "the righteousness of God" to be a statement about God's own personal character rather than a reference to what God does, either in righting wrong or in putting people right with himself. Most persons continue to think that the reference to God "hardening the heart of Pharaoh" means that God was making Pharaoh insensitive to the plight of the Israelites. In a sense this is true, but the Hebrew idiom means that God was making Pharaoh stubborn and obstinate.

In the Fulani language of Africa the biblical idiom "hardening the heart" can only be understood correctly when translated as "hardening the head." A literal translation of the Hebrew expression also makes sense, but it is the wrong sense, for in Fulani "to harden the heart" means "to be courageous" (Kassühlke, 1982, 156).

A word such as *phylacteries* (borrowed from Greek and meaning literally "charms") is rarely understood even by better educated lay persons. And the expression "poor in spirit" in Matthew 5:3 remains almost totally obscure to most persons who read traditional translations.

The use of marginal notes (textual, exegetical, historical, and cultural), glossaries, references, indices, and concordances can all be of help, but rarely do they suffice to "correct" the meaning of an otherwise misleading term. Rather than incorporate obscure, ambiguous, and potentially misleading expressions into the text of a translation, it is far better to provide receptors with a meaningful equivalent in the text and possible alternatives in the margin, including, if necessary, literal renderings if this will help the reader understand better the significance of the original.

Role of the Message

The role of the message is usually taken for granted, for it is equated simply with the content or the purpose of the writer, but the situation is not quite as simple as first imagined. In dealing with any text, whether secular or religious, there are several important questions which must be asked if one is to determine the role of the text in the broader context of communication.

The first question is especially relevant to a religious document, Does the text take history seriously? Or put somewhat differently, Is the content related to historical events or is it merely a set of moralizing utterances?

To appreciate some religious literature it is obviously not necessary to know anything about the author or the original receptors or the circumstances of the writing, but the Scriptures are essentially unique among religious documents in that God's entrance into history is an integral element. For the Bible, God is the one who not only speaks, but acts, usually through particular people.

The second question (or series of questions) relates to the exclusive or universal nature of the message. Is it necessary to know who said what to whom, when, how, under what circumstances, and for what purposes in order to understand the real significance of a statement? Is the content applicable only to a particular person or group, or does it have universal implications, despite the fact that originally the words may have been addressed to one person or to a restricted group? For example, are the statements in 1 Corinthians 11:14–15 about long hair and the restrictions on women speaking in church (1 Cor. 14:34–35) to be understood as universally applicable for all societies at all times, or are these statements to be understood in terms of the particular situation in the city of Corinth? The various books of the Bible differ considerably as to the universality of the message. But for the most part the New Testament makes universal claims. Even the structure of the book of Acts points to the universal implications of the good news.

The third question relates to the difference in emphasis upon ritual enactments and everyday behavior. The basic documents of some religions contain accounts of and specifications for religious observances. Some portions of the Bible are largely of this nature; for example, Leviticus, the last half of Exodus, and parts of Numbers and Deuteronomy. But most of the Scriptures deal essentially with everyday life. The New Testament focuses primarily upon the basic principles for a new way of life rather than upon ritual reenactment of approved customs.

The fourth question relates to the contrast between belief and action, or in other words, the tension between faith and works. In some religious writing, almost the entire emphasis is upon a system of belief, so that religion becomes almost equivalent to a philosophy. But largely because of a realistic approach to history, the Scriptures combine systems of thought with plans of action in such a way as to make the Bible, and especially the New Testament, a uniquely disturbing religious text. As one Buddhist abbot in Thailand said when he forewarned his monks about reading the New Testament, "Do not read this book unless you are prepared to lose sleep!" For the Scriptures, the role of the message provides the essential basis for a theology of translation.

Formal Correspondence and Functional Equivalence

The crucial problems of translation are often stated in terms of a conflict between formal correspondence and functional equivalence. As already noted in the preface, in certain previous discussions of functional equivalence in translation (Nida, 1964; Nida and Taber, 1969), the expression "dynamic equivalence" has been employed. Basically, dynamic equivalence has been described in terms of functional equivalence. The translation process has been defined on the basis that the receptors of a translation should comprehend the translated text to such an extent that they can understand how the original receptors must have understood the original text. The expression "dynamic equivalence" has, however, led to some confusion, since the term "dynamic" has been understood merely in terms of something which has impact and appeal. Accordingly, to avoid misunderstanding such terminology, this text employs the expression "functional equivalence," particularly since the twin bases for effective translation seem to be best represented in a sociosemiotic and sociolinguistic orientation, in which the focus is upon function.

In reference to revisions, one often hears the statement that the form of an existing text must be altered in order to preserve the meaning of the original languages, since receptor languages are constantly in the process of change. But to describe the difficulties of faithful translating merely in terms of the tension between preservation of the form and adherence to meaning is to oversimplify the issues. It is not right to speak of the Greek or Hebrew text (or a literal translation of such) as being merely "the form" and a freer idiomatic translation as being "the meaning." An expression in any language consists of a set of forms which serve to signal meaning on various levels: lexical, grammatical, and rhetorical. The translator must seek to employ a functionally equivalent set of forms which in so far as possible will match the meaning of the original source-language text.

In Amos 1 and 2 there are several instances of the expression "for three transgressions . . . and for four," as the prophet warns various cities and nations of impending disaster because of their repeated acts of wickedness. The Hebrew expression could be understood literally as referring to merely three or four transgressions. In reality, however, the phrases "for three . . . and for four" constitute an idiom meaning "time after time" or "again and again." In fact, the numbers "three" and "four" should be understood symbolically, but the importance of this combination is not in the symbolic significance of the individual numbers, but in the progression from three to four, in order to emphasize a culminating point. Note, for example, the sequence 1 . . . 2 in Psalm 62:11 and Job 40:5, the sequence 2 . . . 3 in Sirach 26:28, the sequence 3 . . . 4 in Proverbs 30:15, and the sequence 9 . . . 10 in Sirach 25:7–11 (Roth, 1962, 300–11).

If in translating one only reproduces the so-called "literal meaning" of the original by clinging to the original form, receptors will be surprised that in Amos 1 and 2 God would punish cities and nations so severely for only three or four offenses. The functional equivalent in English would be "crime after crime" or "committing violence again and again."

Literal correspondences may involve a number of different degrees of intelligibility. The meanings of such phrases as "lifted up his voice" (Gen. 27:38) and "opened his mouth and taught the people" (Matt. 5:2) are more or less guessable, even though they sound strange in English, and they inevitably tend to slow down a reader's or a hearer's rate of comprehension. Curiously enough, no one has ever rendered the parallel Hebrew construction in Genesis 29:1 by translating literally "Jacob lifted up his feet and went." That would have been too ludicrous even for the most literal translator (Orlinsky, 1974, 410).

A statement such as "I will give you cleanness of teeth" (Amos 4:6) is likely to have little meaning or possibly be understood in the wrong sense. This expression is not about dental hygiene but about a state of famine. The idiom "gird up the loins of your mind" (1 Pet. 1:13) will also surely be meaningless if rendered literally. The statement "whose blood Pilate mingled with their sacrifices" (Luke 13:1) has been seriously misunderstood. Some readers have thought that in a sadistic outrage Pilate stood stirring the meat of the animal sacrifices in the blood of the slain people. In reality, of course, Pilate simply ordered those who were sacrificing to be slain in the Temple. The figuratively heightened expression used by Luke would, however, have expressed very effectively the emotional outrage of the Jewish people against Pilate's action.

A close formal correspondence in a receptor language so frequently does not carry the correct meaning of the source text. Though the original receptors could readily recognize that an idiom should not be understood in a literal but in a figurative sense, speakers of a receptor language frequently have no basis for recognizing the nonliteral meaning. Under such circumstances, changes of form can and should be made, but only under certain specified conditions:

1. *When a literal rendering would give an entirely wrong meaning.* The idiom "heap coals of fire on his head" (Prov. 25:22 and Rom. 12:20) has often been seriously misunderstood as a means of torturing people to death.

2. *When a borrowed term constitutes a semantic "zero" and is therefore likely to be filled with the wrong meaning.* Early missionaries to Indians of Latin America usually borrowed the Spanish word *Dios* for "God," but the Indians generally assumed that this was merely another proper name for their own sun god.

3. *When a formal correspondence involves a serious obscurity in meaning.* The expression "circumcision of the heart" (Rom. 2:29) is rarely understood unless people have been specifically instructed as to the figurative significance of circumcision. On the other hand, there are certain important religious symbols which, though often obscure in their meaning, are necessarily important for the preservation of the integrity and unity of the biblical message.

Expressions such as "Lamb of God," "cross," and "sacrifice" need to be preserved, but often with explanatory marginal notes. Readers may not be acquainted with execution by crucifixion, but this would not justify substituting "lynching" or "beheading," nor can one justify the use of "little pig of God" rather than "Lamb of God" merely because in the case of some peoples of Melanesia, pigs are highly praised and sheep are either unknown or despised.

4. *When a formal correspondence would result in an ambiguity evidently not intended by the original author.* A literal translation of Genesis 49:14 could read, "Issachar is a strong ass," if one understands Hebrew *gerem* in the sense of "bony, strong-limbed, strong" and not in the sense of "castrated." Although the explicit mention of "strong" guarantees a better understanding, one may completely miss the significance of the metaphorical use of "ass" because in many languages the associative meaning of "ass" is strongly pejorative. For that reason the recent German translation *(Die Gute Nachricht)* was obliged not only to change the metaphor into a comparison, but to restructure the text:

> Du, Issachar, beugst deinen Rücken
> und schleppst als Sklave schwere Lasten.
> Genauso wie ein dürrer Esel
> brichst du darunter in die Knie.

This German text of Genesis 49:14 may be rendered as:

> Issachar, you bend your back
> and like a slave carry heavy loads.
> Just like a bony donkey
> your knees collapse under the weight.

Most ambiguities in the original text are due to our own ignorance of the cultural and historical backgrounds of the text. It is unfair to the original writer and to the receptors to reproduce as ambiguities all those passages which may be interpreted in more than one way. In the first place, the reader will almost inevitably acquire a wrong impression as to the intent or purpose of the biblical writer, since it would seem to the reader that the biblical writer was not concerned with communicating a message but only with "playing language games." In the second place, the translator places a very heavy burden on the receptor to determine which of two or more meanings may be involved. The average reader is usually much less capable of making correct judgments about such alternative meanings than is the translator, who can make use of the best scholarly judgments on ambiguous passages. Accordingly, the translator should place in the text the best attested interpretation and provide in marginal notes the appropriate alternatives.

5. *When a formal correspondence would result in bad grammar or style in the receptor language.* The avoidance of bad grammar or style is particularly important if such would represent substandard usage or vulgar expressions. There is simply no excuse for "bad language." Usually, however, Bible translators are not fully aware of the manner in which they offend by their improper language or poor style. In one instance a local chief in West Africa prohibited the distribution of a New Testament in his language by saying, "I will not allow our language to be corrupted by the language mistakes in that book."

It is a mistake to assume that all figurative meanings must be automatically changed to nonfigurative expressions. Sometimes a literal translation is perfectly acceptable. Frequently there are closely corresponding figurative expressions in source and receptor languages. For example, in a number of languages in Africa one may use "liver" in most contexts in which the Greek uses "heart," while in several Mayan languages the equivalent is "abdomen." In most European languages joy is experienced in the "heart," but in most Chadic languages of Africa joy is related to the "liver," whereas in Hebrew the "kidneys" are said to experience joy.

In Hebrew the figurative expression "to cover sins" (Ps. 32:1; "Blessed is he whose transgression is forgiven, whose sin is covered") involves far more than "covering up of something that offends the eye" (Kissane, 1964, 141). The expression is essentially equivalent to "forgiving sins." Other languages may use different figurative expressions such as "to wash away" (Timorese), "to turn one's back on sins" (Kpelle), "to heal the neck" (Kipsigis), or "to spit on the ground for someone" (Shilluk). Such expressions are not literal correspondences, but they do involve the closest functional equivalents.

Some persons have argued that translators must translate literally despite the dangers of misunderstanding and must leave to teachers and preachers the responsibility of correcting any wrong impressions or misunderstanding resulting from literal renderings. Such a procedure, however, involves serious problems. In the first place, relatively few readers of the Bible always have available persons who can instruct them as to the proper understanding of the text. In the second place, such efforts in the past to correct misunderstanding have been singularly unsuccessful, since people almost always have greater confidence in the printed word than in supplementary explanations.

This issue of the communicative role of the Bible highlights an important distinction which may be made between exegesis and hermeneutics, although some writers use these terms almost indistinguishably. The translator's task may be described as being essentially exegetical, in that a translation should faithfully reflect who said what to whom under what circumstances and for what purpose and should be in a form of the receptor language which does not distort the content or misrepresent the rhetorical impact or appeal, as specified in the above five limitations on formal adjustments between source and receptor languages.

The responsibility of the preacher or teacher is to take this message and to apply it hermeneutically to the different cultural contexts in which people now live. The function of the preacher and teacher may likewise be viewed as a kind of translation, but it is cultural-historical translation and not a linguistic one.

Languages do not differ significantly in what they can say but in how particular concepts are expressed. Even in so-called "new languages" (those which have only recently been reduced to writing) the real problems for the translator do not consist primarily in manufacturing new expressions but in discovering the various ways in which such languages can speak effectively about the incredibly numerous experiences of human life.

Different Types of Translations

Translations of a particular text may differ radically, all the way from an interlinear word-for-word correspondence to a radical transformation. For the most part, diverse kinds of translations may be classified as: interlinear, literal, closest natural equivalent, adapted, and culturally reinterpreted.

An interlinear translation (usually with an accompanying literal rendering in intelligible syntactic order) may be valuable to ethnologists, linguists, and philologists, who are interested in the original structure or literary devices without themselves having to learn the language in question. Some interlinear translations produced for linguists go so far as to identify all the morphemes and mark certain important grammatical classes. Such translations, however, are relatively rare and of little use to the average person.

Literal translations adhere to the form of the original as much as possible, while still being grammatically possible, though stylistically awkward. Translations such as the American Standard Version, the English Revised Version, and the New American Standard Version are representative of this type of translating.

A translation which is the closest natural equivalent of the original text may be on a literary level or on the so-called "common-language level" (the overlap area between the literary and colloquial). It is also possible to produce a closest-natural-equivalent type of translation on a substandard level, but such is certainly not advisable, since it is generally rejected by the very persons who would be most capable of understanding and identifying with the substandard forms. Such translations are almost always regarded as being paternalistic and hence unacceptable to those who employ substandard forms in daily communication. Actually, such translations are mainly cherished by academics. It is interesting to note that the French Bible in argot *(Le livre des darons sacrés)* has a preface by Jean Cocteau of the French Academy!

Adapted translations are largely of two types: (1) those which must be adapted to an accompanying code, for example, music, literary genres (a different poetic format), or a different language with its distinctive articulation of sounds (the problem of lip synchronization in translating material for television or cinema), and (2) adaptations prompted by different views as to the nature of translating, resulting in additions, deletions, harmonizations, added explanations, corrections, and embellishments.

Cultural reinterpretations involve transferring the cultural setting from one language-culture context to another. Clarence Jordan's *Cottonpatch Version* of most of the New Testament is a typical cultural reinterpretation, in which Pontius Pilate is governor of Georgia, and Annas and Caiaphas are co-presidents of the Southern Baptist Convention. Jesus is born in Gainesville, Georgia, and lynched by a mob in Atlanta.

Another example of a cultural reinterpretation in translation is Roger Parmentier's modern transcription of Amos into French, in which Amos, a suburban laborer, delivers his message to the Christians in France during the coalition of Giscard, in the time of Brezhnev and Carter, and two years before the outbreak of a third world war! The crimes of Chilean generals and of Kampala are denounced and fire is sent upon the palace of Idi Amin, the Kremlin, etc.

These types of translations carry a great deal of impact for certain readers, but their message is largely lost on those who really should read them. Too often people are unaware of or do not want to recognize the striking parallels between the biblical accounts and their own sociopolitical lives.

All of these varieties of translating and adapting have a certain legitimacy for particular audiences and special circumstances. This volume, however, concentrates upon the significance of and techniques employed in producing the closest natural equivalent of the original text, whether on a literary or a common-language level. As a help for those who may be interested in further implications of diverse types of translations and their relation to different theories of translating, Appendix A contains a brief description of the philological, linguistic, communicative, and sociosemiotic theories of translation and how these complementary theories may serve to understand better the history of Bible translating and the nature of functional equivalence.

The Possibility of Translating

Despite the fact that so much effective translating has been undertaken for so many thousands of years (historical evidence goes back to the third millennium before Christ), some scholars have raised serious questions as to the validity of any and all translating, and there are strenuous objections against translating proposed by philologists (Güttinger, 1963). Wilhelm von Humboldt, in a famous letter of July 23, 1796, to August Wilhelm Schlegel, stated that all translational activities only tried to solve an impossible task. More than a hundred years later, Leo Weisgerber has taken up again this axiom which has exercised a tremendous influence, especially in theological circles. The so-called school of the *Sprachinhaltsforschung* ("investigation into the content of speech") has placed major emphasis upon what is linguistically and culturally divergent. Georges Mounin, however, wrote more than twenty years ago that the theory of untranslatability is built entirely upon exceptions (Mounin, 1976; see also Ladmiral, 1979).

There is no doubt about the fact that absolute communication in translating is impossible, but this is true of any and all kinds of communication, whether intralingual or interlingual. There is always some loss in the communication process, for sources and receptors never have identical linguistic and cultural backgrounds. Even two scholars talking about something in their area of particular competence may very well have a loss of at least twenty percent. Accordingly, some loss in translating from one language to another is certainly not unexpected. The translator's task, however, is to keep such loss at a minimum.

The real question, however, is not whether translating is possible but how it is possible that translating is accomplished so successfully in so many instances. For those who assume that people think differently simply because they use different languages, translating may very well appear to be extremely difficult, if not impossible. But translating does go on, and interlingual understanding takes place for several important reasons.

In the first place, there are a number of language universals which are significant in any and all interlingual communication. All languages, for example, exhibit certain important parallel levels of structure; for example, sounds, morphemes, words, phrases, sentences, and paragraphs. All languages have sets of discrete contrasts, and there are numerous genres which are amazingly similar; for example, personal narrative, didactic and epic poetry, proverbs, oratory, and laws. Furthermore, all languages are open systems in the sense of being open not only to new words but to new concepts. In addition, all languages possess figurative expressions, both metaphorical and metonymic.

In the second place, all languages, though in certain respects arbitrary (particularly on the word level in the relationship between sounds and meaning), are only relatively arbitrary, for the structure, whether on the level of sounds, morphemes, words, or phrases, is essentially systematic. That is to say, in no language are words simply thrown together in a haphazard order. There are always classes of sounds, words, and grammatical structures, and rules which make sense within each system. Such rules do not determine what people can think but only the system of signs and signals by which thoughts can be expressed.

In the third place, the intellectual capacities of all peoples are essentially similar. There is no such thing as "primitive mentality," but simply different presuppositions which give rise to very different ways of interpreting events and utterances. Without more understanding of the situation, some people might very well regard the Kaka Christians of the Camerouns as being "primitive" in their thought patterns, since they regard the story of Hagar as being such a central symbol of the grace of God. For the Kaka people, however, their god (symbolized as a spider) never speaks to people, but the God of the Scriptures is described as speaking not only to people but to a second wife (actually the slave of a first wife) and promising that her son will be the progenitor of a great nation. God's address to a slave woman, who has been sent away because of the jealousy of a first wife, is regarded by the Kaka as a sure symbol of God's grace. One of the important shared intellectual capacities of all peoples is imagination, the gift of being able to understand how different people with quite different ideas can both think and act in a meaningful way.

In the fourth place, all peoples share far more cultural similarities than is usually thought to be the case. What binds people together is much greater than what separates them. In adjustments to the physical environment, in the organization of society, in dealing with crucial stages of life (birth, puberty, marriage, and death), in the development of elaborate ritual and symbolism, and in a drive for aesthetic expression (whether in decorating masks or in refining poetic forms), people are amazingly alike. Because of all this, translating can be undertaken with the expectation of communicative effectiveness.

The loss of meaning in translation is largely proportionate to the extent that a meaning is carried by the form. This is the crucial problem of rhetorical meaning, which is treated in Chapters 5 and 6. In reality, translating is amazingly natural for people. Even small children grasp the basic principles of interlingual communication with relative ease, often even better than adults. This is particularly evident in circumstances in which an immigrant family depends on the children for translating on behalf of adult members, who have so much more difficulty learning a new language.

Though the possibility of a translation into a particular language always exists, this does not mean that the people in question always desire to have a translation, even in instances when they may be sympathetic with the content of the message. For a number of years many Christians in Haiti opposed the translation of the New Testament into Haitian Creole. They regarded this universally used language of Haiti as being such a corruption of French as to not be worthy of representing Christian truth. Their attitude toward the language which they used in daily conversation resulted from the low regard which French-speaking people displayed concerning Haitian Creole.

Similarly, in Zaire there was opposition in the early days to producing the Scriptures in Kituba, a widely used *lingua franca* of the Lower Congo. At present, some Zulu speakers are very much opposed to any of the Scriptures being translated into Fanakalo, the widely used adaptation of Zulu employed in the mines in South Africa. Though some American Indian communities in North America continue to use their Indian language for the expression of group solidarity and ritual observance, they often object to translations of the Scriptures in their own language, since all of their reading has been done in English. They see no point in learning to read their own language if the only book printed in that language is the Bible, which they can also read in English. On the other hand, some American Indian tribes which have a Bible in a rather old-fashioned form of language insist upon reprinting the text, since it has strong sentimental value and constitutes a symbol of a time when the language was more widely used and the tribe constituted a more unified and meaningful entity.

3

Basic Issues

There is no way in which translating can be isolated from the total communication act. One must always ask the questions: For whom is a translation being prepared? How will it be used? In what form will it be published? In what language or dialect is it to be made? What level of language will the text represent? And perhaps the most important question of all: Who is to make the translation? For the quality of a translation is directly proportionate to the competence of the translator.

Audience

In the case of Bible translating it is not enough to consider merely the educational level of the perspective audience or the age of the persons involved. Knowing whether the audience is to be primarily upper class, middle class, or lower class may have some relevance as to language usage, but more important is the nature of the religious constituency. Persons may be highly literate and yet know practically nothing about the Bible. They may be relatively open to new ideas in politics and science but be relatively closed to new approaches in religious thought and vocabulary.

Before preparing a revision or a new translation of the Scriptures for a constituency that has had the Scriptures for some years, it is important to know (a) what translation or translations are in use, (b) how they are regarded, and (c) what suggestions a constituency may have as to the improvements which can or should be made. The presuppositions which such persons have about translating may determine the acceptance or rejection of any revision or new translation. Do people, for example, insist that a translation be more or less word-for-word and that any departure from this is mere paraphrase and therefore theologically unacceptable? In producing a functionally equivalent translation, one must be concerned with the accuracy with which the content is represented rather than the number of words which may be employed to accomplish this. For many people, however, this concept of equivalence is difficult to accept, particularly when it applies to the Bible.

Use

The manner in which a translation is to be used may also be an important factor in deciding principles and procedures of translating. Many readers, for example, appreciate a translation in common language, especially if it is to be used in private reading or for group discussion. Such a functional equivalent translation seems to be particularly appropriate for this type of use. But many persons insist that from the pulpit they wish to hear a translation which seems more traditional, since due to its unusual and often high-level vocabulary it apparently is more awe-inspiring and authoritative. In fact, some people insist that it is more important to have an impressive message rather than an intelligible one, though clearly a translator's aim should be to produce a text which will be not only rhetorically impressive but fully understandable.

Language or Dialect

The language in which a Bible translation is made often represents a serious issue. Should, for example, the Bible be produced in every language and significantly different dialect, regardless of the size of the constituency, even for groups in which there may be less than a hundred speakers? Or should the Bible be produced only in one central dialect with the highest percentage of common vocabulary, and variants from other dialects be provided in footnotes, as has been done, for example, in the latest Basque translation of the New Testament? Should one possibly refrain from producing a written Bible text at all and improve upon current oral Bible translating through special handbooks, as has been proposed for the Bamileke area in the Camerouns (Fueter and Voorhoeve, 1963, 242–52; and de Waard, 1968, 131–43)?

Should one translate the Bible in order to erect tribal monuments, as has frequently been done, or should one take the entire communication situation into account? To what extent should the interest and the desires of local people be considered in determining whether to produce a translation of the Scriptures in a particular language or dialect?

A decision to translate the Scriptures should not be based upon the size of the constituency but upon the religious and linguistic need. One must always determine the extent of dialect variation and the attitudes which people may have with regard to differences of pronunciation, grammar, and vocabulary. One should also carefully note political attitudes of local authorities and the language policy of national governments. In one region of Africa, in spite of expert advice, central dialects were rejected and an insignificant dialect was chosen for Bible translation, simply because it had no prestige and there were no imperialistic overtones!

There also needs to be a religious justification for translating the Bible. Is there, for example, an actual or potential constituency to use a translation? On the island of Kusaie in Polynesia there are only about fifteen hundred Kusaien speakers, but there has been an active church for fully a hundred years, and there is no other language which the Kusaien people can use meaningfully. There is no reason to doubt the validity of publishing the Scriptures for such a group. Even when there is a good deal of bilingualism, as in the case of Central Eskimo of northern Canada, there is a real need for the Bible in this form of Eskimo. At least ninety percent of the population are active churchgoing Christians, the services are always in Eskimo, and most of the people are literate in their own language. Furthermore, they have a number of well-trained people who are competent to translate for a church that shows increasing interest in the use of the Scriptures.

In many parts of the world there are bilingual or multilingual societies. Frequently there is a dominant language in an area in which there are a number of minority languages. Some of these minority languages may be widely used as a kind of second language and thus serve as trade languages in an area. In general, one may classify such languages on the basis of four different functional levels: primary, secondary, tertiary, and quaternary.

The primary languages are the so-called "international languages," usually with a long literary tradition. They always serve as instruments of higher education and are employed widely for technological information. Such languages include English, Spanish, French, Russian, Chinese, Japanese, and German.

Secondary languages are used for general education, constitute a national language, usually have considerable literary tradition, but may be employed only marginally for technological information. Such languages would include Icelandic, Persian, Marathi, Indonesian, and Afrikaans.

Tertiary languages are those in which education is strictly limited (usually only primary). The literature may be only recent, but the language is used extensively for in-group identification. Such languages would include Yoruba (Nigeria), Swahili (East Africa), Shona (Zimbabwe), Pilipino (Philippines), and Cusco Quechua (Peru). A number of so-called trade languages also fall into this class, for example Lingala (Zaire), Fulani (West Africa), and Hause (West Africa).

These trade languages are normally of great importance for the strategy of Bible translating. High quality translations in these trade languages will considerably improve translations in quaternary languages. The new translation of the Bible in Fulani, for example, is not important for native Fulani speakers in the churches, since there are practically none. It is, however, of extreme importance for thousands of Christians speaking quaternary languages and who primarily or exclusively have access to Fulani as a second language.

Quaternary languages are the so-called "primitive" languages of tribal groups. These have either only recently been reduced to writing or are still in an unwritten form. Such languages include Pacaas Novas (Brazil), Piro (Peru), Kiyanzi (Zaire), Subanum (Philippines), Miao (southeast Asia), and Enga (New Guinea).

Between dominant and subordinate languages there are a number of different degrees of interdependence and numerous patterns of relationship. In the German-speaking areas of Switzerland, High German carries considerable prestige because of its association with education, literature, and religion, but the language of solidarity is not High German but various forms of Swiss German. Furthermore, the prestige of certain of these dialects is growing rapidly as more and more books are published in Swiss German.

In some situations a minority language acquires important political value as it becomes increasingly a symbol of ethnic solidarity. This is conspicuously true of Welsh in Great Britain and Catalan and Basque in Spain. A sense of self-determination may also be an important factor, as in the case of Maltese. This language of Malta belongs to the Southwest Semitic languages, but it is a separate form because of its long historical severance from Asia Minor and its exposure to non-Semitic influences (Moscati, 1969, 15). In modern times it is gaining rapid prestige despite the fact that most of the people in Malta also speak English and Italian.

In some instances a minority language has won out over a more prestigious international language in terms of the number of speakers, though not necessarily in terms of status. Many early Spanish-speaking settlers in Paraguay gradually gave up the use of Spanish and adopted the Guarani Indian language as the medium of communication. As a result, at the present time in Paraguay many more people are able to communicate effectively in Guarani than in Spanish, despite the fact that Spanish is the language of the educational system and the language of official national life, but it is not the language of everyday conversation.

One would assume that educational policy would inevitably eliminate minority languages, but this is by no means always the case. In Haiti, the French language has been the official language of the country and the language of education for at least 150 years, but probably less than 25 percent of the population are able to use French effectively, while almost everyone speaks Haitian Creole. In view of the fact that so many Haitians have lived and worked in the United States or other English-speaking areas for periods of time, there are probably more Haitians who can converse effectively in English than in French. This is certainly true of the million or more Haitians now living in English-speaking countries.

For a number of years there was strong official opposition to Haitian Creole as a language for publications. This has gradually changed, however, as more and more books have been produced in Haitian Creole, particularly as the result of more and more persons reading the Scriptures in that language.

In view of the many differences in relationships between competing languages and in view of the complex patterns of interrelationship between dominant and subordinate languages, it is not easy to determine in which language one should translate or how much should be produced in a particular form of language or dialect.

Level of Language

As difficult as it is to determine just what language or dialect into which a translation should be made, it is even more complex to determine what level of language should be employed in a particular text. There is always a tendency for people to embellish whatever is regarded as being of high value, and this has often led to embellishing the style of Bible translating in order to make it seem to fit the elevated character of the content. This was certainly the tendency in translating at the time of the Reformation, and as a result a number of translations from that period established more or less a norm for Bible translating. This was true of the King James Version, which in its vocabulary and grammatical forms was somewhat obsolescent in its own day, but it did possess certain rhythmic patterns which commended it for public readings; and despite its excessive punctuation, many preachers have been able to learn to dramatize the text in reading.

The famous preface of the King James Version, entitled "The Translators to the Readers," contains some rather modern ideas in defense of the work of the committee which produced the text. This introduction was the work of Miles Smith. Unfortunately, it is normally not reprinted in editions of the King James Version. The following statement about translation principles is particularly revealing:

> Lastly, we have on the one side avoided the scrupulosity of the Puritans, who leave the old Ecclesiastical words, and betake them to other, as when they put *washing* for *Baptism*, and *Congregation* instead of *Church*; as also on the other side we have shunned the obscurity of the Papists, in their *Azimes*, *Tunike*, *Rational*, *Holocausts*, *Praepuce*, *Pasche*, and a number of such like,

whereof their late Translation is full, and that of purpose to darken the sense, that since they must needs translate the Bible, yet by the language thereof, it may be kept from being understood. But we desire that the Scripture may speak like itself, as in the language of *Canaan*, that it may be understood even of the very vulgar (Dufour, 1983, 103–15).

The problem with the King James Version and other translations of the same type is that no attempt has been made to fit the level of language to the diverse genres. The kind of language to be found in the book of Job or the Song of Songs is not the same as should be found in the Gospel of Mark, nor is the style of Leviticus something which should be carried over in the translation of the Pauline Epistles. A special problem is posed by 1 and 2 Peter, since 1 Peter represents highly polished rhetorical Greek, but 2 Peter contains quite a different type of language and a very different style.

One of the curious features of the style of 2 Peter is the tendency to employ iambic rhythm. Whereas the vocabulary of 1 Peter is dignified, that of 2 Peter inclines to the pompous. This is not to say that 1 and 2 Peter do not have certain stylistic features in common. Both, for example, frequently repeat the same lexical items instead of employing synonyms, but the differences in style should be noted and reflected in a translation (Turner, 1976, 140–44).

The problem, however, is not primarily a matter of the level of the language in the source text, but the level that is likely to be understood by receptors when the text is either heard or read. In other words, the level of language must also involve the channel capacity of the audience in comprehending the text.

There are three basic dimensions which are involved in matters of language level: present-day/archaic, literary/common/substandard, and formal/informal. In each of these dimensions there are a number of gradations. For example, in the temporal dimension one may have present-day, old-fashioned, obsolescent, obsolete, and archaic. In the dimension of literary, common, and substandard one may also add technical and vulgar at the extremes, and for the formal/informal dimension there are probably at least five significant levels, often spoken of as ritual (or frozen), formal, informal, casual, and intimate.

These five levels of language on the formal/informal dimension are well illustrated by the following series of names and titles which could be used in speaking to or about the same person, but in quite different circumstances: *Your Honor, Mr. Thomas Jackson, Jackson, Tom, Red*. Invitations to eat may also be classified in terms of a formal/informal series, for example, *the guests may now enter the dining room, you are invited to dine, let's go eat now, let's eat,* and *soup's on*.

Material to be Translated

In addition to studying problems posed by diversity of receptors, use of the text, languages and dialects in which to translate, and the levels of language, one must also give consideration to what should be translated. Undoubtedly the competence, interest, and need of receptors are the primary considerations. If one is to begin with a series of selections from the Holy Scriptures (as is often the case), one needs to consider not only the inherent difficulties of the text itself but the matter of cultural relevance.

People living in the Sahara are unlikely to be especially interested in Paul's harrowing experience of a storm and ultimate shipwreck on Malta. Similarly, people living in an environment which has been heavily influenced by "historical materialism" will not first of all be attracted by a miracle story from the Bible. Likewise, most people will find it difficult to understand some of the subtle symbolism in the signs which constitute such important elements in the Gospel of John, nor will they be able to appreciate certain features of the Johannine style which reflect what is known as "stream of consciousness" ordering.

Even in the translating of selections there are some problems because the setting of the selection depends on the total discourse. Therefore, one must often add phrases from a preceding section to provide an adequate setting. Furthermore, it may be necessary to eliminate certain expressions at the end of a selection, which in reality introduce the following episode, and which are therefore confusing if they introduce something that does not follow in a given publication. Even the translation of a single book of the Bible often presents problems. For example, calling the first Gospel simply "Matthew" may be completely confusing. A fuller title such as "The Good News about Jesus According to Matthew" will certainly convey much more meaning. In addition, it is important to have some kind of supplementary information with regard to the relationship of this book to other parts of the Holy Scriptures.

The issue of the canon poses no special problems in the case of the New Testament, although the order in which translators should undertake to translate the various books of the New Testament may be an important matter to consider. Some translators assume that a book such as John is easy to translate, since it has such simple sentence structure. However, the discourse structure of the Gospel of John is extremely complex, and the highly generic vocabulary and the amount of symbolism, in vocabulary as well as in events, make this book an extremely difficult book to translate satisfactorily. Translators are certainly well advised to begin work on a book such as Mark, possibly to be followed by Acts and then perhaps one of the more popular epistles, (for example, James and Philippians) before tackling the rest of the New Testament.

The issue of the canon involves serious problems in the case of the Old Testament. The Septuagint text used by the early Christian church contained a number of books (called generally "apocryphal" or "deuterocanonical"), which were later rejected by the Jewish community toward the end of the first century A.D. (the oldest Jewish enumeration of the canonical writings can be found in the second century A.D. in the Talmud, *Baba Bathra* 14b). As a consequence of this rejection, the Jews in the Hellenistic diaspora rejected the Septuagint as a whole and replaced it with a new Greek translation made by Aquila.

The Councils of Hippo (393) and Carthage (397) essentially accepted the canon presented by Augustine, which included the apocrypha or deuterocanon. The same canon is defended in the Decretum Gelasianum (end of the sixth century A.D.), and it includes in addition to the writings of the Jewish canon also the Book of Wisdom, Ecclesiasticus, Baruch, Tobit, Judith, and 1 and 2 Maccabees.

Officially, the Greek church decided at the synod of Jerusalem in 1672 to include only four of these apocryphal or deuterocanonical books in their canon, namely, the Book of Wisdom, Ecclesiasticus, Tobit, and Judith. In the Western Church, which was under the influence of the Latin Vulgate translation (finally declared the authentic Bible text at the Council of Trent in 1546), the situation was again different.

Lutherans accepted the apocrypha as being profitable for reading but not for the establishment of doctrine. The same position was taken by Anglicans and Episcopalians, although these churches accepted a few additional books not included by Lutherans.

At the time of the Reformation almost all translations into various languages included these additional books in one way or another. Whether the Bible Societies now publish these books in any particular language depends upon the need and the climate of cooperation in the area. For a statement concerning the basic principles of cooperation on such issues, one should consult the document on Interconfessional Cooperation in Bible Translating.

In some countries in which these books have been translated, an attempt has been made to get rid of the rather unsatisfactory names "deuterocanonical" and "apocrypha," which to the average reader do not convey any meaning, or they may convey the wrong meaning. In the latest German translation *(Die Gute Nachricht)* it was unanimously decided to use the expression *Die Spätschriften des Alten Testaments* ("The Late Writings of the Old Testament") with the traditional designations in parentheses.

As in the case of the New Testament, there are a number of important considerations for those undertaking to translate the Old Testament. In many instances there is a strong demand on the part of churches to translate the book of Psalms immediately after completing the New Testament. Unless translators are particularly well equipped to undertake such a task, it certainly is preferable to begin with some of the significantly easier books to translate, for example, Ruth and 1 Samuel through 2 Kings. To do justice to the poetry of Psalms, and especially to the style of Job, requires outstanding skill and intense effort.

The Text

In addition to the decisions which must be made with regard to the audience, use, language, or dialect, level of language, and canon, it is also essential that translators have a clear idea of the nature of the texts which they are to follow and the underlying principles which have been employed in establishing such texts.

As already noted in Chapter 1, there are some 5000 passages in the Old Testament and at least 1400 in the New Testament in which there are textual alternatives involving differences of interpretation. The fact of such differences is not strange, since biblical and nonbiblical texts from the ancient world are basically no different in this regard. There is simply no technique for perfect transmission of a text. In the process of copying a manuscript there is a tendency to make mistakes. The longer the series of manuscripts which have been copied one from another, the greater will be the departure from the original autographs. This means, of course, that older manuscripts are much less likely to suffer contamination. They probably represent fewer cases of copying and thus are more likely to be similar to the autographs. The age of such manuscripts can be determined by chemical analysis of the vellum or papyri, by the style of writing, and by the degree of conformity of the text of such manuscripts to other texts which can be more or less definitely dated.

Because of the varying degrees of dependency of manuscripts upon one another in view of the process of copying, manuscripts tend to form so-called "families," though as some have commented, there is a good deal of "intermarriage," since copyists may have copied from more than one manuscript in the process of preparing a text. Even in the earliest manuscripts of the New Testament which are available to us, there are no so-called "pure types," for there was early textual contamination. Even the so-called "majority text" (also spoken of as the Byzantine text) is essentially a fifth-century A.D. text, and there are a good many significant differences even within the manuscripts belonging to this class.

In establishing a text of the New Testament which is as close to the autographs as possible, one cannot simply count manuscripts; they must be "weighed" in terms of both external and internal evidence.

External evidence is considered on the basis of the variety of evidence;

that is, a reading which comes from several different families of manuscripts is much more likely to be original than one which exists only in one particular set of manuscripts. The age of the manuscript is likewise important, as well as its reliability; that is, the extent to which a manuscript characteristically employs readings which are known to be early.

Internal evidence in the analysis of manuscripts is also important, for one must consider the probabilities as to whether a particular reading is better explained as added or deleted. For example, in Matthew 5:22 the Greek term *eikē*, "without reason," seems to go so well with the statement about "being angry with one's brother." One can, however, readily see why it would be added, for without *eikē* the harsh condemnation must have seemed unwarranted to early scribes.

In analyzing internal evidence, one must always be alert to the possibility of harmonization. In Matthew 5:43–44 some later manuscripts have a number of phrases evidently borrowed from Luke 6:27–28. The statement about loving one's enemies in Luke 6:27–28 is somewhat longer than the passage in Matthew 5:43–44. In the Lukan section there are no significant differences in textual evidence in the various manuscripts. But in Matthew various scribes evidently borrowed at different times so that the borrowings occur in different orders and in differing amounts. In addition, the shorter form of the text in Matthew 5:43–44 has some of the best textual evidence and excellent support in the versions.

Many persons are rightly concerned as to the reasons for changes which occur in texts—changes which may be classified in terms of communication theory as "noise." For the most part there are four basic reasons for such alterations of material in a text.

1. *Phonological ambiguity.* No language code is perfect. There are always, for example, certain phonological ambiguities—different words which are pronounced exactly alike. One of the most frequently confused sets of terms in the Greek New Testament are the first and second person plural pronouns, which in Classical Greek were pronounced in quite distinct ways, but by New Testament times these two pronouns were written differently but pronounced exactly the same. In addition to such homophones, there is also a degree of lexical ambiguity. For example, in the New Testament the Greek term *kurios* may refer either to Jesus or to God, and this has given rise to a number of variations in the text.

All languages also contain a certain number of grammatical ambiguities. For example, in John 1:3 the expression "which was made" (or "which came into existence") may go with the preceding clause or with the following clause. The answer to this issue is not to be found in the grammatical structure but in the rhetorical structure.

As already noted, there are different levels of language, so that there is a tendency for scribes to change unusual forms, as in 2 Peter, Jude, and

Revelation, into forms which seem to be more in keeping with standard usage. Note, for example, the way in which different manuscripts attempted to correct the seemingly awkward grammar of Revelation 2:13.

Though all languages are open to change, nevertheless new concepts often result in stretching the language to its limits. This almost inevitably results in expressions which are either ambiguous or obscure, and therefore they are readily subject to what scribes may regard as improvements.

2. *Orthographic ambiguity.* As already noted, any written form of a text is in certain respects highly restricted or truncated. One might even call a written text an impoverished text in comparison with certain features of an oral text, which includes intonational contrasts and differences in pause pitches, quality of voice, and emphasis. For the biblical texts there is also the problem of word division, since ancient scribes normally wrote without spaces between words. In 2 Thessalonians 2:13 early scribes did not know whether *aparkhēn*, "first fruits," should be understood as a single noun or as a prepositional phrase meaning "from the beginning." In 1 Thessalonians 2:7 it would have been difficult for scribes to have always known whether the n-sound belonged to the end of the expression "we became" or whether it should be associated with the following expression, which with the n-sound would mean "children" and without the n-sound would mean "gentle."

Ancient scribes often used abbreviations, particularly for frequently recurring proper names or titles. This practice gives rise to a problem in 1 Timothy 3:16, in which manuscripts read different Greek words meaning "who" or "which" or "God," respectively.

3. *Visual and oral copying.* The manner in which scribes copied manuscripts also explains some of the problems involved in textual variants. If scribes, for example, copied by looking back and forth from an existing manuscript to the one which they were writing, there would be the tendency to skip a line, particularly if the lines began or ended with the same letters or even words. There was also the tendency to duplicate a line or expression, particularly if the resulting phrase or clause made sense.

Very frequent changes in manuscripts occurred because of the practice of having one person read a manuscript aloud while several scribes made separate copies. Since by New Testament times six different vowels or diphthongs in Greek were pronounced exactly alike, a number of words sounded the same even though customarily they were written differently. This explains the problems involved in first and second person plural pronouns (already noted) and also explains numerous instances of itacism, the mistaking of the orthographic form of a word because of similarity in pronunciation.

4. *Inattention.* Words are related to concepts, and in the process of conceptualization there may be lapses in attention, or the reader of a text to be

written down by scribes may also suffer a lapse of attention and either omit or put in words which seem to fit the context.

Certain distortions often arise because of the influence of memory. For example, in Mark 1:2 scribes must have realized that the quoted passage came not simply from Isaiah but from Malachi and Isaiah. Therefore, they almost automatically corrected the text to read "the prophets" rather than "Isaiah." Something similar may very well have taken place in the additions to the Lord's Prayer as recorded in Luke, because the form in Matthew was evidently much better known.

Contextual pressures may also have given rise to substitutions of one word for another. For example, in 1 Corinthians 13:3 the best texts read *kaukhēsōmai*, "that I might boast," in contrast with *kauthēsōmai*, "that I might be burned." The experience of early Christian martyrs may very well have suggested such a change.

In order to appreciate the nature of textual variants, it is important to note something about the direction of change. There are, of course, some errors which appear to be completely random and almost inexplicable. These, however, are relatively few in number. In the case of most variants one can readily detect that there is primarily a leveling principle in which there is a tendency to adjust the form of a text to the immediate context, to other parallel texts, to general usage, and to background knowledge. This is precisely what is found to be the case in all manuscript traditions. In this respect such changes reflect the application of entropy in the so-called second law of thermodynamics. For example, a cup of hot water left in a room of normal temperature will utlimately come to have the same temperature as the room. Similarly in the case of a text, that which is uniquely significant about a text tends to be leveled out so as to fit more readily the context, whether verbal or behavioral.

Adaptation to the immediate context is well illustrated by a textual problem in 1 Corinthians 7:14, in which the better or early texts read *adelphō*, "fellow believer," while other texts have *andri*, "husband." In a context which speaks of a husband and wife, it seemed much better to introduce "husband" in the second part of the verse rather than the unusual expression meaning "fellow believer."

As already noted, adjustment to other texts which are parallel either in form or content occurs frequently as a type of harmonization. In Titus 1:4 there is perhaps a more subtle harmonization in that some manuscripts employ the usual Pauline expression "grace, mercy, and peace," while certain manuscripts have the more unusual expression, "grace and peace."

Certain adjustments in the form of a text are made in terms of general usage. For example, in John 1:18 one can readily understand why the expression *monogenēs theos*, "unique God," would be changed to *monogenēs huios,* "only son." One could also readily understand why in 1 Corinthians 7:15 *humas,* "you," would be changed to *hēmas,* "we" (the two expressions would be pronounced the same), since the final clause of 1 Corinthians 7:15 seems so generic in that God calls believers to live in peace. Compare also 1 John 5:18, 2 Thessalonians 2:3, and 1 Thessalonians 5:28.

The adjustment to general background knowledge is evident in 1 Corinthians 10:9, in which certain texts have changed "let us not tempt Christ" to "let us not tempt the Lord." The latter seems far more in keeping with the reference to the revolt against Moses at the time of the giving of the Law. The introduction of additional background information is typified by the explanation about an angel disturbing the water in the pool of Bethzatha in John 5:4–5.

It is not always possible to determine which particular factor or factors are primary in certain scribal alterations of the text, nor can one always determine whether such changes were intentional or unintentional. What is important is to determine the relative probability of certain readings being as close as possible to the original autographs. There are certain significant differences in the amount and types of evidence available for textual problems of the Old Testament and the New Testament. For the Old Testament there are relatively few differences in Hebrew manuscripts, since at an early date Jewish scribes made every effort to arrive at a so-called "common text," but variants do show up in early ancient translations, especially in the Greek texts of the Septuagint and Aquila and in early Syriac and Latin versions. For the New Testament, however, one encounters a so-called mixed text, even in the earliest manuscripts. Evidently there was no overwhelming concern for the validation of the early textual evidence, since believers must have been convinced of the quick return of Christ.

In order to assist translators materially in problems of the New Testament and Old Testament texts, the United Bible Societies have sponsored two important projects. The first consisted of an interconfessional and international committee of New Testament text scholars who prepared the text of The Greek New Testament and of the Nestle-Aland twenty-sixth edition. The texts of these two editions are essentially the same, although the apparatuses are different in view of the different purposes of the marginal information. For The Greek New Testament the committee selected only those passages in which there are significant differences of meaning, and in each instance further data is supplied. For the Nestle-Aland text the apparatus contains all types of variants in order to provide more information on the history of textual development.

In The Greek New Testament text the variants are rated A, B, C, D to assist translators in evaluating the significance of the textual variants. A rating of "A" indicates that the text is quite certain; "B" indicates that there is some doubt as to the validity of the reading assigned to the text. "C" indicates a considerable measure of doubt, and "D" indicates a high degree of doubt. A fourth edition of The Greek New Testament text is now in preparation in which there will be certain differences in the selection of apparatus items, further data, and the correction of data based on the examination of manuscripts rather than dependence upon edited texts. And finally, there will be a measure of upgrading in the rating of readings occurring in the text.

For the Hebrew Old Testament, likewise, an international and interconfessional committee of Old Testament text scholars studied some five thousand textual variants of the Old Testament and prepared a series of five preliminary volumes which indicate degrees of probability, likewise based on a scale of A, B, C, and D. A series of five volumes representing the full report of the committee are in process of publication in French and in English.

Translators working with the United Bible Societies are not obliged to follow in every instance the text adopted by the respective committees. But if translators depart from A or B type readings for the text, they must be certain that they do so for good and sufficient reasons.

It is obviously essential that in any translation of the Scriptures adequate attention should be given in marginal helps to the problems of textual variations. To fail to recognize manuscript differences inevitably falsifies the textual base for any translation. Some persons object to such notes on the basis that they may suggest doubt about the reliability of the Bible itself, but one who fails to recognize some of the basic textual problems will ultimately destroy reader's confidence in the integrity of the translation process.

Translators

In a sense, translators are born and not made, though it is equally true that skills can be improved with training and practice. If, however, a translator is to be qualified to do a first-rate piece of work, there are certain fundamental characteristics which he or she must possess. Perhaps one of the most important of these is verbal facility, or, the capacity of a person to express ideas accurately, clearly, and with seeming ease. A translator must have the intelligence which comes from mental alertness, the capacity to catch on rapidly, and a retentive memory. There must also be a creative capacity for verbal expression. This is especially important in the translation of poetry, and any experience which such a person has had in creative writing will certainly pay rich dividends.

Knowledge of the subject matter, both general and specific, is also a basic requirement. No matter how skilled a translator may be, if he is not aware of the implications of the subject matter, he is certainly going to make serious mistakes.

Verbal facility, intelligence, creativity of expression, and knowledge, however, are not adequate if one does not possess intellectual honesty and integrity. Unless a translator is willing to let an author speak for himself, the results are inevitably going to be skewed. A translator who feels that one must embellish or jazz up a text will certainly distort the true implications of divine inspiration.

If a translator is not able to work with others in welcoming and accepting criticisms, his participation in any translation program will be a disaster. On one occasion a member of a translations committee was so adamant about his superior knowledge of Hebrew that he insisted that when the committee did not follow his advice, he would have a heart attack. Fortunately, this person became so discouraged with his role in the committee that he resigned after a few days.

One thing is certain: the choice of a translator to undertake any task of translating must be based upon the individual's personal capacity and not upon political or social connections. The translating of the Holy Scriptures is too important and serious a task to be made a political football for competing constituencies.

4

Translating Means Translating Meaning

Before undertaking the study of rhetorical, grammatical, and lexical meaning, it is essential to understand some of the underlying principles in the structure of codes. The study of codes considers why languages seem to be structured the way they are, how verbal signs are related to thought processes, and the isomorphic relationships between utterances and the referents of which the utterances are signs.

Basic Principles in the Function of Verbal Signs

Everything in the world is different and also in the process of change—a principle enunciated by the famous Greek philosopher Heraclitus, who declared *panta rhei*, literally "everything flows." There are no two stones alike, no two flowers the same, and no two people who are identical. Even so-called "identical twins" are not completely identical. Although the structures of the DNA in the nucleus of their cells may be the same, such persons nevertheless differ as the result of certain developmental factors. No two sounds are ever exactly alike, and even the same person pronouncing the same word will never utter it in an absolutely identical manner.

Ours is a universe of infinite variety of objects, events, and features of objects and events. Our senses are able to distinguish almost an infinite variety of objects and features of objects. For example, the human eyes can distinguish some fourteen million different shades and hues of color. But it would be hopeless for us to insist on a vocabulary of fourteen million words in order to identify all color contrasts. We could not manage a world in which separate names would be required for the infinite variety of objects, events, qualities, and quantities with which we must constantly deal in interpersonal relations. Accordingly, it is essential to classify and to categorize, so we can talk about classes of objects, types of events, various kinds of features, and diverse relations.

This process of categorizing and attaching names to various kinds of phenomena means that there is inevitably a degree of artificiality and arbitrariness about the way in which we segment or divide different sets of phenomena. The arbitrary character of such classifications, as marked by our terminologies, is abundantly evident when we examine the ways in which different languages have segmented reality. For example, many European languages use anywhere from a dozen to fifteen basic color words, ranging from violet to red. But in some African languages there are only three basic color words, namely, "black," "white," and "red." This does not mean, however, that one cannot describe other colors in these African languages. One can always liken a color to the color of some flower, butterfly, leaf, or well-known mineral pigment. In the Lamba language of Zambia, there is only one genuine term for color, namely, the verb *kasika*, "to be red." In order to indicate blackness, one has to use the verb *fita*, meaning "to be dark," whereas for whiteness a verb *tuwa*, "to be light," is employed. The color green can be expressed through a comparison with the color of malachite. The dark blue color can be designated by a phrase "dark like the sky," and light blue may be rendered as "light like the sky." The color of yellow is indicated by a reference to a baby's excreta. The term for gray is *uwulelu*, "marsh water," whereas the colors of different wild animals serve to indicate brown and tawny.

In spite of these many possibilities in a language like Lamba, Hebrew color terms may present some real problems. Hebrew distinguishes, for example, *shasher*, "red" (Jer. 22:14); *shani*, "scarlet" (Exod. 25:4); *'argaman*, "purple" (Exod. 26:11); and *'adom*, "reddish brown" or "crimson" (Num. 19:2). Where there is some emphasis on the distinctive features of color, translators may have to use a basic word for "red" and modify it with terms for "light" and "dark," respectively, to render the Hebrew words *shani* and *'adom*. To translate *'argaman*, some kind of intensifier can be used. In other instances some association with the word for "blood" may have to be made (Doke, 1958, 62).

In treating problems of category there is a tendency for people to look for so-called "perfect types." Accordingly, variations from such perfect types are regarded as departures from the norm. One must recognize, however, that such "normal forms" are really only statistical or conceptual abstractions. Even in language there is no ultimate norm of usage, and there are no completely ideal speakers or hearers. In life we are all awash in a sea of lesser or greater indeterminacy. Nothing in language usage is ever hard and fast, fixed for all time, but it is this very indeterminacy which allows for creativity. Without indeterminacy there would be no poetry.

If the concept of norms does not prove satisfactory, people tend to look for neat distinctions in classes. They wish to be able to pigeonhole objects, events, and features into various categories. They struggle hard to discover the "necessary and sufficient features" of which Aristotle spoke. But life is made up of fuzzy sets of continuums that are not easily subdivided. One only needs to compare certain Hebrew and Greek terms used in speaking about various aspects of human personality to see how difficult it is to distinguish readily between areas of meaning or to relate certain Hebrew terms to specific Greek terms. Compare, for example, the Hebrew terms *nephesh*, "soul, life, person;" *ruah*, "spirit;" *leb*, "heart, mind;" *shem*, "name;" and *basar*, "flesh, body," and the Greek series *pneuma*, "spirit;" *nous*, "mind, thought;" *kardia*, "heart, mind;" *sōma*, "body, person;" *onoma*, "name;" *psukhē*, "soul, spirit, life;" and *sarks*, "flesh, human nature."

In present-day scientific studies (and particularly in biology), scholars have given up looking for neatly defined species and subspecies. It seems much more realistic to talk about "family resemblances," "gene pools," and "transitional phenomena." Frequently the variation within a species appears to be far greater than differences between species. Who is likely to assume without special training that rose bushes, apple trees, and strawberry plants belong to the same family of plants? In the same way that there are different degrees of gene compatibility, there are also differing degrees of acceptability in sentence structure.

Another mistake which many persons make is to assume that if there are words, there must be certain corresponding realities. Since the Bible speaks of "body, soul, and spirit," many people assume that there must be three quite distinct parts of human personality. Other persons assume that there are only two, namely, the physical and the spiritual, and therefore a conflict arises between the trichotomists and the dichotomists. In some languages there are still additional terms used in speaking about human personality, so that there are expressions not only for "body," "soul," and "spirit" but also for "name" and "shadow." When pressed to explain the differences between these five aspects or "parts of a person," an African responded, "These are not five parts of me, but only five different ways of talking about me." This observation is in many respects far closer to conceptual reality than many attempts of systematic theologians to explain the meanings of different terms relating to human personality.

An additional mistake is made by many persons in trying to classify concepts on the basis of different grammatical parts of speech. They assume that if a word is a noun, then it obviously must refer to a thing, but a word such as English *name* is only a sign of a language event which is characteristically associated with a particular person. The term *demon* is essentially a conceptual deduction from a series of events, and a *mermaid* is a conceptual deduction from pure fantasy and imagination. Verbs are supposed to mark events, but in many instances they may mark only features of events. For example, the verbs *begin, stop,* and *continue* only signal aspects of other events, as in the phrases *begin to speak, stop working,* and *continue reading.* Though the verbs *begin, stop* and *continue* are the so-called principal verbs of the grammatical construction, they are semantically only qualifiers of the events which follow.

Despite the fact that life has so many complex sets of relations between objects, events, and abstracts, and the fact that these are classified in so many different ways, many persons still insist upon single answers to the issues of multiple classifications. They feel that in some way or another a single theory will or should explain everything. Such a holistic approach almost inevitably leads to dogmatism. It may seem awkward to have to live with multiple hypotheses, but if one is to deal with the issues of inter-lingual communication in a realistic way, one has to recognize that answers are not always in black and white but in varying shades of gray. In other words, they are based upon probabilities and not upon verbal certainties.

The entire process of naming (that is, associating verbal signs with objects, events, abstracts, and relations) reflects largely the human cognitive motivation to look for and recognize similarities and contrasts. Objects or entities are generally classified (or segmented) in terms of their features, arrangements, and roles, while events are often classified on the basis of types of movement, sense perception by which events are noted, and the relationship of certain events to others, especially in terms of cause and effect. Abstracts fall into various classes determined by such features as shape, size, number, and quantity, as well as their relationship to objects and events. This categorization simply allows the recognition that language signs make sense of the external world around us and the internal world of our thoughts and sense perceptions. Perhaps this may seem to have little to do with Bible translating, but as will be demonstrated increasingly in various chapters of this volume, these are the crucial factors which help to explain some of the otherwise overlooked aspects of communication.

Isomorphs

Isomorphs, as features of similarity and contrast, are fundamental to the study of verbal communication, and they may be described as consisting of two basic types: those which are information-preserving and those which are information-altering (Hofstadter, 1980).

An isomorphic set that preserves information involves the possibility of mapping two complex structures, one on the other, despite certain formal differences. This is possible since each part of one structure corresponds in some way to a related part of another structure. For example, the Roman numerical series I, II, III, is isomorphic with the Greek series α, β, γ, as well as the English series 1, 2, 3. The forms employed for the first three numbers of the three distinct codes are formally different, but they are functionally equivalent, for they occupy the same relative positions within the respective codes. One may also say that the series 2, 4, 8 is isomorphic with the series 16, 32, 64, even though there is no form in common; the relationship of doubling from one number to another involves a functionally isomorphic relation.

Sets of formal shapes may also be regarded as isomorphic, as in the illustration below.

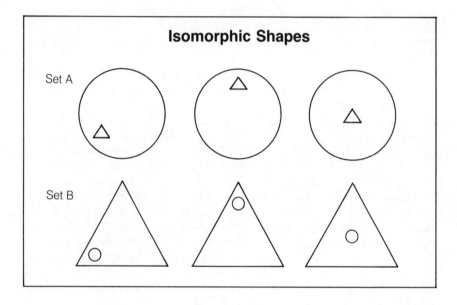

Set A may be said to be isomorphic with Set B in that the relative positions of the circles and triangles correspond, and a very simple rule can be employed to derive Set B from Set A.

In a discourse, corresponding parallel and chiastic sets can also be regarded as isomorphic if an accompanying rule can state the relationship between the parallelism of A B C / A B C and the chiasm A B C / C B A.

Isomorphic sets that are completely repetitious, and hence completely tautological, are structurally uninteresting. In language it is important that there be certain formal differences, which at the same time preserve certain functional similarities.

Outside of the area of language, there are numerous isomorphic sets. For example, the relationship between a segment of the DNA of a living cell and the RNA (a type of template of the original) is isomorphic. Similarly, in electronic recording there is an information-preserving process of isomorphs between the voice mechanism, the patterns of the resulting air waves, the vibrations of a receiver, the electrical impulses recorded on a tape, and finally the reversal of this process until an individual ultimately hears a recording. The physical forms of air waves, electrical impulses, magnetic recording, etc. involve isomorphic patterning. The particular forms differ appreciably, but the functional relationship is such that the process is largely information preserving, except for such disturbances as may be caused by certain inadequacies of the recording mechanism or by noise.

The record is the information bearer and the player is the revealer. One must not expect the information bearer to be perfect, nor should one try to pull out of a record more information than is actually there. This applies specifically to the problem of biblical exegesis versus biblical eisegesis, by which latter process people attempt to read into a text more than is actually there.

A verbal written text is essentially a record of the meaning indicated by a series of signs, but the text is never a perfect transcript. It is always devoid of certain features of intonation, voice quality, and as already noted, lacks very important elements of paralinguistic and extralinguistic features. Decoding devices (principles of exegesis) should attempt to obtain from the text all the meaning that resides in it, but it is certainly dangerous to attempt to introduce more into a text than it contains.

In the case of the biblical texts, some of the isomorphisms which would be recognized by the original audience may no longer be recognized by a present-day audience. The fact that Jesus normally sat down to teach is usually not understood by the average present-day reader as being symbolic of his adopting the role of a rabbi. In Jesus' day rabbis customarily sat down to expound religious doctrines, and hence this behavior on the part of Jesus would be immediately understood as symbolizing his role as a bona-fide religious teacher.

Ignorance as to the original isomorphic potential of a message can be supplemented by footnotes, but there is no excuse for qualifying the Law in John 1:17 by adding "rigid demands and merciless justice," as is done in the Living Bible. Such a characterization of the Law is nowhere to be found in the Old Testament or in the New Testament, and certainly not in the text of the Gospel of John.

Information-altering isomorphic series are not functionally equivalent, for they involve certain significant dissimilarities. For example, there are similarities between parents and children, and one may speak of certain isomorphic relations, but certainly not of identity, for in the process of conception there is a redistribution of genes. In grammar one may encounter an isomorphic relationship on one level but not on another level of analysis. For example, the two sentences *John hit Bill* and *John heard Bill* are isomorphic on one level of syntax—the level of noun-verb-noun structure and the subject-predicate structure—but the functional relationship of agent and experiencer is reversed. In the statement *John hit Bill*, *Bill* is the experiencer of the hitting and *John* is the agent, but in *John heard Bill*, *Bill* is the agent in producing the noise and *John* is the experiencer of such a noise.

Similarly, different-sized units in grammar may be isomorphic on one level but not on another. Compare, for example, the two subject-predicate constructions: *the man died* and *the old man living next door died yesterday in his sleep.* Both consist of subject-predicate constructions, and both may relate to the same event. But one carries far more information than the other.

Certain isomorphic relations on the level of rhetorical figures may be formally quite distinct and yet be functionally very similar. In English one may very well say *do not lead a bad person into temptation*, but in Tsonga (a language of South Africa) a functional equivalent would be "don't throw a mouse into a granary of monkey nuts." In the Ndonga language there is an interesting functional equivalent of the famous refrain of the book of Judges, "Everyone did what was right in his own eyes" (Judg. 21:25) in the proverb, "Everyone was a lone-grazing goat."

Parallel and dependent literary developments may also be regarded as isomorphic in certain respects. For example, the expression "our father who is in heaven," occurring in the Lord's Prayer, was also used in its Hebrew form in the Palestinian synagogue in the second half of the first century A.D. This may be regarded as one of the isomorphisms between the early church and the synagogue. No doubt the original audiences, in contrast with today's receptors, were aware of this similarity. In fact, for the Lord's Prayer there are a number of significant similarities in the ancient prayer of the synagogue known as the Kaddisch, "May his great name be magnified and sanctified in the world which he has created according to his will. And may he cause his sovereignty to reign . . . in your life and in your days." (Dalman, 1898), and in the talmudic prayer in *Berakoth* 60b, "And bring me not into the hands of sin, nor into the hands of iniquity, nor into the hands of temptation." (Taylor, 1970). There are, however, a number of problems involved in dating the sources, and this makes it difficult to draw conclusions as to the original audience.

People often assume certain isomorphic relations when none actually exist. Imitative magic is filled with such mistaken interpretations. For example, some people in Cuba believe that by bathing a sick person in water and then throwing the water into the street, the sick person's disease will be carried away by the next person who walks along. Statements about the sun rising and setting reflect a misunderstood isomorphic relation. The traditional view of the earth as the center of the universe is a misconception about relationships. Perhaps the most serious misinterpretation of presumed isomorphic relations is the extent to which people equate suffering or happiness with having done evil or good, as is so well illustrated in the book of Job. If people are prosperous, they must have been righteous, and if successful, they must be the special object of divine blessing.

Distinct cultural presuppositions about causality and reality often lead to serious misunderstanding. For example, in many parts of Africa almost all accidents and disease are regarded as having a double cause. If a tree falls and kills a person, the immediate cause is the falling of the tree, but there must also be a secondary cause which somehow made the person be in a particular place so that the tree would fall on him. This second cause is often interpreted as sorcery or black magic.

In many instances the presumed isomorphic basis for relations of cause and effect has been lost. Hence the behavior seems not only inexplicable to foreigners but even somewhat mystifying to persons who participate in the culture in question. Note, for example, such beliefs as: breaking a mirror brings seven years of bad luck, carrying a rabbit's foot increases one's luck in gambling, and, by throwing small coins into a pool of water, one may somehow realize a wish.

Increasing isomorphic awareness is one of the important ingredients in education. A child may speak of any plant with pretty petals as being a flower. Only later does he or she learn to distinguish between roses, lilies, daisies, etc. Possibly only at a much later stage does one begin to distinguish between various kinds of roses with names such as Peace, Paradise, Double Delight, and Mr. Lincoln. This is a process of recognizing diversities within classes of similarities, in other words, distinctiveness within isomorphic classes.

The process of recognizing similarities is a somewhat more subtle procedure. Some children, for example, never speak of grass as a flower, for it has no petals, even though it has all the other essential features, but students of botany soon learn that grasses are flowering plants. Similarly, most people do not associate porpoises with whales. They are much more likely to think of them as somehow related to seals or sea lions. Only as one learns to distinguish the relevance of isomorphic features does one begin to recognize the distinction between basic structures and superficial ones. In fact, scientific development may very well be described in terms of the recognition of valid functional isomorphisms; for example, Mendelian genetics and the chemical tables.

In trying to interpret the meaning of some otherwise obscure expression, a person almost inevitably looks for certain isomorphic relations. A headline in *The New York Times* of November 28, 1982, read, "Price fixers get creamed." Such a statement carries little meaning until one realizes that this is a statement about dairy suppliers being fined for price fixing. This, then, makes sense of the idiom "to get creamed,"—"to experience a significant loss."

Translating involves a constant process of discovering valid functional isomorphs between languages on all levels, in other words, signs and series of signs which will be functionally isomorphic. One must always be on the lookout for so-called "equivalent" words, grammatical structures, and rhetorical features, but in moving from one language to another the equivalences are essentially functional rather than formal. This is precisely why the concept of isomorphic relations becomes so important, since the significance of isomorphs is not their formal resemblance but their functional equivalence.

Once an isomorphic pattern has been found, the next task is to determine its meaning—the function which it performs in the sense of signaling to a receptor certain referents, whether objective or subjective. Note, for example, the double parallelism in Psalm 108:3–4 (Revised Standard Version):

> I will give thanks to thee, O LORD, among the peoples,
>   I will sing praises to thee among the nations.
> For thy steadfast love is great above the heavens,
>   thy faithfulness reaches to the clouds.

The fact of poetic phraseology and format immediately signals to the average reader that there is something special and elevated or elegant about such a patterning. The thematic parallelism in the two verses certainly signals the importance of the themes, and the repetitions of the doublets *peoples/nations, heavens/clouds, give thanks/sing praises,* and *steadfast love/faithfulness* signal an aspect of totality or inclusiveness.

Though receptors differ somewhat as to the designative meanings of such rhetorical structures, they may differ even more radically as to their associative meanings. Anyone familiar with and appreciative of the liturgical value of parallelism will certainly react favorably to this type of structure, but a person who has no such experience, or who may be emotionally allergic to such traditional poetic forms, may react very negatively to this type of parallelism. In fact, Ronald Knox so disapproved of Hebrew parallelism in the Psalms that he attempted in his own translation to eliminate such structures.

Meaning and Mind

As already noted in the previous section, there are a number of isomorphic relations in the patterns produced by series that preserve information in the process of recording speech. It is useful, however, to note in more detail the series of isomorphic patterns in the reception of a recorded message. A loudspeaker, for example, produces a number of air waves which then strike the ear drum of a person, setting up an isomorphic set of vibrations of a diaphragm. This is then extended through the bones of the ear to the liquid of the inner ear, and these vibrations are then picked up by the cilia and transmitted by electro-chemical impulses to the brain itself by means of the auditory nerves. Up to this point, the isomorphic patterning is information-preserving. The interpretive process, however, involves memory, various routines, and ultimate synthesis, which includes the matching of diverse kinds of information. The final concepts which are derived from the physical events of verbal communication are never exactly the same as the concepts of a source.

The brain may be regarded in certain respects as similar to the hardware of a computer, while the mind corresponds to the software program. The differences of background information stored in the memory, the diverse routines through which the interpretive process proceeds, and the distinctive cultural and personal grids all contribute to the altering of information.

The brain itself can be congenitally flawed, damaged by an accident, or debilitated by drugs, but it is essentially a logically organized structure with more or less ten billion neurons, each with some two hundred thousand entry ports and numerous exits. It can interpret information with amazing speed, since each neuron can fire more than a thousand times a second. In addition, there are some one hundred billion glial supporting cells.

Though memory apparently is coded in various places in the brain, it seems to be triggered primarily in one place. But each brain is in a sense somewhat different, even as the fingerprints on the hand are different.

In contrast with the brain, the mind, which consists of memory and program, is not necessarily rational. The rules for mental operations seem to be mixed with the signs, and they are sorted largely by context, so that a person quickly realizes, for example, that *can* has quite different meanings in the expressions *I can, the can, can him, can it!*, and *can the peaches*. Impulses come into the mind on what may be regarded as the lower level, but they are put together on a considerably higher level. The statement in Genesis 49:11 about Judah "washing his garments in wine" must certainly not be understood on the lower level of literalness but on a higher, metaphorical level of being exceptionally prosperous and therefore able to engage in "conspicuous consumption." The story of the Good Samaritan (Luke 10:30–35) is on its literal, lower level a brief drama with three episodes, but on a higher level it is immediately recognized as an effective account of the callous insensitivity of established religion.

Similarly, the story of Jacob and Laban (Genesis 29–31) comes in on the lower level as a clever story in the setting of a herding culture, but on the higher level it is soon identified as an effective account of family deceit. In the very first sentence of the sixth scene (Gen. 29:15), Laban sets a trap in which he is to catch Jacob, the fox, for some twenty years (Fokkelman, 1975, 126), a typical story of "the deceiver deceived."

Since there are no strict isomorphisms on the higher levels of mental operation, one can well understand the reason for quite different interpretations of verbal signs: these signs must pass through so many neural grids, both personal and cultural. As persons we tend to interpret expressions on the basis of inbuilt attitudes of aggression/passivity, hostility/friendliness, optimism/pessimism, and paranoid/open. Some persons, for example, almost always interpret what is said in the best possible light, while others seem confirmed in their tendency to always look for hidden motives and thus to suspect the intentions behind what is said.

In interlingual communication the inculcated cultural grids are even more important than the personal grids. For example, in some societies there is a concept of "the limited good," the idea that there are strict limitations as to success, acquisition of wealth, and the potentiality to control others. In many cultures there is the constant and overwhelming fear of "spirit" power, while in other societies it is the unpredictability of fate or chance, or even the inevitability of a deterministic universe.

The concept of limited good is an important factor in understanding what may seem to be completely irrational behavior, at least in terms of the typical attitude in the Western world. For example, in order to better himself financially, a Shilluk young man put out an orchard of mango trees, which he carefully cultivated for some five years to the point where they were just beginning to bear fruit. But some close members of his family proceeded one night to chop down all of his trees, since they believed so implicitly in the concept of limited good and that anyone who rose too high above the rest of the group had inevitably done so at the expense of others.

A young scholar from one of the countries in Southeast Asia went abroad for further study and distinguished himself to the point of obtaining a doctorate. But his return to his own country was thwarted by persons who simply could not afford to have anyone rise too high above them. This was also the experience of Jesus, who was rejected by the people of his own town; they simply could not understand how a carpenter's son could have become such an influential teacher and miracle worker.

The mind is constantly in the process of change as the result of new information, new paradigms for intellectual activity, and new value systems. But for effective communication there must be some measure of partial isomorphism between communicating individuals or communities. In other words, people must be speaking, at least to some extent, on "the same wave length." In part, what makes communication possible are such features as (1) the similarity of the neurophysiological reactions in smiling, laughing, frowning, and grimacing, whether in pain or in anger (typical extralinguistic features), (2) the fact that all peoples have sufficient imagination as to be able to comprehend another system and to be able even to lie (if it were not for imagination and thus the potentiality for lying, there would be neither possibility of forming hypotheses nor scientific progress), (3) the universality of semantic classes of objects, events and related states, abstracts, and relationals, (4) model perception, so that people may speak of events as being possible, probable, and certain, as well as impossible, improbable, and uncertain, (5) beliefs which have no evident perceptual basis, as in the case of spirits, demons, God, and quarks, and (6) even the ability to hold what many regard as contradictory views, for example, predestination and moral accountability, evolution of physical matter but not of biological species, and atheism and Christian ethics.

The Automatic Nature of Verbal Processing

One of the reasons why it is so difficult to analyze the function of language and the processes of translating is that so much of the processing of language signs by the mind is automatic, that is, much of this processing is "buried in the brain." This results in remarkable efficiency. One can speak without thinking of all of the processes which are involved in selecting words, putting them into grammatical structures, and finally pronouncing the right sounds. It is also true that the automatic processing of the brain and mind can lead to false ideas about meaning and quite incorrect concepts about how language operates.

Much of the phonological structure of any language operates without conscious awareness on the part of a speaker. English speakers, for example, are usually quite unaware of the fact that voiceless initial stops normally occur with an aspiration, while the corresponding series that are voiced have no aspiration and are often unvoiced, though lenis (soft) in articulation. On the other hand, voiceless stops preceded by an s approximate very closely the phonetic features of initial voiced stops. Compare, for example, the following series:

till	dill	still
pill	bill	spill
kill	gill	skill

It is also true that most English speakers are unaware of the fact that in the case of final voiceless and voiced stops, what is really distinctive is not so much the voiceless or voiced features but the length of the preceding vowel. Compare, for example, the set *rip/rib, bat/bad,* and *lock/log.* In many pronunciations of these series, the final so-called voiced and voiceless stops are phonetically very similar, if not identical, but the preceding vowels differ significantly in length.

On the semantic level of language there are likewise numerous differences of meaning which are normally unrecognized. For example, in the statement of John 1:1, "In the beginning was the Word, and the Word was with God, and the Word was God," the Greek verb for "to be" has three quite distinct meanings. In the first clause it means "to exist," but in the second clause it means "to be in a place," for the Greek verb, together with the following preposition and the accusative, has to be considered as a Semitism answering the question "where?" (Bultmann, 1953, 16). In the third clause, however, the Greek verb marks membership in a particular class, and in this instance, a class consisting of only one member, namely, God.

People may speak a language with complete accuracy and still be unable to define differences of meaning. For example, English speakers have no difficulty in using the words *run* and *walk* in describing actions which they see, but most people are unable to define the diagnostic or distinctive differences in the referents; namely, the fact that in the case of *run* there is an instant in which neither foot is on the supporting surface, while in the case of *walk* there is always one foot in touch with the surface.

The differences in the use of the word *of* as a marker of relations are something which many speakers simply take for granted. They seldom realize how many different relations are marked by *of.* Compare, for example, the following phrases: *day of graduation* (time of an event), *man of character* (quality of an entity), *the country of Mexico* (identity), *house of brick* (substance of an object), *leg of a table* (part of a whole), *management of the office* (action and affected entity), and *the statutes of the king* (verbal formulations by an agent).

It is scarcely any wonder, therefore, that people have considerable difficulty in understanding a number of biblical phrases containing the marker *of.* Note, for example, the following expressions in Ephesians 1:3–14: *the foundation of the world, the purpose of his will, the praise of his glorious grace, the forgiveness of our trespasses, the riches of his grace, the mystery of his will, the fullness of time, the purpose of him, the counsel of his will, the praise of his glory, the gospel of your salvation,* and *the glory of our inheritance.*

In order to discover the meaning of expressions which one has not heard before, it is almost always necessary to set up certain hypotheses based on possible isomorphic relations, a matter already briefly noted above. If one already knows that a certain person is very studious, it does not take much imagination to realize that the foreign-language expression "he is a book swallower" applied to this person is equivalent to saying in English "he is a bookworm." But a statement such as "Can a man's mind be washed without bleaching his soul?" takes a much more elaborate set of isomorphic hypotheses. In the same way it may be rather easy to see how the South-Toradja expression "to fathom the river of marriage" can mean "to commit adultery," but far more isomorphic hypotheses are necessary to understand how the Conob expression "entering something into one's stomach" is the functional equivalent of "to believe."

Unusual behavior in a different culture likewise means attempting to find meaning by means of possible isomorphic relations. How is it, for example, that a Guatemalan Indian may object to explanations of religion, since this would rob religion of its true character? How is it that the Fon of Gabon who participate in fertility cults do not normally discuss their meaning; only the old men seem to be interested in the meaning? Or why is it that in so many parts of the world it is dangerous to praise a child, since this may cause an evil spirit to pay too much attention to the child? Rather, it is often safer to give a child a bad name so as to discourage attacks by jealous demons.

A Sociosemiotic Approach to Meaning

As already suggested at certain points in preceding sections, a sociosemiotic approach to meaning seems particularly useful in Bible translating in view of the following: (1) semiotics is the most all-embracing system for the analysis of signs, (2) a sociosemiotic approach to the meaning of verbal signs always involves the total communication of an event within the social context; in other words, a text cannot be isolated from its context, despite the fact that some persons have tried to insist that texts have "an independent existence." In such a sociosemiotic approach to meaning there are very close relationships to sociolinguistics (Hymes, 1974). (3) A sociosemiotic view of signs involves the interpretation of signs in terms of the structure of which the signs themselves are a part. In other words, any individual verbal sign can only be interpreted by means of other related signs.

Considering verbal signs together with other signs in a broad structural framework has significant value for a Bible translator, since in translating one must deal not only with the meaning of words and sentences but also with the meaning of events. For example, in the account of Jacob and Laban in Genesis 31:51–54, eating together was not simply a matter of satisfying hunger. Eating was a symbolic event to solemnly establish the validity of the covenant which had just been made. It was a sacrificial meal which Jacob had to prepare since he was the one to make the solemn promise. Not only Laban and his people were invited, but even God who sanctioned the covenant was regarded as taking part in the meal as an invisible guest (Westermann, 1981, 610; von Rad, 1968, 318). In addition, the symbol of "eating bread" serves to reflect the promise that God had given Jacob when Jacob was a lonely refugee (Gen. 28:20).

In many parts of the world eating together constitutes a similar kind of symbolism. In some universities in West Africa it is difficult to get students from different clans or tribes to eat together, since the process of eating together would seem to annul traditional enmities.

From a sociosemiotic perspective there are always three elements in any meaningful relationship: the sign, the referent, and the interpretant. The interpretant is essentially the means by which the relationship of the sign to the referent is established through the system of signs which segments and symbolizes reality in a particular way. For example, the meaning of *run* cannot be understood apart from a set of semantically related signs such as *walk, jump, hop, skip,* and *crawl.* Similarly, a gesture in any language-culture can only be understood in terms of a set of related gestures.

In the Western world, one way of pointing is to employ the index finger of the right hand, but in some parts of Zaire this is regarded as an erotic symbol; any polite, cultured person will point with the lower lip. When the tax collector in Luke 18:13 "beats his breast," this gesture expresses sorrow and contrition. However, the Batswana people of South Africa also beat the breast, but only to express self-assurance and aggressiveness. The equivalent gesture (and therefore the functional equivalent) in their culture is "to take hold of the beard," but in some other languages of Africa, one may say "to club one's head."

Signs always occur in clusters of related signs. Hence any one sign must be interpreted by means of other signs which cluster together in segmenting experience.

This interpretive process of identifying the significance of a sign by means of other signs involves essentially a kind of infinite progression, or regression, depending upon one's point of view. It is impossible to know the meaning of any one sign without discovering the meaning of other signs which help to define the sign in question. Accordingly, in order to know the meaning of any one word, one must look to other words in the same semantic domain in order to understand the particular area of meaning covered by that one word. To determine the meaning of any one word one must also determine the meanings of related words, which must in turn be defined in terms of still other words. Thus defining meaning is theoretically endless, although from a practical standpoint there is a point of diminishing returns. There can be no ultimate definitions and no absolute verbal formulations. This should come as a relief to theologians, even though it may appear to be a disappointment to some. The fact that the definition of any sign depends on other signs is also the reason why no translation can ever be absolute or definitive.

The interpretation of signs, particularly those of an elaborate nature, may be done on three different levels, perhaps best termed immediate, analytical, and synthetic. The immediate reaction to an African proverb such as "they built a bridge over the stream after the chief's son fell into the water" is to regard it as a very clever saying. The meaning is evident, and it even sounds somewhat like the English idiom, "They locked the barn door after the horse was stolen."

A more analytical approach to this proverb would mean a close analysis in terms of the genre requirements for this type of proverb. The fact that there is a reason/result relationship, but that the result is stated before the reason, certainly adds poignancy to the comment, for it is the last clause which bears the impact of the social situation.

The synthetic level of interpretation of this proverb involves seeing by means of the proverb the implications of the social structure of many African societies. This can lead to even broader implications, for there are parallels in many societies, namely, the fact that activity takes place only when there is some threat of danger or loss to those in power.

This same type of interpretation on three levels can be applied to a story such as the Prodigal Son. In first reading the story of the Prodigal Son, one is immediately impressed with the return of the prodigal and the continued hostility of the older brother. But an analytical approach to the story reveals amazingly subtle features. In fact, this story has sometimes been acclaimed as the best short, short story ever written. Nothing essential to this story is left out, and everything that is important is expressed with unusual subtlety and poignancy.

On the synthetic level of analysis, this story has many important theological implications. In a most effective fashion, Jesus' teaching about repentance, forgiveness, acceptance, and the hostility of self-righteous legalism becomes evident. Clearly there is more than one crucial element in the story (Fiebig, 1912, 27). Some scholars have regarded this parable as a type of "gospel within the gospel." As early as Tertullian (second century A.D.) a symbolic interpretation of the parable was suggested in which the younger son was regarded as representing the Gentiles and the elder son as representing the Jews.

The interpretive process can only be done by interpreters, so that any logical operation of interpretation must reckon with the fact that persons with different presuppositions often come to quite different conclusions. Some tribesmen in the northern Philippines have reinterpreted the story of the Prodigal Son as being totally the fault of the father, who should have known better than to give his younger son a part of the estate. Some tribesmen of New Guinea failed completely to understand the pitiful state of the prodigal son when he was working as a herder of pigs, for in New Guinea society this is a very prestigious job.

Without awareness of the cultural presuppositions that underlie the biblical accounts, radical reinterpretations of the message of the Scriptures are almost inevitable. For example, the K!ung Bushmen regard the biblical practice of fasting as insulting rather than worshiping God, since anyone who refuses a gift is insulting the giver, and anyone who refuses to eat what God has provided is obviously insulting the provider.

Part of the background which any interpreter brings to the process of interpretation depends upon his knowledge of similar types of discourses, that is, his knowledge of certain literary genres (sometimes spoken of as the factor of intertextuality). This often means that attitudes toward certain passages in the Scriptures differ appreciably because of the way in which people interpret the respective literary genres. For many people in the Western world there are serious problems involved in knowing how to interpret the first eleven chapters of Genesis. Are these to be regarded as literal accounts of particular historical events, or are they to be thought of as symbolic and, in a sense, types of parables? For many so-called "primitive peoples" no such question ever arises. They assume that such accounts fit neatly into their category of cosmological legends, and therefore they arrive at the theological implications of the accounts without being at all concerned as to their "facticity." In some languages, however, one has to mark grammatically by means of tense/aspect affixes or particles whether or not history is involved.

A sociosemiotic approach to the process of translating is particularly useful in highlighting the fact that practically everything about a translation carries meaning, in the sense that anything that constitutes a sign of something is meaningful. This approach to "meaning" is not the usual one, but from a sociosemiotic point of view meaning is not to be found merely in words or grammatical constructions. Signs have meaning whether on a lexical, grammatical, or rhetorical level, and whether paralinguistic or extralinguistic. Sociosemiotics is also concerned with the meaning of phonetic symbolism (in onomatopoeic expressions), the associative meaning of so-called "purple prose," the meaning of emphasis and impact in rhetorical structures, and even the meaning of "a jazzed-up style."

A sociosemiotic approach to meaning involves not only the evident meaning of verbal utterances but even the disguised meanings, as in the book of Revelation, in which the city of Babylon substitutes for Rome. Even the absence of lexical elements may be meaningful; that is, even what is not written may carry significance, since it may be interpreted as a zero, a significant absence of something. For example, the fact that the book of Acts ends on such a positive note suggests a number of questions. Did Luke originally desire to write a third book? Was the book of Acts written before the end of the trial in which Paul was involved? Was there originally a description of Paul's martyrdom, which for one reason or another was later removed from the book? Or did Luke presuppose Paul's death without mentioning it in order to counteract the spirit of martyrdom? (Conzelmann, 1963, 150; Haenchen, 1957, 664). A sociosemiotic approach to interpretation inevitably raises such questions.

One particularly significant value of a sociosemiotic approach to translating is that it meshes so neatly with the sociolinguistic orientation in language description, for both look to the communication context for ultimate validation. While the sociosemiotic approach focuses on the linguistic structures and the codes which provide a key to meaning, the sociolinguistic approach looks to the social structure of the users of the language for keys to the significance of any element in a discourse.

5

Rhetorical Functions

Rhetorical meaning is signaled by patterns of selection and arrangement. The selection may involve anything from the level of similar or contrasting sounds to the level of major themes or from the level of embedded aphorisms to the level of a major literary genre, such as dramatic poetry in the book of Job. Arrangement may involve the level of words within a clause to the level of major sections of a book.

The factors of selection and arrangement also apply to the level of syntax, but rhetoric differs from syntax in involving several important elements: (1) normally larger patterns, (2) less rigidly rule-governed structures, that is, having a greater range of optional features, and (3) involving both digital and analogical relations. Rhetorical structures may be not only "right or wrong" but may involve varying degrees of emphasis, appropriateness, acceptability, and appeal.

The same structures may be analyzed from the standpoint of their rhetorical patterns as well as in terms of their syntactic constructions. For example, one may analyze the three third person imperative structures of Matthew 6:9e–10b first on the basis of the syntactic form and secondly on the basis of their rhetorical significance. From the standpoint of the syntax, the phrases (*to onoma sou*, "your name;" *hē basileia sou*, "your kingdom;" and *to thelēma sou*, "your will") constitute the subjects, and the three verbs (*hagiasthētō*, "be hallowed;" *elthetō*, "come;" and *genēthētō*, "become") constitute regular, third person structures, which are completely normal for petitions addressed to deity in Koine Greek. From the rhetorical standpoint, however, these three lines are especially noteworthy in terms of parallelism, order of words, and the number of syllables:

> *hagiasthētō to onoma sou,*
> *elthetō hē basileia sou,*
> *genēthētō to thelēma sou.*

The subject-predicate relationship is inverted in order, which thus calls special attention to the verbs in initial position. Note that in each instance, the nouns are preceded by articles, and the second person singular personal pronoun occurs in final position. In addition, each line consists of nine syllables, assuming that the vowel sequence *iota alpha* in *hagiasthētō* is a diphthong.

In general, one may say that the rhetorical structures begin where the syntactic structures leave off. Stated somewhat differently, the rhetorical structures are above the level of the syntax because they are generally more inclusive.

Rhetorical structures normally involve a number of diverse features, so that the meaning of a rhetorical pattern often consists of a number of distinct elements such as unusual order, parallelism of form, novelty of expression, rhythmic features, and repetitions. Furthermore, the significance of a rhetorical pattern often depends upon the total context. For example, in Matthew 5:14 the Greek expression *humeis este to fōs tou kosmou* (literally, "you are the light of the world") contains a very emphatic form. In the first place, *humeis* occurs in initial position, and the pronoun is not only an emphatic second person plural pronominal reference, but the significance of its position is reinforced because *humeis* also occurs in an initial position at Matthew 5:13: "You yourselves are the salt of the earth." This expression modifies the usual Old Testament claim that the Scriptures, including both the Law and the prophets, were a light to the Jewish believing community as well as to the Gentiles. This statement by Jesus that his followers were indeed the light of the world no doubt serves to highlight the importance of Jesus' declaration in Matthew 5:17 that he had not come to destroy the Law and the prophets but to fulfill them.

The reinforcement of a rhetorical pattern by repetition is conspicuous in the introductions to six sections occurring in Matthew 5 (beginning at verses 21, 27, 31, 33 38, 43), in which the text begins with a statement about "you have heard it said" or "it has been said," which is then contrasted with a statement by Jesus introduced by "but I say to you." The significance of such structures cannot be treated merely in terms of traditional rules of syntax, but requires a more inclusive level of structure, namely, the rhetorical.

Unfortunately, the terms *rhetoric* and *rhetorical* are regarded by many persons as having pejorative meanings. People associate such words with statements such as "that is pure rhetoric" and "nothing but rhetorical babbling," meaning that the utterance may have an attractive form but little or no content. This deprecation for the words *rhetoric* and *rhetorical* derives in part from the abuse of rhetoric by the panegyric orators of late Greek and Roman times, who employed many rhetorical devices in the praise of unworthy rulers and despicable events. However, in the true sense of rhetoric as developed by outstanding Greek and Roman rhetoricians, the effective exploitation of selection and arrangement of formal features of discourse was designed to produce impact and appeal. Though such techniques can certainly be misused, they are also capable of effective employment in producing a style that is compatible with the elevated thematic content of divine revelation.

To appreciate more fully the significance of rhetorical meaning, it is important to recognize the major functions of rhetoric. These include wholeness, aesthetic appeal, impact, appropriateness, coherence, cohesion, focus, and emphasis.

The function of *wholeness* involves the aspects of completeness and unity. Completeness means that a text will contain all that is relevant for its particular purpose, but this does not mean that a text is ever fully explicit in every detail. Discourses are primarily suggestive rather than logically detailed and fully explicit. Much is always left covert in any discourse, since it is generally regarded as inappropriate for a source to communicate information that both receptors and source already know. In other words, one of the important maxims of communication is not to tell people what they already know or, in other words, to make explicit what is generally regarded as shared knowledge. For a Bible translator to add a great deal of supplementary information can result in serious distortion, since it would imply that the original receptors of such a communication did not share with the source the background data.

In some instances a text may appear to be unnecessarily complete, even to the point of repetition which seems overdone and even tautological, but this also may have a rhetorical meaning. For example, in the book of Job the various so-called "comforters" repeat more or less the same themes in slightly different form, which may well be part of the calculated rhetorical meaning of the repetitions: that the theologies of established religious systems are conspicuously lacking in fresh insights.

The aspect of unity involves the manner in which a discourse or a section of a discourse combines elements that fit together and form a united whole. Though John 1:19–28 involves a number of different elements, the unity is carefully marked by a reference to John in verse 19 and also in verse 28. The unity is further emphasized by a series of questions posed to John the Baptist, first by the priests and Levites and secondly by the Pharisees. The first series of questions relates to the theme of "Who are you?" and the second series asks "Why are you baptizing?" The unity of the book of Job is accomplished not only by the thematic content but is highlighted by the dramatic setting in the prologue (Job 1:1—2:13) and the conclusion (Job 42:7–17), in which Job is more than compensated for all of his losses.

The *aesthetic appeal* of a discourse is a far more important factor than is often recognized. The Matthean form of the Lord's Prayer (Matthew 6:9–13) is far more often quoted than the Lukan parallel because of the differences of rhetorical structure. The better Greek manuscripts of Luke 11:2–4 do not have the expanded reference to "the Father." There are only two third-person imperative expressions: "hallowed be your name" and "your kingdom come." Moreover, the following three expressions in Luke do not contain the same rhetorical balance that occurs in the Matthean form of the Lord's Prayer.

The first five verses of John 1 also have significant aesthetic appeal because of balance in length, rhythmic form, and largely chiastic shifting between old and new information, in that the new information in the predicate of each clause immediately becomes the old information as the subject of the following clause. First Corinthians 13 is certainly a favorite chapter, largely in view of its unusually effective rhetorical patterning, involving parallelism, repetition, compactness, and rhythm.

The function of *impact* involves two important elements, novelty and relevance. Impact based on novelty is well illustrated in the Beatitudes. To declare that the poor in spirit are truly blessed and that they will participate in the kingdom of heaven would certainly have seemed to the original receptors as completely contrary to all expectations. In fact, all of the Beatitudes have a ring of the unexpected, especially the beatitude which declares that those who are persecuted for the sake of righteousness are truly blessed.

In so many of the parables of Jesus there is an unusual and novel element; for example, a Samaritan taking pity on a wounded man, in contrast with a priest and a Levite, who certainly should have been concerned for the plight of a victim of violence. Or consider Jesus' statement about the fact that so few people find the narrow gate and the rough road which leads to life (Matt. 7:14). Most religious leaders try to give the impression that everyone will want to follow them.

The function of *appropriateness* is a particularly subtle factor of rhetorical meaning. Matching the literary genre to the nature of the content is very important. This has certainly been done effectively in the Song of Songs, in which idyllic love is described in appropriate poetic form, which is realistically sensual while avoiding vulgarity. Paul's use of the epistolary form to communicate important spiritual truths provides a realism which no type of essay would have communicated. Likewise the fact that most writers of the New Testament evidently chose to use a more or less common Koiné level of vocabulary and grammatical structure is indicative of the Christian community's use of language and the manner in which they evidently sought to reach out to the masses who would employ a similar form of communication and level of language.

The rhetorical function of *coherence* is a particularly complex one. It involves various types of "fit," that is, the manner in which a text fits or coheres to the world view of the participants in the communication, the setting in which a communication takes place, and the existence of other similar or diverse texts (often spoken of technically as "intertextuality").

As one would expect, the biblical texts cohere very closely to several important aspects of the ancient world view: miracles, a three-tiered cosmology (the heavens, the earth, and a region beneath the earth), suffering as payment for one's sins, taboo (both negative and positive), ordeals, and curses and blessings which could not be altered or retracted.

Since many persons in the so-called scientific or sophisticated Western world do not share this same world view, there are problems for translators, some of whom feel that the text must be changed so as not to violate present-day ideas. For example, some translators wish to make the days of creation into eons of time and others want to add psychosomatic explanations to miracles of healing.

Coherence to the setting almost always constitutes a problem for translators, since the original biblical setting of a discourse and the present-day use of a translation of such a discourse are almost always significantly different. The documents of the Scriptures were employed primarily by members of the believing community. In general, they were read to people and explained, but at the present time the Scriptures are often distributed to people who are not members of the believing community, and they are frequently read to people (especially by radio and television) who have little or no means of receiving explanations.

The function of coherence in respect to other religious texts is a particularly complex matter. For the Old Testament, three grades of canonicity were evidently recognized in early times—the law, the prophets, and the writings. For the New Testament the Septuagint obviously played a very important role, since it formed the basis for more than half the quotations, some of which differ appreciably from the Hebrew text. In many ways the Old Testament served as background for New Testament outgrowth and fulfillment.

At the present time some of the same issues continue, although in a slightly different form. Although most Christians do not make distinctions in degrees of canonicity, nevertheless for most people there is almost inevitably a kind of "canon within the canon." There are even those who claim to be Bible translators but who make it a policy to translate only the New Testament rather than the entire Bible.

The problems of intertextual coherence are for many people the result of the amazing variety of literary genres which occur within the Bible. Apocalyptic writings seem so strange as to be out of place, and others find the skepticism of Ecclesiastes representing a discordant note, while the references of romantic love in the Song of Songs seem better reinterpreted as some relationship between God and the believing community or between Jesus Christ and the church.

Progression and *cohesion* may be regarded as two sides of the same discourse. Progression marks the manner in which the discourse moves from one episode to the next, from one argument to the next, or from one item in a description to the next. Cohesion involves the ways in which the various units in any discourse are connected one with the other.

The major types of progression are: (1) a series of related events (usually with some continuity of participants); (2) a spatially organized description of an object (for example, describing a person from head to toes); (3) a description by categories (for example, describing a building by the number of its windows, rooms, floors, and doors); (4) logical progression in terms of (a) consequence (for example, cause-effect, reason-result, condition-result), (b) dialectic, that is, thesis, antithesis, and synthesis (for example, Job, with certain significant differences), (c) generic-specific (for example, taxonomic hierarchies), and (d) stream of consciousness, in which some item of new information becomes the old information in a subsequent section (note, for example, how in James 1:2–8 terms such as *hupomonē* "patience," *telios* "perfect," *leipō* "to lack," *aiteō* "to ask," and *diakrinō* "to doubt" serve as links in a concatenation of ideas); (5) dialogue, in which a following statement is conditioned in form by a preceding one, primarily involving questions and answers or affirmations and negations.

The decision as to the nature of a dialogue may radically change the interpretation. For example, in 1 Kings 19:20 Elisha says to Elijah, "Let me kiss my father and my mother, and then I will follow you." And Elijah answers, "Go back again, *ki mah 'asiti lak* (literally, 'for what have I done to you?')." If this dialogue is interpreted as an affirmation and a negation, the answer means, "You can go back to your work. Did I ask you anything?" If, however, it is interpreted as a question and an answer, it means, "You can go quietly back to your house, for I have done nothing to you which would prevent you from saying farewell to your parents." Or, shorter, "Go and return, for you know what I have done to you." The second interpretation probably is the correct one, the first one having been influenced to a large extent by Luke 9:59–62.

These types of progressions also imply cohesion, for the ways in which the events, descriptions, logical relations, and dependencies of form are organized not only mark the progression but also tie the elements of content together. In addition to this structural cohesion of progressive units, however, there are also various kinds of linkage which are overtly marked: (1) by reference, in which, for example, pronouns may refer back to an antecendent or ahead to something which is to come in the discourse, or (2) by such transitionals as conjunctive expressions, for example, *therefore, hence, moreover, in this way, because of this, as the result of,* and *in view of;* or (3) by catchwords. Note, for example, the effective use of the catchword *r'osh*, "head," in Micah 2:13 and 3:1, which should not be considered as a purely formal device to overcome a semantic discontinuity. One sometimes has the impression that the game of continuities and discontinuities has been played by the redactor of a book in a far more subtle way than has been done by modern commentators (de Waard, 1979b, 511–12).

The function of *rhetorical focus* involves three different kinds of relationships: (a) foregrounding and backgrounding, (b) new and old information, and (c) topic in contrast with comment.

In many respects the contrast between foregrounding and backgrounding is one of the most complex and subtle aspects of focus. In Ephesians 1:3–14 God is the causative agent of all that is mentioned, but the Greek term *theos*, "God," occurs only once, while Christ, who is the immediate agent, is specifically named five times. In this brief discourse, God is obviously backgrounded, while Christ is foregrounded. In Luke 15 the events associated with the lost coin, the lost sheep, and the lost son are clearly foregrounded, but the rejoicing in heaven is an underlying theme, and though specifically mentioned only twice, it is certainly an important background element.

In the Joseph story, God's provision for the family of Jacob is an essential factor, but it is backgrounded in contrast with the foregrounding of the tension between Joseph and his brothers.

In a majority of languages, old information tends to precede new information in lineal order; that is, a person normally begins a statement with something that is known from the immediate physical or literary context, and then proceeds to say something new about such a topic. For various rhetorical purposes, however, the order can be reversed with a significant increase in impact. For example, in John 1:1 *ho logos*, "the Word," is in the so-called predicate position in the first clause, but it becomes the subject of the second clause. It is now old information in the sense that *ho logos* has already been identified and the new information is contained in the predicate, but in the third clause there is a reversal of order following a type of chiastic arrangement of words, but by placing *theos*, "God," before the verb, the emphasis upon the deity of the Word becomes heightened.

In the third type of focus, almost any element of a statement may be made the topic and then be followed by a statement concerning the topic. For example, in the sentence *in the closet, that's where you will find the sweater* the topic is clearly *in the closet*, and the comment is the rest of the utterance. In the sentence *for fifty cents you can buy three bananas* the focus is upon the topic, *for fifty cents*. The comment concerns what could be bought for that amount. In English, emphasis and focus are often combined in a sentence such as *Peter is the one I am looking for*.

The function of *rhetorical emphasis* or highlighting involves giving some feature of a discourse special prominence. In an oral text this emphasis is easily accomplished by extra loudness, precision in pronunciation, setting off a portion by pauses, or by lengthening the pronunciation of a word or phrase. Even whispering a phrase may add emphasis. In written texts emphasis may be marked by an unusual position in the discourse, repetition, or by various intensifiers, or, modifying terms that highlight the importance or relevance of some feature. The emphasis of *makarioi*, "blessed," in Matthew 5:3-11 is accomplished not only by the unusual position of the predicate adjective but by the fact that it occurs in this position nine different times.

6

Rhetorical Processes

To accomplish the rhetorical functions of wholeness, aesthetic appeal, impact, appropriateness, coherence, progression-cohesion, focus, and emphasis, various rhetorical processes are employed. The principal ones are: (1) repetition, (2) compactness, (3) connectives, (4) rhythm, (5) shifts in expectancies (primarily order, syntactic structures, and semantic content), and (6) the exploitation of similarities and contrasts in the selection and arrangement of the elements of a discourse.

These rhetorical processes may involve any and all levels and types of discourse structures, but in actual practice they are far more frequent at the micro-level of discourse structure rather than at the macro-level of the larger units.

For example, parallelism may apply to two successive lines of poetry, to two parables (the Lost Coin and the Lost Sheep), or to the structures of two separate books (the gospels of Mark and Matthew). Compactness may apply to a brief paragraph, such as the Lord's Prayer, or to an entire letter, as in the case of Colossians. Similarly, repetition may involve individual words or even entire events, as in the case of the triple descriptions of Paul's conversion experience in Acts.

In discussing these rhetorical processes there are, however, a number of terminological problems, because we often lack an adequate metalanguage to deal with these various processes. It is quite possible, of course, to talk about some features of these processes in purely descriptive terms. For example, one may speak of occurrence in initial position as being a matter of emphasis, but this type of description can be misleading. If certain classes of words tend to occur first in an utterance, then their occurrence in such a position does not particularly indicate any special emphasis. Emphasis by initial position occurs only when a term not normally occurring in such a position is placed at the beginning of an utterance. What is important, therefore, is not so much the actual initial position but the shift in expectancy of such a term with regard to position.

It is for that reason that the numerous detailed rhetorical features (which have been given such names as epanaphora, symploke, anastrophe, isocolon, parison, zeugma, and sullepsis) are treated in terms of types of processes rather than as special rhetorical devices.

Repetition

Repetition is perhaps the most obvious of all rhetorical processes. For the most part it serves the functions of emphasis, unity, and cohesion, in which it is particularly useful in marking transitions. Repetitions can, however, be misleading in some languages. In English the repetition of *Lord, Lord* would certainly mark emphasis, but a similar type of repetition in some of the Philippine languages seriously detracts from emphasis. Similarly, in some languages the repetition which occurs in the thematic parallelism of the Psalms is regarded in bad taste since it seems like tautology, saying the same thing twice and thus depreciating the intelligence of readers.

Repetitions may be regarded as of two basic types: those which occur within the same discourse and those which involve two or more discourses, as in the case of quotations. In some instances the repetitions are not direct quotations but allusions, sometimes arranged in a kind of pastiche of echoing phrases, as in the case of the song of Mary (Luke 1:47–55) and the prophecy of Zechariah (Luke 1:68–79).

Repetitions within the same discourse involve sounds, individual words, phrases, syntactic constructions, propositions, and even entire sections, though in some instances the repetition of extensive content may be given in summary form (Gen. 10:1–31 is summarized in Gen. 10:32).

The repetition of sounds may have no particular relationship to the meaning of the words involved. For example, in Hebrews 1:1 there are five words beginning with the sound *p*. In this same verse there are five occurrences of the sound *l* and two adverbial endings in -ōs. So many such features would seem to indicate clearly an intentional repetition of sounds. In the New Testament, however, there is relatively little of this type of phonemic repetition. Far more of this type of repetition occurs in the Hebrew text of the Old Testament. Note, for example, Ecclesiastes 2:25: *umi yaḥush ḥuts mimmenni*, "and who can enjoy himself without me?" The syllables with similar sounds even show a chiastic arrangement: *mi . . . ḥush . . . ḥuts . . . mi*. More frequently, however, repetitions are on other levels, and they involve words, phrases, and even sentences. This is particularly true of Hebrew verse. An example of simple word repetition is Psalm 106:10a and 10b:

wayoshi 'em miyad śone'
wayiga'lem miyad 'oyeb
He saved them *from the power* of the one who hated them;
He redeemed them *from the power* of the enemy.

Specifically there is the repetition of the preposition *min* and a noun *yad*, and on another level there are the sound repetitions in the last syllable of the first and in both syllables of the last word.

In the New Testament similarity of sound frequently involves similar or contrastive meanings. Note, for example, the following sequences: *phthonou, phonou*, "jealousy, murder" (Rom. 1:29); *asunetous, asunthetous*, "without a conscience, failing to keep promises" (Rom. 1:31); and *limoi kai loimoi*, "famines and plagues" (Luke 21:11). The same is also true for the Old Testament. One should, however, eliminate from the discussion the phenomenon of so-called *figura etymologica*, that is, the use within a definable distance of two words from the same root. This figure does not represent a wordplay, and it does not belong with the structural device of repetition. So, in spite of sound repetitions, the Hebrew expression *sogeret umesugeret* in Joshua 6:1, literally "closing and closed," does not present a wordplay. It is therefore unjustified when the *Traduction Oecuménique de la Bible* renders the expression with *fermée et enfermée* in French, explaining in a footnote that a special effort has been made to maintain the Hebrew pun in the translation. The grammatical doubling of forms of the same verbal root is simply an idiomatic device to express intensification, and one may represent the meaning by "all the gates of the city of Jericho were tightly closed."

The greatest challenge to the translator and the greatest possibilities for creative imagination are provided by those wordplays in which only a degree of sound resemblance involves a difference of meaning. In the impressive series of sound repetitions found in Amos 5:5: *haggilgal galoh yigleh*, the consonantal sequence *gl* is repeated four times, and each word either starts or ends with the consonant *h*. A literal rendering like "for Gilgal shall surely go into exile" or even a more dynamic rendering like "her people are doomed to exile" cannot claim to be a functional equivalent in English because of the undertranslation and loss of impact. It is difficult to make the message in a translation as forceful as it was in the original. The original readers shared information which will be new to many readers today, such as Gilgal having been a place where the land was symbolically given to Israel. Nevertheless, some inspiring renderings can be noted, such as Wellhausen's German translation, *Gilgal wird zum Galgen gehen*, "Gilgal will go to the gallows." In German there is also the now almost classical contrastive pair *Rechtsspruch/Rechtsbruch* "legal decision/violation of the law" as a rendering of the Hebrew *mishpat/mispaḥ* in Isaiah 5:7.

The awareness of the presence of sound repetitions may also help identify obsolete forms. For example, in Isaiah 47:1:

redi ushebi 'al-'apar	Come down and sit in the dust,
betulat bat-babel	O virgin daughter of Babylon,

betulat is a grammatically unusual form. Traditionally, this term has been explained as a construct with the genitive apposition *bat*. But it is, however, very doubtful whether such a genitive ever existed. The form probably is an archaic feminine absolute, deliberately used to secure the *taw* alliteration (Boadt, 1983, 353–63).

Rhyme is not a part of Greek poetic structuring, but it does occur to some extent in Hebrew as, for example, in Judges 16:24, which is built on a single rhyme occurring four times: *beyadenu . . . 'oyebenu . . . 'artsenu . . . halalenu*. This phenomenon is rather frequent in other Semitic languages but rare in Hebrew. Moffatt tried to transpose the rhyme into English:

> Our God has now put
> the foe in our hands,
> who wasted our lands
> and slew us in bands!

But this attempt to reproduce the Hebrew rhyme structure by such an English jingle results in a serious loss of dignity.

In Judges 14:18 one can note the rhyme between *be'eglati*, "my heifer," and *hidati*, "my riddle," which Moffatt also tried to render in English as:

> Had you not used my heifer for your plough,
> You never would have guessed my riddle now!

It is clear that not all translations which try to match the Hebrew form can be considered functional equivalents. Frequently, the result is rather artificial and therefore does not recreate the original impact. A more successful example is the way in which Alonso-Schokel has rendered the sound repetitions and the threefold rhyme of *shu'alim . . . getannim . . . keramim* of the Song of Songs 2:15 into Spanish:

> Agarradnos
> las raposas,
> las raposas
> pequeñitas,
> que destrozan
> nuestras viñas,
> nuestras viñas
> florecidas.

This Spanish poem may be translated into English rather literally as:

> Grab for us the foxes,
> the little foxes
> that destroy our vines,
> our flowering vines.

The repetition of grammatical constructions involving either lexically distinct or similar elements is quite common in the New Testament. In Matthew 7:7 there are three parallel grammatical constructions, beginning in each case with an imperative and followed by a future form of a verb. In two instances the verbs are in the passive form and in one case the form is active, but it may be regarded as semantically passive since the subject is the beneficiary of the event: *aiteite, kai dothēsetai humin; zēteite, kai heurēsete; krouete, kai anoigēsetai humin,* "Ask and it will be given to you; seek and you will find; knock and it will be opened to you." One additional interesting feature about this set of three parallel constructions is that the imperative in each case functions like a conditional, so that in some languages it is essential to translate, "If you ask for anything, it will be given to you; if you seek for something, you will find it; and if you knock, it will be opened to you."

In 1 John 2:12–14 the first two words in each principal line are identical with the exception of the tense, and the third word in each case belongs to the same semantic domain. The lines introduced by *hoti,* "that," differ to some extent in content, but there is a good deal of grammatical and thematic repetition. In fact, this series of six expressions is almost monotonously repetitive in its grammatical structures:

> *graphō humin, teknia,*
>   *hoti apheōntai humin hai hamartiai*
>   *dia to onoma autou.*
> *graphō humin, pateres,*
>   *hoti egnōkate ton ap' arkhēs.*
> *graphō humin, neaniskoi,*
>   *hoti nenikēkate ton ponēron.*
> *egrapsa humin, paidia,*
>   *hoti egnōkate ton patera.*
> *egrapsa humin, pateres,*
>   *hoti egnōkate ton ap' arkhēs.*
> *egrapsa humin, neaniskoi,*
>   *hoti iskhuroi este*
>   *kai ho logos tou theou en humin menei*
>   *kai nenikekate ton ponēron.*

I write to you, children,
  because your sins have been forgiven
    on account of his name.
I write to you, fathers,
  because you have known him who is from the beginning.
I write to you, young men,
  because you have been victorious over the evil one.
I wrote to you, children,
  because you have known the father.
I wrote to you, fathers,
  because you have known the one who existed
    from the beginning.
I wrote to you, young men,
  because you are strong
  and the word of God remains in you
  and you have been victorious over the evil one.

The most frequent repetition of lexical units consists of single words, which may occur contiguous with one another or noncontiguous but in corresponding structural positions. In a number of instances, however, the same word is repeated but with a strikingly different meaning. Though the repetition of a word in corresponding structural positions carries more impact, most repetitions are not of this type. There are a great many different patterns of repetitions, but the following are those which occur most frequently.

The repetition of single words, which are contiguous to one another and in the same grammatical construction, is clearly emphatic, as in the case of *kurie, kurie,* "Lord, Lord" (Luke 6:46) and *staurou, staurou auton,* "crucify, crucify him" (Luke 23:21). Words are often repeated in noncontiguous positions but in corresponding structural positions, as in 1 Corinthians 13:7, in which *panta,* "all things," is repeated in an initial position with four verbs: *panta stegei, panta pisteuei, panta elpizei, panta hupomenei,* "bears all things, believes all things, hopes all things, endures all things." The final position in corresponding clauses is not as emphatic as the initial position, but it is certainly significant in the oratorical style of Hebrews 2:16: *ou gar dēpou aggelōn epilambanetai, alla spermatos abraam epilambanetai,* "for clearly he does not help the angels, but he helps the descendants of Abraham."

In some instances repetition occurs in both initial and final positions, as in 1 Corinthians 10:21: *ou dunasthe potērion kuriou pinein kai potērion daimoniōn; ou dunasthe trapezēs kuriou metekhein kai trapezēs daimoniōn,* "you are not able to drink the cup of the Lord and the cup of demons; you are not able to share in the table of the Lord and in the table of demons."

One important rhetorical device in Greek consists of ending an expression with a word and beginning the following expression with the same word. This is done with some slight variation in Romans 5:3b–5a: *hē thlipsis hupomonēn katergazetai, hē de hupomonē dokimēn, hē de dokimē elpida; hē de elpis ou kataiskhunei,* "trouble produces endurance, endurance produces approval, and approval produces hope, and hope does not disappoint." In Romans 8:30 the repetitive series of verbs form a structure of the type A B B C C D, while the pronominal markers *hous . . . toutous* occur three times: *hous de proōrisen, toutous kai ekalesen; kai hous ekalesen, toutous kai edikaiōsen; hous de edikaiōsen, toutous kai edoksasen,* "whom he set apart, he called; and those he called, he put right; and those whom he put right, he glorified."

A word may be repeated frequently within a particular section of a discourse without occurring in certain corresponding structural positions. For example, the Greek term *sōma,* "body," occurs seventeen times in 1 Corinthians 12:12–26 (an average of more than once in each verse), and in 1 Corinthians 15:12–19 the verb *egeiromai* occurs nine times. Such repetitions not only mark a theme but add emphasis.

In Psalm 106:37–38d there is a threefold repetition of *dam,* "blood," a twofold repetition of the verb *zabaḥ,* "to sacrifice," and a twofold repetition of the sentence *benehem we ('et) benotehem,* "their sons and their daughters."

The repetition of so-called "function words" may be quite distinctive of certain styles. For example, in Mark 3 only three sentences out of twenty-three do not begin with *kai,* "and." Though it is true that in the works of some of the best Greek writers almost all sentences begin with some kind of conjunction (whether initial or postpositional), this excessive use of *kai,* almost to the exclusion of such typical Greek conjunctions as *de* "and, but," *gar* "for," and *oun* "therefore," suggests a kind of semiticized Greek under the influence of Hebrew *vav.* Since Hebrew *vav* must appear first in the sentence, Mark seems to prefer *kai* to the second place conjunctions in Greek. In fact, Mark has a *kai/de* proportion of 5:1. A comparative statistical analysis of translation Greek and original Greek shows that Greek which is a translation of Hebrew or Aramaic will have at least two or more *kai* for every *de,* while original Greek will have considerably fewer *kai* than *de* (Martin, 1974, 19).

The repetition of the same word but with a different meaning is also a device for rhetorical emphasis. Compare, for example, the use of *pneuma* in John 3:8, which occurs first in the meaning of "wind," but at the end of the verse it designates the Holy Spirit.

In some instances the same words may be repeated but in different grammatical constructions. In Mark 2:27 two clauses are contrastive with the order reversed, thus providing a chiastic structure: *to sabbaton dia ton anthrōpon egeneto kai oukh ho anthrōpos dia to sabbaton,* "the Sabbath was made for man and not man for the Sabbath."

The use of different words with closely related meanings may be a device for enlarging somewhat the scope of reference of a statement. In 1 John 1:1, for example, *heōrakamen* and *etheasametha* are closely related, though not identical in meaning. They do, however, mutually reinforce the notion of visual experience. In Matthew 5:45 the phrases *epi ponērous kai agathous,* "upon the evil and the good," and *epi dikaious kai adikous,* "upon the righteous and the unrighteous," clearly refer to the same types of persons on whom God makes the sun rise and the rain fall, though in the order of words there is a chiastic arrangement of the semantic parallels.

In Hebrew it also frequently happens that repetitions of words having similar sounds involve a play on associated or contiguous meanings. The second lexical unit may then function as an intensifier of the first. An example of this can be found in Isaiah 29:2, *ta'niyah . . . wa'aniyah.* This combination has been strikingly rendered in *Français Courant* by the word pair *tristesse et détresse,* "sadness and distress" (König, 1900, 157).

In a number of instances words within the same semantic domain are simply piled up one on the other, as in Ephesians 1:19: *kata tēn energeian tou kratous tēs iskhuos autou,* "according to the power of the strength of his might." The three nouns do not refer to three entirely different potentialities or degrees of power; they are simply repeated to emphasize the greatness of the power.

The use of close synonyms, however, may be designed primarily for the sake of variety rather than for any emphasis or distinctiveness in meaning. Such repetition of words which are closely related in meaning is typical of Johannine writings. Compare, for example, *legō* and *laleō,* "to speak," *oida* and *ginōskō,* "to know," and *horaō* and *blepō,* "to see." In John 21:15–19 the shift from *agapaō* to *phileō* seems also to reflect the use of close synonyms for the sake of variety. One should, however, not speak of "a pointless variety in style" (Turner, 1976, 76). The avoidance of monotony certainly is not pointless. It only means that in the absence of the same kind of stylistic requirements in the receptor language, the translator does not have to match the close synonyms of the original in his renderings.

The use of terms with completely contrastive meanings but within the same semantic domain is also a significant rhetorical device, and in the New Testament considerable use is made of such contrasts, for example, *fōs,* "light;" and *skotia,* "darkness;" in John 1:5 and 1 John 1:5; *pseustēs,* "liar;" and *hē alētheia,* "truth;" in 1 John 2:4; and *ho arnoumenos,* "one who denies;" and *ho homologōn,* "one who confesses;" in 1 John 2:23. Note also

94 FROM ONE LANGUAGE TO ANOTHER

thanatos, "death," and *zōē,* "life;" *enestōta,* "things present;" and *mellonta,* "things in the future," and *hupsōma,* "height;" and *bathos,* "depth" in Romans 8:38–39.

Sometimes there is significant rhetorical impact by the use of different words based on the same root. For example, in 1 John 2:18–27 there is an important interplay between *antikhristos,* "antichrist," *khristos,* "Christ," and *khrisma,* "annointing."

Even the repetition of the same morphological formations in words may be rhetorically significant, as in 1 Corinthians 15:44–49: *psukhikos,* "natural," *pneumatikos,* "spiritual," *khoikos,* "earthly," and *epouranios,* "heavenly."

In some instances the repetitions are complex in that they may involve significant syntactic similarity and repetition of certain words, though there are sometimes different words within the same semantic domain. Compare, for example, the two statements in 1 Corinthians 12:17: *ei holon to sōma ophthalmos, pou hē akoē? ei holon akoē, pou hē osphrēsis?* "If the whole body were the eye, where would the hearing be? If the whole body were hearing, where would be the sense of smell?"

Some syntactic repetition involves a reversal of roles. In 1 John 4:10, for example, there is a repetition of lexical units, but the respective roles are reversed: *oukh hoti hēmeis ēgapēkamen ton theon, all' hoti autos ēgapēsen hēmas,* "not that we love God, but that he loves us." Compare also 1 John 4:16b: *en tō theō menei kai ho theos en autō menei,* "he remains in God and God remains in him."

In some instances the use of different terms for the same referent involves purposeful verbal avoidance. The use of *ouranos,* "heaven," as a substitute for *theos,* "God," or the use of *pantokratōr,* "Almighty," as a title for God no doubt reflects the positive taboo which was associated with the Hebrew term YHWH "Yahweh" (Jehovah) and which was later extended to Hebrew *Elohim,* "God," and in turn to Greek *theos,* "God."

Some propositional repetition involves positive/negative contrasts, which is a conspicuous feature in the Johannine writings, for example: *panta di' autou egeneto, kai khōris autou egeneto oude hen,* "all things came into existence through him, and without him not anything came into existence" (John 1:3) or *kai hōmologēsen kai ouk ērnēsato,* "and he confessed and he did not deny" (John 1:20).

One of the conspicuous features of Hebrew poetry is thematic repetition in parallel lines; for example, "he gives me victory over my enemies; he subdues the nations under me" (Ps. 18:47). In some instances synonymous parallelism with reversal of roles also occurs; for example, "He loved to curse—may he be cursed! He hated to give blessings—may no one bless him!" (Ps. 109:17). Direct antithesis may also occur, as in Psalm 1:6: "For the Lord knows the way of the righteous, but the way of the wicked will perish." Some so-called parallelism in the Old Testament is simply sequential (or perhaps better termed "consequential") as in Psalm 68:1, "God rises up and scatters his enemies; those who hate him run away in defeat."

Within consequential parallelism, one often faces considerable rhetorical complexity. For example, one may find a repetition of words from the same root but arranged in a chiastic pattern A B B A, as in these two lines in Ezekiel 15:4a:

> hinneh *la'esh* nittan *le'akela*
> *'et shene qetsotaw 'akela ha'esh*
> Lo! to the *fire;* it is given as *fuel;*
> *The fire consumes* its two ends.
> (literally, "its two ends consumes the fire.")

The reversal of order in the two roots *'esh* and *'akal* underscores the fact that *'akela* changes from nominal to verbal use. An important number of examples of this phenomenon can be found in the book of Ezekiel (Boadt, 1975, 693–99).

Within consequential parallelism one can also have the repetition of the same initial verbs occurring in a chiastic pattern. In Psalm 105:25–29 there is the following order: *hapak* "he changed" . . . *shalah* "he sent" . . . *samu* "they placed" . . . *shalah* "he sent" . . . *hapak* "he changed." The rhetorical meaning of such a pattern is emphasis on God's total control of Egypt's attack (Clifford, 1979, 420–27).

Repetitions in consequential parallelism may also involve chiastic word order and consonantal similarity of sounds. In Genesis 27:36, for example, the following text marked only for consonants has the form:

| *'t bkrty lqh* | he took away my birthright |
| *whnh 'th lqh brkty* | and look, now he has taken away my blessing. |

In this case there is an interesting interchange of consonants in the two nouns (Kselman, 1977, 219–23).

Quotations may be regarded as a type of repetition, though the repetition is intertextual. Nevertheless, this is an important rhetorical device to validate what has been said and to emphasize its continuity with previous authoritative statements. Quotations carry particularly great impact if there are certain additional shifts from the expected order or from negative to positive content. For example, in Haggai 1:10 the text reads: "The heavens have withheld the dew / and the earth has withheld its increase." Zechariah 8:12 quotes this text, but in a significantly different manner, for the order of the text in Haggai is inverted and the negative statement is changed into a positive one: "The earth shall give its increase / and the heavens shall give their dew." In fact, there are four different levels of inversion: (1) the order of letters within the Hebrew word for "dew" has been reversed (the initial *mem* having correctly become a final *mem*), (2) the chiastic structure of the text in Haggai has become a parallel structure in Zechariah, (3) the order of the two sentences has been reversed, and (4) a semantic inversion has taken place, the verb *kala'* having been replaced by its opposite *natan*.

The phenomenon of an inverted order of quotation, but without any negative-positive transformation, is rather frequent as, for example, in the quotation of Isaiah 52:11 in 2 Corinthians 6:17. It also happens that a certain number of words from a specific text may recur in a passage with the same theme but in a different sequence. (Compare, for example, Mic. 5:9–13 and Isa. 2:6–8.) In all these instances the same aim can be detected, namely, that through the change of sequences in traditional wording, a special impact is created (Beentjes, 1982, 506–23).

The repetition of whole sections of a discourse may likewise be regarded as a type of repetition. Such repetitions may have some liturgical value, for they emphasize the importance of certain events or objects. Compare, for example, the repetition of materials in Exodus 25–31 and in Exodus 35–40. The last chapters simply relate how the instructions given in the first chapters were carried out by Moses and the Israelites. In many instances there is a verbatim repetition of the wording of the former chapters with only a change in the aspects of the verbs from incompletive to completive.

Certain repetitions, however, are not a matter of rhetorical emphasis but are related to problems of text. For example, Isaiah 36–39 is almost identical with 2 Kings 18:13—20:19. There are three possible explanations for this fact: (a) these chapters originally belonged to 2 Kings and they were added to the Isaiah text; (b) they were originally part of Isaiah and were inserted into 2 Kings; and (c) they were a separate document introduced in 2 Kings as well as in Isaiah. The first possibility has found the most defenders. Such repetitions, however, present a very special problem to translators. They should be anxious not to harmonize the two texts wherever there are differences, nor should they try to reconstruct in a translation a common ancestor text (Preliminary Report of the Hebrew Old Testament Text Project, Vol. 4, 1979, 83).

Repetitions always produce certain problems for translators. When the repetitions involve strict parallelism of thematic elements (that is, the type of synonymous parallelism so frequently found in the Psalms), they may cause strongly adverse reactions on the part of receptors. To state the same thing twice, even with a change of vocabulary, may be interpreted by some people as an insult to their intelligence. But when parallelism does not exist in the source text, translators have sometimes been forced to produce a parallel statement to translate "correctly," since in some languages the very essence of poetry is the occurrence of parallel lines. In certain instances parallelism exists in a receptor language, but the parallel line must always contain some additional information. The translator therefore has problems in dealing with synonymous parallelism in which no new information is added.

In some languages the repetition of particular words in the same context is frowned upon as stylistically unappealing. In such instances receptors demand the use of different words for the same referent.

The repetition of sounds in a receptor language to match those of the Greek and Hebrew texts is practically impossible. Nevertheless, the first Greek translator of Isaiah frequently tried to give a "phonological" translation of the Hebrew. For example, he rendered Hebrew *sas* with Greek *sēs*, both meaning "moth" in Isaiah 51:8, Hebrew *pah*, "snare," with Greek *pagis* in Isaiah 8:14, 24:17, and 24:18, and Hebrew *por* by the Greek root *por-* in Isaiah 24:19 (de Waard, 1981, 551–61). It is usually only a matter of chance that there is some kind of phonological correspondence.

Rather than seeking to reproduce repetitions that may occur in the biblical text, a translator needs to determine first what functions such repetitions have. Are they primarily for emphasis? Or do they merely highlight some particular feature? Do they possibly act as a cohesive element in order to show the connection between juxtaposed sentences or paragraphs? Or is it possible that the repetition only marks the thematic unity of a section? Only after one has determined the function of the repetition can one attempt to reproduce the functional equivalence of this rhetorical process.

Compactness

Compactness as a rhetorical device includes primarily ellipses, nominalization, the use of generic expression, gnomic utterances, and poetic language.

In 1 Corinthians 13:4–7 there are thirteen possible omissions of *kai*, "and." The loss of such a connective does not impair the meaning, and in fact makes possible the juxtaposition of terms which highlight both similarity and contrast. In Hebrews 1:5–10 there are several highly significant contractions in the markers of direct discourse. Note how the full expression (*tini gar eipen pote tōn aggelōn;* "for to whom of the angels did he ever say") is drastically reduced later to *kai palin*, "and again," and in verse 8 to *pros de ton huion*, "but to the Son." In verse 10 the reduction is simply to *kai*, "and." In this type of contraction there is no significant loss of information, for the necessary semantic "fillers" are available from the larger context. Ellipses of certain function words (primarily pronouns, auxiliaries, and conjunctions) are quite common in many languages.

The use of nominals derived from verbs introduces a particular type of ellipsis in which the participants in such events are frequently not identi-fied. For example, the statement *the wages of sin is death* (Rom. 6:23) in-volves the nominals *sin* and *death*. These involve events in which persons participate, and the term *wages* implies an event of payment. In some lan-guages it is simply not possible to employ such a succinct expression. An equivalent may be a considerably expanded expression such as "if a per-son sins, the pay he will receive for that will cause him to die."

Highly generic terms also involve a degree of compactness, since the terms cover such a wide range of meaning condensed into a single lexical unit. Note, for example, in 1 John 1:5–10 such generic nominals as *fōs*, "light;" *skotia*, "darkness;" *alēthia*, "truth;" *koinonia*, "fellowship;" *adikia*, "unrighteousness;" and *haima*, "blood," as a symbolic reference to sacrifi-cial death.

Such gnomic utterances as proverbs and credal formulas are typically compact in their structure; with only a few words a great deal of wisdom is communicated. Note, for example, two typical proverbs: "Fear an an-gry king as you would a growling lion; making him angry is suicide" (Prov. 20:2) and "Better to live on the roof than share the house with a nagging wife" (Prov. 21:9). The credal formula in 1 Timothy 3:16b is re-markably compact:

> *hos ephanerōthē en sarki,*
> *edikaiōthē en pneumati,*
> *ōphthē aggelois,*
> *ekērukhthē en ethnesin,*
> *episteuthē en kosmō,*
> *anelēmphthē en doksē.*
> Who appeared in human form,
> shown to be right by the Spirit,
> seen by angels,
> proclaimed among the nations,
> believed on in the world,
> taken up in glory.

It is the very succinctness of this formulation which has led to necessary expansion in various translations. Note, for example, Today's English Ver-sion:

> He appeared in human form,
> was shown to be right by the Spirit,
> and was seen by angels.
> He was preached among the nations,
> was believed in throughout the world,
> and was taken up to heaven.

One of the almost universal characteristics of poetry (with the exception of certain types of epic poetry) is the compactness with which information is carried. Perhaps no literary tradition illustrates this better than the poetry of the Old Testament. Psalm 101 is particularly compact, and in terms of word count, syllable count, or line length, it is conspicuously shorter than any translation into English.

Compactness is a factor in several different functions. Not only is a compact expression seemingly easier to remember, therefore having more mnemonic value, but the elimination of unnecessary words suggests something which carries both authority and the weight of tradition. It is interesting to note that most of the Old Testament quotations in the New Testament are precisely of this type. Compactness also permits the juxtaposition of expressions which normally would not be found together, but which in such positions may reinforce the respective meanings or highlight their contrast. Compactness also signals the fact that someone has evidently given careful and serious thought to the formulation of an utterance. It therefore has a greater claim on a receptor's time and energy.

Connection

Connection involves primarily reference, linkage, and transition. By means of various pronouns one may refer to objects or events which have already occurred in the text or which may occur later in a text. The reference may be back to something already mentioned (anaphoric) or ahead to something to be mentioned more specifically (cataphoric). The so-called deictic pronouns are particularly useful, as in English *this* and *that*, and in connection with location in a discourse, the expressions *the latter* and *the former*. In English the definite article *the* serves a type of reference function in that it often indicates that the object in question has already been mentioned in the discourse.

Linkage involves both coordinate and subordinate relations. The coordinate relations are primarily additive *(and, both . . . and)*, appositional *(namely, that is)*, alternative *(or, either . . . or)*, and contrastive *(but, except)*. Subordinate relations are marked by such conjunctions as *if, while, when, so that, because,* and *in order to.*

Transitions are marked by such conjunctions as *therefore, moreover,* and *accordingly,* and by conjunctive phrases such as *as a result* and *in view of this*.

Some languages make extensive use of connectives, while others use relatively few. Greek, for example, employs an abundance of connectives; some writers of Classical Greek practically never wrote a clause or sentence without indicating its connection with what preceded. Isocrates even began a book with a postpositional conjunction. In contrast with

Greek, Hebrew uses relatively fewer connectives, and accordingly the structures are regarded as largely paratactic in contrast with the hypotactic structures of Greek. This does not mean, however, that the logical or temporal relationships do not exist in such texts. It is simply that such relationships are implied but not explicitly marked.

In translating from Greek into English, it is necessary in many instances to reduce the number of explicit connectives, for English simply does not use the abundance of such forms as does the Koine Greek of the New Testament. On the other hand, English employs a number of explicit connectives which are normally missing in Hebrew. In translating from Hebrew into English, it is necessary to add a number of such connectives if the style of the English translation is to be satisfactory.

Rhythm

Rhythm consists of a pattern of periodically recurring peaks and troughs of prominence. Such peaks and troughs may be phonological, syntactic, or semantic.

The most common type of phonological rhythm is based upon loudness. This is a feature of poetry in many languages, in which different combinations of stressed and unstressed syllables are described in terms of poetic feet and arrangements of such feet (for example, iambs, trochees, dactyls, spondees, and anapaests). Such rhythmic stress by means of contrasts in loudness is also an important element in prose; for example, the avoidance of too many potentially unaccented syllables in a row, or the avoidance of too many accented syllables in a row.

In a number of languages rhythm is based not upon loudness but upon length of syllables. This is true, for example, of Classical Greek, in which the various types of poetic feet depend upon the length of the vowels and accompanying consonants. In some languages the rhythmic units are based entirely upon the number of syllables and in other instances upon the number of long or short vowels. But units of length are not based upon words as such, unless the words count only as individual syllables or as sets of syllables.

In some cases the rhythmic length is based on rhythm lines, but in such instances the underlying patterns are essentially breath units, and one may therefore speak of chant patterns.

In some languages in the Orient, rhythm is based not upon alternating loudness of stress or even length of syllables but upon certain types of tonal contrasts. Tones in Mandarin Chinese, for example, have been traditionally divided into two classes. The ways in which these tones alternate in rhythmic patterns of succeeding lines are complex and intricate.

In the case of poetic rhythm in Hebrew, there is a vast and confusing literature. It is possible, however, to discern the broad outlines of different schools of thought: the traditional one (Bellermann, Budde, Sievers), the semantic parallelism school (Lowth, Gray, Robinson), and the alternating meter school (Ewald, Mowinckel, Segert). The latest developments stress particularly the importance of syllabic meter, but the symmetry does not depend upon theories of internal stress. The number of syllables per colon will always be a precise measure of couplet and triplet length. When a couplet consists of two lines of eight syllables each, it is the number of syllables involved which is important, rather than their arrangement in certain kinds of poetic feet, whether iambic, trochaic, anapaestic, or dactylic (Stuart, 1976).

There may also be significant rhythm in syntactic constructions. The length of phrases and the alternation between content and function words can be important elements in syntactic rhythm. This usually means that good syntactic rhythm avoids too much apposition and parenthetical interruption, which tend to break the rhythmic flow.

One may speak of semantic rhythm as a kind of "content rhythm," in the sense that there should be a rhythmic peaking of content relevance. This means that important features of content should be rhythmically spaced. Another closely related element of rhythm involves rhythmic peaks of difficulty in decoding. These would then contrast with troughs of decoding, which would represent periods of ease in decoding. In other words, difficult and easy units of decoding should be rhythmically alternated so as to avoid semantic overloading or underloading.

Classical rhetoricians were keenly aware of the problem of rhythm and discussed these matters in terms of variation and frequency in the use of various rhetorical devices. Discussions of these issues were often dealt with under the heading of *varietas*, "variety," implying a principle of balance and rhythm in the variety of rhetorical devices and in their rhythmic spacing in a discourse.

Rhythm is no doubt one of the most subtle factors in rhetoric, but it is also one of the most important. Its significance in oral utterances is usually admitted, but some persons assume that it is relatively irrelevant in written discourse. This, however, is not true. Even though persons may read a text silently, there nevertheless seems to be a kind of internal playback which is sensitive to the rhythmic patterns of an implied oral form. Good writers have always been sensitive to such matters, but some translators have been so preoccupied with semantic and syntactic correspondences between source and receptor languages that they tend to overlook some of the more important and subtle factors of rhythm.

It is often difficult to analyze the precise nature of rhythmic poetry and/ or prose, but violating certain principles of rhythm certainly lessens the appeal of a text.

To produce a text with good rhythm is not easy, but it is not at all difficult to ruin the rhythm by a number of means; for example, long strings of
unaccented words (especially clusters of so-called function words, e.g.,
because in order to, wherewith when, or *down in under beside*). Heavy series of
preposed content words can also play havoc with content rhythm. Fortunately, the Bible does not have expressions typical of bureaucratese; for
example, *California State Environmental Protection Authority* as the name of a
government department. But one does often find renderings which are
too long and involved and hence violate patterns of rhythmic decoding;
for example, Ephesians 2:19b–22, "but you are fellow citizens with the
saints and members of the household of God, built upon the foundation
of the apostles and prophets, Christ Jesus himself being the cornerstone,
in whom the whole structure is joined together and grows into a holy
temple in the Lord; in whom you also are built into it for the dwelling
place of God in the Spirit" (Revised Standard Version).

Two or more syntactic embeddings in a sentence can also readily destroy rhythm. Compare, for example, the sentence *since though in order to
help he had left, the others refused to cooperate.* Discontinuous immediate constituents likewise violate patterns of rhythm, for example, *he left the room
with his friend from China quickly.*

Perhaps the best way to describe a text which does have rhythm is to
describe it as "a text which flows." The rhythmic structure of John 1:1–5 is
such as to make it almost poetry, and the same is characteristic of 1 John
1:1–4. In the latter passage the clauses do not resemble each other so
much in terms of length, but the relationship between function and content words reflects a good periodicity and rhythm. In Psalm 101 the parts
of the lines preceding the break (caesura) tend to be of approximately the
same length, particularly in couplets, and the same is true for the parts of
the lines which follow the caesura. Furthermore, in each instance the portion following the caesura is significantly shorter than the portion that
precedes the caesura.

Shifts in Expectancies

Shifts in expectancies are of numerous types, for they include order of
expressions, anacolutha, play on the multiple meanings of a word, shifts
of meaning based on similar or identical sounds, shifts from syntactic to
rhetorical meaning, paradoxes, irony, differences of degrees, symbolic
language for esoteric purposes, and figurative expressions. There is no
doubt but that these shifts in expectancies cause the greatest number of
problems for translators. They are also extremely important in a number

of functions of rhetoric, including especially impact, aesthetic appeal, coherence, and emphasis.

Shifts of order may involve words, phrases, sentences, and even episodes, and are largely for the purpose of highlighting and creating impact. The key positions for emphasis by means of order are (1) the beginning of an utterance or, somewhat less so, the beginning of an embedded sentence, or (2) the end of an utterance and similarly, the end of an embedded sentence or unit. Actually, any order which is non-normal carries a measure of impact. For example, one would expect a story to begin with the first episode and then proceed to the end. However, it is also possible to begin a story at a crisis point and then introduce a series of flashbacks to bring the reader "up to date" in terms of the series of events which have prompted the crisis. Such a shift in expected order provides greater initial impact.

A good example of this in Hebrew is what has sometimes been called "the broken construct chain," as in Ecclesiastes 10:10b, *weyitron haksher hokmah*, "but the advantage of wisdom is success," which can be analyzed in this way. *Yitron*, "advantage," is the construct and *hokmah*, "wisdom," is the dependent noun, whereas *haksher*, "success," is the element that separates the primary noun from the dependent noun. Therefore, this is a type of rhetorical device which forbids any kind of transposition in the text (Frendo, 1981, 544–45). This, however, is just one example of a wider phenomenon which has been termed "literary insertion." When such a rhetorical device is not recognized by translators, they may be led astray and produce a wrong translation, or follow the rendering found in one of the ancient versions which also did not recognize the rhetorical device.

For example, in the case of Psalm 24:6 there are three stages in the development of the text: (1) *zeh dor ya'aqob doreshaw*, "this is the generation of Jacob, those who seek him"; (2) *zeh dor doreshaw ya'aqob* (literary insertion: A X B); and (3) *zeh dor doreshaw mebaqshe paneka ya'aqob* (literary insertion and expansion: A X X B). Failure to recognize this phenomenon has led to the variant reading "God of Jacob" in some Hebrew manuscripts and in some of the ancient versions. As a result, this variant reading went into many modern translations. It also led to the proposal in the Preliminary Report of the Hebrew Old Testament Text Project that one should translate "those who seek your face, O Jacob," a proposal hard to follow by any translator. In fact, the correct translation can only be found in Buber-Rosenzweig, "Dieses ist das Geschlecht derer, die nach ihm fragen. Die dein Antlitz suchen, Jacob ists," and in the recent German translation, "So sind die Menschen, die nach Gott fragen und in seine Nähe kommen dürfen. So sind die wahren Nachkommen Jakobs." This may be rendered in English as, "Such are the people who seek for God and would come into his presence. Such are the true descendants of Jacob."

The inserted element can be a verbal phrase as in Psalm 109:10, a noun phrase as in Psalm 46:2, or even a bicolon as in Psalm 86:12 (Tsumura, 1983a, 468–83). The same phenomenon has been described in a less appropriate way in terms of "double duty modifier" (Dahood) or "pivot pattern" (Watson).

In James 1:2 the occurrence of *pasan kharan*, "all joy," at the beginning of the paragraph which speaks of "all kinds of difficulties" clearly carries considerable impact. The unexpected shift in order highlights the paradoxical nature of the content in James 1:2. Something of the rhetorical effect of the Greek text of James 1:2 may be brought out in an English translation such as "how completely fortunate you should consider yourselves, my brothers, when you encounter all kinds of trials."

One must not assume, however, that all unusual orders of words to be found in the New Testament are intended as rhetorical devices to perform some function. In Hebrews 5:5, for example, the unusual and awkward word order of the quotation from the Septuagint (based on a strictly literal rendering of the Hebrew text) is simply the result of faulty translation procedures and principles.

In some instances there is a shift of a word or phrase outside of its normal position within a clause. This type of shift in order clearly heightens its significance. In Matthew 6:28b, for example, the phrase *ta krina tou agrou*, "flowers of the field," occurs outside the clause *pōs auksanousin*, "how they grow." This order actually serves to focus greater attention upon the flowers.

Embedded parenthetical material occurs in an unexpected order and at the same time it disrupts the syntactic structure. Its unexpectedness in such a position obviously increases the impact. Note, for example, the phrase, *en aphrosunē legō*, "I am speaking like a fool" (2 Corinthians 11:21b), which is parenthetically related to the preceding and following expressions. The phrase carries considerable impact not only because of the order and interruption of syntactic structure but also because of the unusual content.

Anacolutha, shifts within the grammatical structure of a sentence, are often regarded simply as grammatical errors. When a sentence begins with one type of structure, one expects that the same type of structure will continue until the end. When, however, a structure is broken off and another structure takes over, one can conclude that either there is a grammatical mistake or that the shift may be intentional and serve some rhetorical function. In the case of the Pauline writings, such shifts in sentence structure may reflect Paul's overwhelming involvement in the subject matter. Being so full of the subject and so impressed by the urgency of the message, Paul may have shifted sentence structure without intentionally doing so. This may well be the case in Galatians 2:6:

apo de tōn dokountōn einai ti—hopoioi pote ēsan ouden moi diapherei; prosōpon ho theos anthrōpou ou lambanei—emoi gar oi dokountes ouden prosanethento "from those who seem to do something—it makes no difference to me what sort of person they were; God does not judge by outward appearances—for those who seem to be something made no new suggestions to me."

A similar type of grammatical shift occurs in Romans 5:12–13. These anacolutha may very well indicate Paul's feeling of urgency, but they may also represent merely the types of problems that occur in dictation.

In Acts 1:4, however, there seems to be a clear instance of a shift in grammatical structure for the sake of emphasis. In the first part of verse 4 the reference is to the third person, but in the clause *hēn ēkousate mou* "which you heard from me," the shift is to the second person, and this provides the basis for a shift to the second person in verse 5. Acts 1:4–5 may be more or less literally translated as "And when they came together, he announced that they should not depart from Jerusalem but wait for the promise of the Father, about which you have heard from me, that John baptized with water, but you shall be baptized by the Holy Spirit in a few days." Most translations smooth out this shift by rendering the entire statement by Jesus as direct discourse rather than shifting from indirect to direct discourse, but the shift from third to second person in the Greek text certainly increases the impact of the concluding part of this introduction to the book of Acts.

Reproducing an anacoluthon in the Greek or Hebrew text by a literal rendering into a receptor language is normally a very risky procedure, for it may simply be interpreted as a syntactic or stylistic error. If an anacoluthon carries a significant rhetorical function, it is this function which should be reproduced. There is no reason to reproduce the grammatical anomaly simply for the purpose of formal consistency as, for example, in the case of Acts 24:5f, in which the form of the initial construction is forgotten. Although one may speak of such structural shifts as anacolutha, the usage is in reality simply popular language (Blass-Debrunner, 1961, 294–98). What should be rendered in translation is the rhetorical function of an anacoluthon, and this must usually be done by employing quite different structures.

Shifts in expectancies involving multiple meanings of a word may be regarded as a type of fluctuating semantic shift. In John 3:3, for example, the ambiguity of *anōthen*, "from above," or "again," sets the stage for the initial misinterpretation of the meaning by Nicodemus and the later explanation by Jesus. A similar ambiguity occurs in John 4:10 in the phrase *hudōr zōn*, "living water," which the Samaritan woman interprets in its literal sense of "spring water." This misinterpretation leads to a fuller explanation by Jesus in verse 14. There is likewise an important double meaning assigned to *pneuma*, "wind/spirit," in John 3:8.

A similar type of double meaning of a term occurs in Amos 4:13, which may be rendered as:

> God is the one who makes the mountains,
>   and creates the winds.
> He makes his thoughts known to man;
>   he changes day into night.
> He walks on the heights of the earth.
> This is his name: the Lord God Almighty!

In this sequence the line "He makes his thoughts known to man" seems to suggest a very radical break between statements about God's creation of the mountains and the winds, and his making his thoughts known to people. In Hebrew, however, the sentence "who creates *ruah*" is really ambiguous and provides a deliberate play on the two distinct meanings of the Hebrew word *ruah*, namely, "wind" and "spirit." The meaning "wind" connects this sentence with the preceding one about the creation of such natural phenomena as the mountains, whereas the meaning of "spirit" or "spirit of man" connects it with the following sentence about the revelation of God's thoughts.

In Amos 4:13 there is the possibility of providing a double translation:

> God is the one who makes mountains and winds.
> He creates the spirit of human beings,
> and makes his thoughts known to them.

This type of double translation would not be possible in the case of *anōthen*, "from above" or "again," in John 3:7, for it is the mistaken interpretation of one meaning of *anōthen* which leads to the following explanation.

Many examples can be given for the use of different meanings of the same word or root. Quintilian (Inst. 9.3,68) used the word *antanaclasis* for this: *cui confinis est antanaklasis, eiusdem verbi contraria significatio*, "akin to this is antanaclasis, where the same word is used in two different meanings." A good example is the use of different meanings of Hebrew *matsa',* "to find, to reach, to overtake, to meet, to grasp," etc. For example, in Job 11:7 the meaning may be, "Can you *find out* the designs of God?" or "Can you *reach* the perfection of the Almighty?" In the Song of Songs 3:2-3 *matsa'* occurs at the end of verse 2 and at the beginning of verse 3 and thus highlights in a particular way the differences of meaning (Ceresko, 1982, 551-70):

> I sought but did not *find* him;
>   they *met* me, the watchmen.

This phenomenon has been called "the Janus figure." With varying degrees of probability, a number of examples of this figure have been proposed by scholars. So in the text of Nahum 1:8 one may have the following:

> But with an overflowing flood
> he will completely destroy mqwmh
> and will pursue his enemies into darkness.

The grapheme mqwmh could be vocalized as *meqomah*, "its place," referring probably to a city, or as *meqawmah*, a feminine abstract noun meaning "rebellion" and therefore referring to "rebels." However, there does not seem to be sufficient evidence to introduce a double translation in this case (Tsumura, 1983, 109–11). In some languages, for example, Japanese, a similar poetic device seems to exist.

In some instances the double meaning of a single term may in fact be intended, so that one may be justified in a double translation. Such appears to be the case with *katalambanō* in John 1:5, which may mean "to overcome" or "to understand" or possibly both meanings at the same time, so that one might legitimately translate: "the light shines in the darkness, and the darkness has neither overcome nor understood it." The validity of such a translation is partially justified because the gospel of John employs a number of words with double meanings.

Plays on the meanings of words having similar or identical sounds are particularly difficult to reflect in translating. Even trying to reproduce Hebrew *'ish*, "man," in contrast with *'ishah*, "woman," by using English *man* and *woman* still does not carry the same impact as the sequence in Hebrew, for the feminine formation in Hebrew is a regular one, and there is no such regular formation in the sequence *man/woman*. Such problems of multiple meanings of the same or similar forms must usually be dealt with in marginal notes.

In Jeremiah 17:13 the expression *miqweh yisra'el yahweh* is generally rendered as "Lord, the hope of Israel." However, there exists a homonym *miqweh* with the meaning "pool," and the figurative usage of that homonym could have been intended here with the meaning, "The Lord is the pool of Israel." This seems to be justified since at the end of the same verse (and in a chiastic arrangement), the Lord is identified with "the fountain of living water" (Dahood, 1967, 40–49).

A whole series of passages in Genesis can only be understood if the Hebrew wordplay is made clear: *hawah . . . hay* in 3:20; *qayin . . . qaniti* in 4:1; *peleg . . . niplegah* in 10:25; *'abraham . . . 'ab-hamon* in 17:5, etc. Preference should first be given to a rendering that can be incorporated into the text, but frequently only a footnote can be employed, since it is rare indeed that a textual equivalent can be found. The Greek Septuagint translation of Genesis 3:20, *zōē mētēr pantōn tōn zōntōn*, literally "life the mother of all living things," is an exception.

Although in a majority of cases one can only note resemblances in sounds, in a few instances scholarly consensus exists as to the different meanings. In Genesis 17:5, for example, the typical West Semitic phrase-name *Abram* meaning "my father (that is, "God") is great," is changed into *Abraham*, meaning "father of a great multitude." This play on the meaning of words should certainly be mentioned in a note.

Shifts from syntactic to rhetorical levels of meaning involve primarily rhetorical questions, declarative forms for imperatives, and imperatives employed as conditionals.

A question normally suggests that a source is eliciting information. In reality, however, a rhetorical question may be employed as an emphatic way of making a declaration. In Romans 8:31–35 there are a number of rhetorical questions. In verse 31, for example, Paul writes *ti oun eroumen pros tauta?* "Therefore, what shall we say with regard to these things?" But this is not a request for information. In fact, the immediately following question is in essence an answer, but it is given likewise in the form of a question, "If God is for us, who can be against us?" Paul is not asking for a response but making an emphatic declaration equivalent to, "If God is for us, no one can be against us." In 1 John 3:17 the question "How can the love of God remain in him?" is an emphatic way of saying that such a person cannot really be loving God.

The use of a declarative statement with imperative content is another instance of a shift in expectation between content and intent. In 1 John 2:6, for example, the statement "whoever says he remains in union with him ought to live as that one lived" is formally a declarative statement, but the intent is clearly imperative and may be rendered in some languages as "if you say you remain in union with him, live as that one lived."

In Ephesians 4:26 the imperative *orgizesthe*, "be angry," is not a command but a type of concessive condition meaning "even if you do get angry," followed by the result, "still, you must not sin." Several proverbs employ an imperative expression as a conditional. Note, for example, Proverbs 27:22, "crush a fool in a mortar with a pestle along with crushed grain, yet his folly will not depart from him." The meaning is simply, "Even if you should crush a fool . . . his folly would not depart from him."

Classical rhetoricians particularly favored apparent contradictions, or paradoxes, which could be resolved by the larger contexts. In this way a writer can highlight the significance of something which otherwise might seem impossible. Such an apparent contradiction occurs in 2 Corinthians 3:10, in which the statement *gar ou dedoksastai to dedoksasmenon*, "for that which has been made glorious has not been made glorious," is clearly contradictory, but this is resolved by the rest of verse 10.

Sometimes the paradoxical element in a statement results from a strange shift in logical relationships. For example, in 2 Timothy 2:12b–13, the first part of verse 13 seems to involve a contradiction if one employs a more or less literal interpretation, namely, "if we deny him, he will deny us; and if we are not faithful, he remains faithful, for he cannot deny himself." There seems to be no logical relationship between the conditional clause *ei apistoumen*, "if we are not faithful," and the conclusion *ekeinos pistos menei*, "he remains faithful." But this seemingly illogical relationship is resolved by the final line, in which *arnēsasthai*, "to deny," has quite a different meaning from what it has in verse 12b, and therefore in verse 13 it should be rendered as "to be false to oneself." Furthermore, the conditional expression rendered "if we are not faithful" should be treated as a type of concessive conditional, so that a more accurate rendering of this passage would be: "If we deny him, he will deny us; but even if we are not faithful, he nevertheless remains faithful, for he cannot be false to himself."

Irony involves an important shift between literal content and actual intent. Compare, for example, Paul's statement in 2 Corinthians 12:13, "for how is it that you were treated worse than the other churches, except for the fact that I myself was no burden to you? Forgive me for this injustice." Paul obviously does not regard his treatment of the believers in Corinth as being a case of injustice, but in speaking this way he is taking the position of some persons in Corinth who evidently had accused Paul of taking advantage of the believers.

In Mark 7:9 the adverb *kalōs*, "fine," is used in an ironical sense, for Jesus certainly did not mean literally "you have a fine way of setting aside the commandment of God in order to maintain your tradition." Since in many instances it is not possible to use a term meaning "fine" or a way in which the irony can be overtly marked, it may be better to render *kalōs* as "clever."

The striking shifts in degree by employing expressions which differ radically in literal content and evident intent are well illustrated by understatement (litotes) and overstatement (hyperbole). Such expressions of inverse degree become emphatic by virtue of their obvious understatement or overstatement. For example, in Luke 1:37 the statement *hoti ouk adunatēsei para tou theou pan rhēma*, "because with God everything is not impossible," is really a declaration that "God can do anything." In Romans 10:16 there is likewise an understatement based on negation: *all' ou pantes hupēkousan tō euaggeliō*, "but not all were obedient to the good news," while the actual meaning is "only some were obedient to the good news."

Overstatement seems to be more common than understatement. The statement in Mark 1:5 that all of the people in Judea and Jerusalem went out and were baptized by John in the Jordan is clearly a case of literary exaggeration. Similarly, the statement in Mark 1:33, "and the entire city was gathered at the door," also appears to be a typical overstatement for dramatic effect.

Jesus himself frequently used hyperboles in his teaching when he spoke of straining out a gnat and swallowing a camel (Matthew 23:24) or a beam in one's own eye in contrast with a speck in the eye of another (Luke 6:41–42) or the camel going through the eye of a needle (Matt. 19:24).

The use of figurative language is an important rhetorical device which not only creates impact and aesthetic appeal but often suggests important new insights. Metaphors and metonymies are, of course, always a part of larger verbal contexts which serve to mark their meanings as figurative. The actual differences in meaning between *snake* as a reference to a reptile and as a reference to Dan in Genesis 49:17 is a matter for analysis by techniques employed in lexical semantics, but the use of *snake* in referring to Dan is part of the rhetoric. The marking or contextual conditioning of figurative meanings is also an aspect of the rhetorical structure, but determining the distinctive features of meaning of a figurative expression is an aspect of lexical semantics, treated in Chapter 9.

The use of highly figurative and symbolic language for strictly esoteric purposes in communicating to a particular ingroup, as is true of apocalyptic writing, often leads to purposeful obscurity. To speak of Babylon (Rev. 14:8) when the reference is actually to Rome is a device by which a writer of apocalyptic can communicate to a restricted in-group without those in an out-group knowing what is being communicated. Likewise in Revelation 13:2 the references to a leopard, a bear, and a lion would certainly have meaning to persons familiar with the context of Daniel 7:4–6, where a lion, a bear, and a leopard are mentioned, but this reference in Revelation would be purposefully obscure to persons not familiar with the passage of Daniel.

Figurative language involves a radical shift in semantic domains while preserving a psychological awareness of the respective literal and figurative meanings. This means that one needs to distinguish carefully between figurative meanings and noncentral (or peripheral) meanings of lexical units. The occurrence of *alōpēks,* "fox," (Luke 13:32) as a reference to King Herod is figurative since there is a radical shift in the semantic domain of an animal to a person, and there is at the same time obvious psychological awareness of both the literal and the figurative meaning in that Herod is likened to a fox in terms of craftiness. In the case of a word such as *coat,* however, the three meanings occurring in such phrases as *he put on a coat, a coat of dust,* and *to coat something with paint* do not involve radical shifts, since all of the meanings are related to the domain of close covering. The use of *coat* in the meaning of a garment may be regarded as central and the meaning in *a coat of dust* may be regarded as peripheral, while *coat* in connection with applying paint is a peripheral derivative meaning involving a significant grammatical shift but not a radical alteration of semantic domains.

Psychological awareness is a matter of varying degrees depending upon the freshness of the figurative expression. When a figure of speech is used frequently, the awareness gradually diminishes to the point where the expression becomes "a dead figure of speech." As such, it is simply one of the peripheral meanings of a semantic constellation. There are certain figurative expressions for which the original basis of the figure of speech has been completely lost. For example, the biblical idiom *heap coals of fire on the head* (Prov. 25:22 and Rom. 12:20) is obviously not to be understood in a literal sense but in a figurative sense, probably indicating that one should be so kind to someone as to make him ashamed, but the original basis for such an expression is no longer known.

Figurative meanings are essentially of two basic types: metonymies and metaphors. Metonymies are based upon associations and metaphors are based upon similarities. Figurative language, however, exists not only in single words or idioms but in larger units, for example, proverbs ("wisdom builds her house but folly tears it down," Prov. 14:1), parables ("The Sower," Matt. 13:1–8), and visions (Acts 10:9–15, Ezek. 1:4–28, Daniel 7–8, and much of the book of Revelation).

Some typical lexical metonymies include *peritomē*, "circumcision" (Gal. 2:9), as a reference to the Jews, *psukhē*, "soul," (Acts. 2:43) meaning the entire person, and *sarks*, literally "flesh" (Rom. 9:3), as a designation for "race."

In contrast with such metonymies, which are based on association, metaphors involve a principle of similarity, whether of form or function. For example, when Jesus designates Peter as *satanas*, "Satan," (Mark 8:33), he is simply pointing out that in certain respects Peter's behavior is similar to that of Satan, and in John 8:44 the term *patēr*, "father," is used in referring to the devil as the spiritual progenitor of the Jewish leaders.

These metonymies and metaphors are all typical of active conventional figurative expressions, but many figurative expressions are much less conventional. Note, for example, Paul's extensive use of *klados*, "branch," and *rhiza*, "root," in Romans 11:17–19, in which he employs these two figurative expressions in referring to the experience and function of the Jews in relationship to the promises of God. This less conventional use of figurative expressions is typical of primary religious language, since fresh insights can seldom be expressed adequately by means of traditional semantic formulas. The equation of Hagar with the covenant made at Mount Sinai, and the identification of that with the city of Jerusalem in contrast with the heavenly Jerusalem (Gal. 4:24–25), is an instance of quite unconventional figurative usage.

Full idioms consist of two or more words whose meaning is not to be derived from the sum total of the parts. Both the Old Testament and the New Testament abound in such expressions. Idioms typical of the New Testament are "girding up the loins of your mind" (1 Pet. 1:13), ''do not blow a trumpet ahead of you" (Matt. 6:2), and "it shall be preached on the housetops" (Luke 12:3). For these idioms one can readily determine the relation between the literal, and the figurative meanings, but it is not so easy to determine the relation for such expressions as "his eyes shall be red with wine, and his teeth white with milk" (Gen. 49:12) as a means of referring to the future wealth and status of the tribe of Judah.

In addition to the figurative meaning of verbal expressions, one must also reckon with the figurative meaning of events. To regard the cursing of the fig tree (Mark 11:12–14 and 11:20–25) as only a case of Jesus being irritated at not finding fruit is to miss the symbolic and figurative significance of the event. Even if one does not wish to read the story as a symbolic event or as an acted parable, the truth remains that Mark in his record intended this as an illustration of the divine power of Jesus. Similarly, the account of Jonah has its true meaning not as "a big fish story" but on the higher level of a dramatic illustration of God's grace.

Probably the most serious problems for translators occur in attempts to do justice to figurative expressions. This results largely from the fact that figurative expressions depend so much upon local cultural settings. Unless the figurative significance of an expression is rather obvious from the context, it is often necessary to make some change in the form to reflect the functional equivalence. If that is neither possible or expedient, it may then be useful to add some clarifying marginal note.

Exploitation of Isomorphic Features

Any two or more events, entities, or concepts are likely to have certain features of similarity and contrast. Similarly, any multiple references to such events, entities, or concepts are also likely to show certain similarities or contrasts, and even a single event, entity, or concept may have various features which exhibit significant similarities or contrasts.

As already noted briefly at the beginning of this chapter, in Matthew 5:21–48 there are six brief discourses about anger, adultery, divorce, oaths, retaliation, and love for enemies. In each case there is a significant contrast between traditions and the teachings of Jesus. The parallelism is highlighted by the fact that in each instance there is first a statement about the tradition and then an introduction to the teaching of Jesus by the emphatic form "but I say to you." In order to avoid unnecessary repetition, the introductory statements about the traditions vary slightly, but the focal feature, namely the expression "but I say to you," is the same in each instance. This is an excellent illustration of the way in which similarity and contrast are effectively marked.

In Matthew 7:24–27 the description of the houses built on bedrock and then on sand is likewise both parallel and contrastive. The arrangement of the constituent parts is parallel, but the vocabulary is contrastive, and at the end of verse 27 the contrast is made even more effective by adding the clause "and the fall of it was great," which might well be translated into English as "it collapsed with a crash."

The contrast between (1) the wide gate and easy road and (2) the narrow gate and the rough road is heightened by making the two statements essentially parallel in arrangement. The order of primary elements, namely, *gate, road,* and *direction,* is the same in both instances, while the contrast is brought out by qualifiers, *broad* versus *narrow, easy* versus *rough, many* versus *few,* and *destruction* versus *life.*

In Matthew 7:6 the contrast between giving what is holy to dogs and throwing one's pearls before swine is accentuated by a chiastic arrangement in Greek, which is traditionally translated as "do not give what is holy to dogs, nor throw your pearls before swine, lest they trample them underfeet and turn and rend you." However, it is the pigs that do the trampling and it is the dogs that turn and attack. This chiastic arrangement is missed by a great many readers, and so it may be necessary to shift from a chiastic arrangement to parallelism and thus translate as "do not give to the dogs what is holy, for they will only turn and tear you to pieces; and do not give your pearls to pigs, for they will trample them into the ground."

In Matthew 7:3 there is a very effective use of chiasm to highlight the difference between seeing a speck in someone else's eye and failing to recognize a beam in one's own eye. The principal constituents in the Greek text of Matthew 7:3 are "see," "speck," "eye," "eye," "beam," and "notice." In English, however, it is impossible to preserve this kind of chiastic arrangement, but the contrast can be indicated by a parallel structure using contrastive words, for example, "how can you notice a speck in someone else's eye and not be aware of the log in your own eye?"

In some instances parallelism may be so great as to almost hide certain significant contrasts. The Beatitudes (Matt. 5:3–10), for example, are so alike in general structure that one sometimes misses the fact that in the first and last beatitudes the tense of the verb in present, while all of the intervening beatitudes are in the future. Evidently the focus is upon the fact that the kingdom of heaven (essentially the rule of God over believers) is a present reality and not simply a future blessing.

Any break in otherwise parallel structures may be highly significant. For example, in Luke 15 the stories of the lost sheep, the lost coin, and lost son have a number of important parallel features, namely, loss of something, its being found, and the rejoicing. In the first two parables there is also the echo of rejoicing in heaven over any sinner who repents. In the story of the lost son this rejoicing in heaven is implied by what happens on his return. Note, however, that the estrangement of the older son is not resolved. This is precisely why this third parable is such a significant answer to the Pharisees and scribes who were grumbling about the fact that Jesus had received and eaten with tax collectors and religious outcasts.

Matthew 6:24 is an instructive model as to how both similarities and contrasts can be effectively highlighted. The first clause is a simple, straightforward statement to the effect that no one can serve two masters. This is then followed by the alternative conjunctions $ē$ . . . $ē$ "either . . . or." In the following alternative set the order of "the one . . . the other" remains parallel, but notice the shift in order between "hate . . . love" / "be devoted to . . . despise." In the final clause the contrast between God and money is highlighted by separating them by means of a verb meaning "to serve." There is even a parallelism in the beginning of the first and last clauses in the words meaning "no one can" and "you cannot."

In the Old Testament parallelism is extensively used, particularly in poetic utterances such as in Job, Psalms, and the prophets, but chiasm is also a frequently employed rhetorical device. In many instances the chiasm occurs with a so-called pivot or hinge between the two chiastic sets. Note, for example, Amos 5:4b–6a as rendered in the Revised Standard Version:

> "Seek me and live;
>> but do not seek Bethel,
> and do not enter into Gilgal
>> or cross over to Beer-sheba;
> for Gilgal shall surely go into exile,
>> and Bethel shall come to nought."
> Seek the Lord and live.

This chiastic pattern in this case would be A B C D C B A. Some scholars see in any such pivot or hinge a crucial or focal element in a discourse, but this is not necessarily always the case.

Perhaps one of the clearest discourse structures involving a relatively elaborate chiastic structure is to be found in the book of Joel. One may describe the organization as a type of program and antiprogram, the shift taking place in the center in 2:18. The following division and display of semantic markers can be made (English Bible numerations are in parentheses):

Major Divisions

A Invasion of locusts and drought		1:1–14
B The Day of God's Judgment		1:15–20
C The army of the Enemy as the instrument of God's punishment		2:1–11

D Returning to God	2:12–14	
E Praying to God	2:15–17	
E' God's Answer	2:18–27	
D' God will pour out his Spirit on everyone	3:1–5	(2:28–32)
C' God will punish the enemies of his people	4:1–13	(3:1–13)
B' Promise to Jerusalem	4:14–17	(3:14–17)
A' Prosperity of Judah	4:18–21	(3:18, 21)

Semantic Markers

1:15	The day of the Lord is near
2:1	blow the trumpet in Zion; for the day of the Lord is coming, it is near.
2:11	for the day of the Lord is great
2:12	yet even now
2:15	blow the trumpet in Zion
2:18	(a thematic break)
3:1	it shall come to pass (2:28)
3:5	it shall come to pass (2:32)
4:1	for behold, in those days and at that time (3:1)
4:14	for the day of the Lord is near (3:14)
4:17	it shall be (3:17)
4:18	it shall come to pass in that day (3:18)

The probability that this pattern is the primary structure of the book is heightened by the fact that recursions of vocabulary, motifs, and thematic content take place in pairs: A/A', B/B', C/C', D/D', and E/E'. In so far as possible a translator should maintain the structural transparency of this pattern in a translation. Unfortunately, some of even the most recent translations do not reflect these distinctions in their discourse divisions.

It is even possible to see both parallel and chiastic arrangements within certain discourse units. The story of the tower of Babel in Genesis 11:1–9 may illustrate some of the problems associated with such a patterning:

I. *Parallel Structure*

  A *saphah 'ehat udebarim 'ahadim* "one language and the same words" (11:1)

   B *habah* "come let us" (11:3)

    C *nibneh* "build" (11:4)

     D *na'aseh shem* "let us make a name for ourselves" (11:4)

      E *pen naphuts 'al-pene kol ha'arets* "lest we be scattered upon the face of the whole earth" (11:4)

     A' *'am 'ehad wesaphah 'ahat* "one people and one language" (11:6)

      B' *habah* "come let us" (11:7)

       C' *libnot* "to build" (11:8)

        D' *shemah babel* "its name Babel" (11:9)

         E' *hephitsam 'al pene kol ha'arets* "he scattered them over the face of all the earth" (11:9)

II. *Chiastic Structure*

   A *kol ha'arets saphah 'ehat* "the whole earth one language" (11:1)
    B *sham* "there" (11:2)
     C *'ish 'el re'ehu* "to one another" (11:3)
      D *habah nilbenah lebenim* "come, let us make bricks" (11:3)
       E *nibneh lanu* "let us build ourselves" (11:4)
        F *'ir umigdal* "a city and a tower" (11:4)
         X *wayered yahveh lir'ot* "and the Lord came down to see" (11:5)
        F' *'et ha'ir we'et hamigdal* "the city and the tower" (11:5)
       E' *'asher banu bene ha'adam* "which the sons of men had built" (11:5)
      D' *habah . . . wenablah* "come . . . let us confuse" (11:7)
     C' *'ish sephat re'ehu* "one another's speech" (11:7)
    B' *misham* "from there" (11:8)
   A' *sephat kol ha'arets* "the language of all the earth" (11:9)

In the chiastic arrangement the X marks the pivot or hinge of the structure.

From a strictly linguistic standpoint, however, this type of analysis is open to certain criticisms. In the first place, not all of the features listed are of the same thematic or semantic value. For example, *habah* "come let us" is primarily an exhortative particle in the semantic structuring, and the term *sham* "there" is a deictic particle. Furthermore, there are certain significant omissions. For example, in the parallel structure there is nothing to represent the crucial contents of verse 5, and in the analysis of the presumed chiastic structure there is no reference to the contents of verse 6.

Radday (1981, 101) employs a heavily reductionist approach to this account of the tower of Babel and speaks of a pattern which is chiastic and in the following form:

A Action	(1–2)	by men
B Speech	(3–4)	
C Action	(5)	divine intervention
B' Speech	(6–7)	by God
A' Action	(8–9)	

This type of structuring is appealing, but it can only be the result of a rather extensive reductionism. In reality, verse 1 simply describes a state of affairs and verse 2 describes an action which sets the stage for the following events. Verses 3 and 4 do contain two important direct discourses, but in reality these substitute for action, for the resulting action is implied and not specifically described.

Even verse 5 is not direct divine intervention, but simply inspection. The divine intervention does not actually occur until verse 8. Verses 6 and 7 are primarily cognitive in function, for they represent a process of decision making put into the form of direct address. Verses 8 and 9 do involve action, but there is an embedded popular etymology explaining the derivation of the name of Babylon. The final part of verse 9 simply repeats the first part of verse 8, but in doing so summarizes the entire account.

From a strictly literary standpoint, this story is a typical etiological or "so why" story, for it is designed to explain why people have different languages, are scattered all over the earth, and also why Babylon has the name that it does. Rather than a chiastic structure it might be much better to treat this as most narratives are treated, namely, in terms of a pattern of steady state, complicating factors, crucial decision, decisive action, resolution, and final steady state.

It is possible to treat the Joseph story (Gen. 37:1—46:7) as a case of inverted parallelism or chiasm in which the elevation of Joseph from the prison to a position as governor of Egypt becomes the central point, but this type of approach seriously overlooks the nature of narrative, which normally continues to build the tension of its major themes up to a point of climax, at which point a crucial decision and the subsequent action begin a process of resolution or denouement.

The story of Joseph consists of six acts:

Act 1: from a steady state in 37:1–2a to the complications involved in Joseph being sold as a slave to Potiphar (37:36).

Act 2: from Joseph's success with Potiphar to his being forgotten by the butler as he languishes in prison (39:1–23).

Act 3: from Pharoah's dreams to the prosperity followed by famine (40:1—41:57).

Act 4: from the first journey of Joseph's brothers to Egypt to Jacob's insistence that Benjamin will not return (42:1–38).

Act 5: from the decision to return to Egypt to the point where Joseph reveals himself (43:1—45:15).

Act 6: the resolution and return to a different steady state in Egypt (45:16—46:7).

Note that each act except the last ends with a subcrisis which anticipates further developments and complications. For a narrative such as the story of Joseph, it seems far more relevant to handle the material in terms of a scenario or schema than as a chiastic structure which must depend in most instances on a high degree of selectivity.

In connection with the Joseph story there is always the issue of the thirty-eighth chapter of Genesis. This chapter involving Judah and Tamar has a structural validity in the Joseph story in that it permits a lapse of time for Joseph to be established in Egypt and also introduces an account with a similar theme; namely, the manner in which, despite human actions, the integrity of the family is maintained.

It would be quite wrong to give the impression that all larger units of discourse structure can be handled either in terms of parallelism/chiasm or in terms of narrative scenarios. There are a number of different possibilities for discourse structures, and one which is significant in the Bible involves the patterning of statement and response. This structure is typical of a number of the Psalms but also occurs in a rhetorically elaborate discourse in Ephesians 1:3–14, the longest sentence in the Greek New Testament. This sentence is not, however, merely "a sentence which didn't know when to end," as some people have suggested. Rather, it is a very subtly organized antiphonal structure based on the double meaning of the stem *eulog-* meaning "to praise" and "to bless" and contains seven blessings and four expressions of praise.

The seven blessings include being chosen, being predestined, being delivered, being made known the mysteries, being called, having heard the truth, and being sealed by the Spirit. In all of these blessings God is the causative agent. However, as already noted, God is merely named once (verse 3) and is clearly placed in the background, while Jesus Christ is the effective agent, named five times, and is clearly emphasized in the foreground. The Holy Spirit is introduced in verses 13 and 14 as the guarantee that the promised blessings will come to the believers. The addition of the role of the Holy Spirit makes this antiphonal hymn an important reference to the trinity.

The text begins with a word of praise and thanksgiving followed by two blessings, then another expression of praise followed by three blessings, a third expression of praise followed by two blessings, and finally an expression of praise at the very end. This remarkable structure suggests immediately a kind of theological hymn. To do justice to the intricate structure, a translator is well advised to attempt by the format arrangement to highlight these relationships and thus reproduce by format an isomorphic equivalent of the formal and thematic structure:

3Praise the God and Father of our Lord Jesus Christ,
    for in Christ he has blessed us
        with every spiritual blessing in the heavenly world!

4God chose us in Christ before the world was created,
    so that we would be holy and blameless before him.
Because of his love, 5God had already decided to make us his children,
        through Jesus Christ,
    for this was his pleasure and purpose.

[6]Praise God for his glorious grace,
    for the free gift he gave us in his dear Son!

[7]In Christ we have deliverance through his sacrificial death,
    the forgiveness of our sins [8]through his overwhelming grace.
In all wisdom and insight [9]God made known his purpose in Christ,
    his secret plan for the fullness of time
        [10]to make Christ the head of all things,
            those in heaven and those on earth.
[11]In Christ we have been called
    in accordance with the prior decision of God,
    who does all things according to his plan and purpose.

    [12]We, who were the first to put our hope in Christ, should praise
        God's glory!

    [13]In Christ you also heard the true message,
        the good news about your salvation.
    In Christ you put your faith,
        and God put his stamp of ownership on you
            by giving you the Holy Spirit, whom he had promised.
        [14]The Spirit is the guarantee of our inheritance,
            the deliverance of those who belong to God.

    Praise God's glory!

With each of the blessings there is also a statement of purpose, reason, result, and/or attendant circumstance. There are several other significant rhetorical features in this passage, but this should be sufficient to indicate the complexity of this finely tuned structure and the evident purpose in producing "a theological hymn."

In treating rhetorical features it is often useless, and generally unwise, to attempt to match form for form. What one must try to do, therefore, is to match function for function, in other words, to attempt to discover in the receptor language the closest functional equivalent of the rhetorical structure in the source text. The particular set of forms used for different rhetorical functions is largely language specific, but the functions, as already indicated, are universals, and it is for this reason that one can aim at functional equivalence.

As already noted twice, a formal reproduction of the repetition which occurs in the poetic parallelism of the Old Testament can be seriously misinterpreted in many languages as being an insult to the intelligence of the reader or hearer. The function of such parallelism in Hebrew is to suggest cognitive completeness, relevance, aesthetic balance, and emphasis, but if the translator insists upon reproducing such parallelism the intended functions are completely distorted. It is, however, possible in many languages to represent the rhetorical functions of poetic parallelism but by quite different means; for example, by emphatic particles, rhythm, and compactness as a mark of gnomic relevance. Similarly, the unity and structural intricacy of Ephesians 1:3–14 can be destroyed in some languages by insisting upon translating this passage as a single sentence. But the rhetorical functions of this passage can be displayed meaningfully by quite different rhetorical arrangements.

7

Grammatical Meaning

As in the case of rhetorical meaning, grammatical meanings are far more numerous than are the formal grammatical structures. Note, for example, the following so-called "possessive constructions" in English: *his arm, his car, his father, his work,* and *his incarceration.* If we identify the first constituent, namely *his,* as A and the following noun as B, we may then define the relationship in *his arm* as "B is a part of A." In the case of *his car,* "A possesses B." In the case of *his father,* "A and B are kin in direct line of descent." In the case of *his work,* "A does B," and in the case of *his incarceration,* "A experiences B." On a strictly formal or surface level of structure, these constructions all appear to be alike, but they are quite different in underlying meaning, and in some languages quite different formal structures must be employed to mark these diverse meaningful relations.

As will be found throughout this chapter, it is essential to recognize the fundamental differences which exist between underlying semantic relations and surface forms, or what are called by some linguists, the underlying structures and the surface structures.

Grammatical structures are of two basically different types. The first type may be called combinatory or syntagmatic. In this type of grammatical structure the meaningful relationships are between two (and sometimes more) parts. Normally, however, the structures are binary, that is, there are two immediate constituent elements which combine, and the result of such a set of combining features is a hierarchical structure in which there is a tendency for the immediate constituent elements to be contiguous to one another, but this is not always the case. Note the very simple structure in English shown on the next page.

The other type of grammatical relationship is substitutive or paradigmatic. For example, for the sentence *the old man was asleep on the bench* one could substitute *he* for *the old man,* with the resulting structure *he was asleep on the bench.* This type of substitution is specifically referential. There is, however, a different type of substitutive structure in language, which

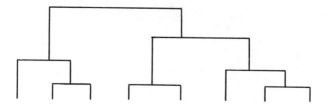

The old man was asleep on the bench.

could be called a type of "class substitute." For example, one can also say *the small dog was asleep on the bench*. Accordingly, *the old man* and *the small dog* may be regarded as belonging to the same class because they can substitute one for another within certain grammatical frames.

To appreciate some of the problems of grammatical meaning, it is essential to explore somewhat more widely the various types of combinatory relations. These are primarily of four basic types: coordinating, delimiting, relation-axis, and propositional. Coordinate relations are easily illustrated by such phrases as *man and woman, he or she,* and *swam and dived*. Delimiting relations may be said to involve one element modifying another, often by qualifying or quantifying, in such phrases as *strong fortress, ran fast,* and *ten men*.

The relation-axis is somewhat more complex. In English the corresponding constructions usually consist of a preposition followed by a noun or of a conjunction followed by a subject-predicate structure or some reduced form of such a structure. Note such phrases as *in the house, above the tree, while sick,* and *if he comes*. The first element in each phrase constitutes the relation, and the second constitutes the axis. For example, one may have a series of phrases such as *in the house, around the house, above the house,* and *under the house,* in which *the house* constitutes clearly the axis and may be preceded by terms representing a number of different relations.

The fourth type of grammatical relation involves propositions and these are primarily of three types: characterizing, identificational, and nucleus-satellite. A characterizing proposition may be illustrated by *the man is righteous* and *the idea seems right*. A statement such as *Jesus is the Messiah* is identificational. A sentence such as *Jael killed Sisera with a tent peg* is best described as nucleus-satellite in that the nucleus is the verb *killed;* the satellites are the agent *Jael,* the affected person *Sisera,* and the instrument *the tent peg*. Such satellites can be related to the nucleus *killed* in various ways. For example, one may say *Sisera was killed with a tent peg,* or *a tent peg killed Sisera,* or *Sisera was killed by Jael*.

On the surface level of grammatical structures most languages have a number of different word classes; for example, nouns, verbs, adjectives, adverbs, prepositions, conjunctions, and pronouns. From the standpoint of the meaningful relations between units in grammatical constructions, the underlying classes are even more important. These may be called semantic classes, and there are four basic types, as already noted: objects, events, abstracts, and relationals. The objects, which may often be called "participants," include such lexical units as *man, house, tree, water, sun,* and *dog,* while events involve such lexical units as *kill, run, think, grow, die,* and *fill.* Abstracts involve lexical units whose semantic contents are always features of something else, for example, *tall, red, good, fast,* and *ten.* The meaning of a term such as *tall* is nothing in and of itself but is always a feature of some object, while the word *fast* is always a feature of some event or activity. There is a special type of abstract which is the result of events, and such abstracts are semantically related to events. For example, *dead* is an abstract of state, but it is the result of the event of dying. Similarly, *full* is an abstract of a condition, and it is related to the activity *fill.*

There is a very special type of abstract called relationals, which relate to space, time, and logic. Spatials involve such prepositions as *in, beyond,* and *above,* while temporal relations may involve such lexical units as *while, when,* and *during,* and logical relationals are characteristic of such lexical units as *if, because, and,* and *or.*

A high percentage of words have meanings which fit into only one semantic class (e.g., *man, run,* and *tall*), but some terms are semantically complex (e.g., *prophet, sanctify,* and *heir*). The term *prophet* identifies not only an object, the person involved but also specifies a particular kind of activity. In *sanctify* there is not only an abstract of holiness but a causative event in making something holy. In the case of *heir,* one is not only speaking of an object, that is, a person, but an individual who will receive or has received something of considerable value, usually as the result of someone else having died.

Designative and Associative Meanings

As in the case of rhetorical and lexical structures, grammatical structures likewise have both designative and associative meanings. The designative meanings simply state relationships between units, whether combinatory or substitutive. For example, in the statement *the promise of God,* the relationship between *the promise* and *God,* which is marked by the preposition *of,* can be stated as "B does A," that is, God is the one who promises. In the statement *the creation of the world,* the semantic relation between the two units *the creation* and *the world* may be defined as "B is the result of A." In stating the substitutive relationship between expressions such as *the man* and *he,* which may occur at different points in a discourse, we may say that *he* "refers to" *the man.*

Associative meanings, however, are quite different. The relationship is not between units but results from the circumstances in which certain grammatical constructions occur. For example, the associative meaning of *he go now* may be described as substandard, and the construction *between you and I* may carry the associative meaning of "traditionally unacceptable but increasingly employed." A question such as *What right hath my beloved?* has an associative meaning of old-fashioned and is certainly out of place in any contemporary setting. Particular grammatical constructions become so typical of certain kinds of discourse that we almost inevitably associate these structures with what we call legalese, bureaucratese, or academese.

For the translator there are a number of special problems relating to designative meaning. For example, in the biblical expression *God and Father of our Lord Jesus Christ* the conjunction *and,* which normally coordinates two different persons, in this instance really marks apposition, for God is the Father of our Lord Jesus Christ. If one translates literally "God and Father of our Lord Jesus Christ," in some languages people will inevitably understand that God is one person and the Father of our Lord Jesus Christ is quite a different person.

In structures such as *began to speak, stopped doing,* and *continued working,* the verbs *began, stopped,* and *continued* are regarded as the grammatical heads of the constructions, while *speak, doing,* and *working* are so-called complements. On the surface level, this is an accurate description, but on the underlying level of semantic relations, the verbs *began, stopped,* and *continued* are only aspects of the more important semantic elements, namely *to speak, doing,* and *working.* In fact, in a number of languages these aspects are indicated by adverbs or by affixes.

A phrase such as *answered and said* (occurring frequently in both the Old Testament and the New Testament) must not be translated in such a way as to mean "he answered and then he said," which is precisely the meaning that has been understood in a number of literal translations. The term rendered "answered" is really the primary semantic carrier, and the word translated "said" serves only to mark the beginning of direct discourse. In a number of languages one can better render a phrase such as *answered and said* as "answered" or "answered by saying."

Delimiting combinatory relations occur frequently in Hebrew. When, for example, in Genesis 27:38 it is said of Esau *wayiśa' . . . qolo wayyebk,* "he lifted up his voice and wept," there is a relation in which the first verb delimits the second one with respect to quality. By means of this combination, the weeping is marked as a loud one, and one can best translate such a combination as "he wept loudly" or even "he wept intensely."

On the other hand, in Genesis 29:1 it is said of Jacob *wayisa' raglaw wayelek*, "he lifted up his feet and went." The surface structure is the same as in Genesis 27:38, but in this instance it is the first verb which delimits the second as to phase; in other words, the first event marks the beginning of the second. The result is almost a type of aspect in which the first verb indicates the beginning of the action of going. Fortunately, few translators would render this phrase in Genesis 29:1 in a strictly literal manner. Most modern versions recognize the combinatory grammatical function and they translate, as in the New American Bible, "After Jacob resumed his journey." Even in the case of Genesis 27:38, most translators recognize the qualitative relationship and, as in the case of the New Jewish Version, have translated "he wept aloud" (Orlinsky, 1974, 410).

In the phrase *wayashkimu wayetse'u*, literally "they rose up early and went" (Josh. 8:14), it is the first verb which limits the second one in respect to time; that is, the first verb serves to mark the second event as one which takes place immediately. There is also an implication in the first verb of early action, and from the context of verse 10 one knows that this took place early in the morning. One should not attempt to bring into a translation all of the supplementary information as in the New English Bible, "he and the citizens rose with all speed that morning and marched out." The combinatory function of both Hebrew verbs can easily be rendered as "they went out immediately" or "he hurried out with all his people" (as in the Smith-Goodspeed translation). It is also possible to employ translational glosses for stylistic reasons, as in the case of "he acted quickly" (Today's English Version).

In actual speech, which is the primary form of language, many potential ambiguities are resolved by intonational contours, stress, and pauses, but these features of language which are so important in analyzing combinatory relations in grammar are only partially marked in written texts. Since we so frequently have no way of reconstructing these so-called suprasegmental features of pitch, stress, and pause, we can only select that particular type of arrangement which seems to fit most satisfactorily in the overall context.

Typical Problems Involving Grammatical Meaning

Because of the necessity of expressing numerous relations with a limited number of surface structures, translators are usually faced with a number of problems in finding satisfactory grammatical equivalents. It is neither possible nor practicable to list all the kinds of adjustments which must be made in interlingual communication, but some of the more frequently recurring difficulties include the following types: (1) relationals, (2) derivatives, (3) shifts in focus, (4) transitionals, (5) unspecified relations, (6) unspecified participants, (7) purpose and intent, (8) causative relations, (9) joint participation, (10) quantifying events, (11) time, and (12) personal reference. In dealing with such difficulties it is not possible to limit one's attention merely to grammatical factors, for the meanings of individual words and of rhetorical patterns are frequently also involved, but in this chapter the focus is primarily upon the grammatical restructuring which is necessary in translating.

Relationals. Some translators seem to believe that in translating one should always match word classes, that is, nouns should be translated by nouns, verbs by verbs, and prepositions by prepositions. Such a principle can, however, result in serious mistakes. For example, the expression "Jesus arose from the dead" cannot be rendered literally in some languages since there is no preposition such as *from.* One reason for this is that in some languages all types of movement are expressed by verbs and not by prepositions such as *from* and *into.* The closest equivalent in some languages may be "Jesus got up and left the dead."

Even more serious problems are involved in the grammatical adjustments necessary in the rendering of the preposition *in.* In Bali one cannot say "to believe in someone," but rather one must say "to believe in the mouth of someone," meaning actually to believe in the utterance and character of someone. In many languages one cannot render literally the Greek construction "in Christ," since in so many instances the preposition meaning "in" refers only to space. Accordingly, the closest equivalent may be "in connection with Christ," "in communion with Christ," or even "tied closely to Christ."

Derivatives. One of the problems involved in many derived words, which in their underlying semantic structure belong to more than one semantic class, is that one is not always certain as to what semantic class may be primarily in focus in a particular construction. For example, in the English phrase *good teacher, good* does not usually qualify the object element in *teacher* but normally refers to the underlying action, namely, the proficiency in teaching.

In both Hebrew and Greek there are a good many derivative constructions of lexical units which have important implications for the underlying grammatical relations. Note, for example, the Hebrew series for the verb *ga'al,* "to redeem." The principal derivatives are *go'el,* "redeemer;" *g'ullah,* "redemption;" and *g'ulim,* "redeemed people." The forms *ga'al* (the verb) and *g'ullah* (the corresponding noun) designate the event in question, but *go'el* designates one who redeems, and *g'ulim* designates those who have been redeemed. Since the two forms of *go'el* and *g'ulim* are semantically complex, they are frequently translated into other languages not by nouns but by clauses, for example, "he who redeems" and "those who are redeemed."

In Greek some basic roots have an even wider range of derivatives. For example, for the root *dik-* there is an extensive series of derivatives, including *dikē*, "the goddess of justice;" *dikaios*, "just, right, righteous;" *dikaiosunē*, "righteousness, justification, charitable acts;" *dikaioō*, "to do justice;" *dikaiōma*, "regulation;" *dikaiōsis*, "justification;" and *dikastēs*, "judge." The form *dikaiosunē* presents a number of serious problems. In the first place, it is difficult to know whether *dikaiosunē* in certain passages is a derivative of *dikaios*, an abstract meaning "righteous," or a derivative of *dikaioō* "to do justice" or "to make righteous." Accordingly, in Romans 1:17, which speaks of "the righteousness of God," the serious question is whether *dikaiosunē* is to be related to the abstract *dikaios* or to the verb form *dikaioō*. Is this God's own personal righteousness or is it what God does in putting people right with himself (Today's English Version) or what God does in "righting wrong" (New English Bible)? In Matthew 6:1 there is a highly specialized derivation of meaning in *dikaiosunē*, for the reference is not to causing something to be right or just but to the performance of certain acts regarded as righteous, and preeminent among these would be the giving of alms to the poor.

An extremely difficult problem occurs in the phrase *marturia Iēsou Khristou* occurring in Revelation 1:2, as well as elsewhere. Does this phrase mean "witness concerning Jesus Christ" or is it "the witness which was given by Jesus Christ to John" (Massyngberecle-Ford, 1975, 373)? The answer to this question depends upon a number of considerations, including whether *marturia Iēsou* is to be considered as a technical phrase referring to martyrdom.

Shifts in focus. Indo-European and Semitic languages generally tend to employ as subjects of propositions those terms which normally refer to agents, experiencers, or those who are benefited by some action. This is particularly true in contexts in which there is some animate being involved in the action. Rather than this type of typical subject-predicate sentence structure, some languages often employ what is called a topic-comment structure. In Genesis 24:22 most translations tend to follow the Hebrew text more or less literally by rendering "the man took an expensive gold ring and put it on her nose and put two large gold bracelets on her arms" (omitting in this context the reference to the weights involved). In a language which typically employs certain shifts of focus on the basis of what is regarded as the primary topic followed by a comment, this statement would need to be significantly restructured to read "an expensive gold ring, that is what the man put in her nose, and two large gold bracelets, that is what he put on her arms." What is in focus in this passage is not so much the activity of the man but the expensive gold ring and the two large gold bracelets.

Most translators reproduce more or less literally the statement in Genesis 1:1, "In the beginning God created the heavens and the earth." For some languages this seems to be misleading, since this type of translation would give the impression that the rest of the immediate discourse is about the nature of God. In reality, the first chapter of Genesis is about the creation of the universe. For a typical topic-comment type of language it may be preferable to translate "the heavens and the earth, God created them in the beginning" or even "the creation of the heavens and the earth, that is what God did in the beginning."

The so-called "hanging case" construction in Hebrew (technically identified as *casus pendens*) may be regarded as a type of topic-comment construction. In this construction a noun or pronoun is placed in an initial position and is independent of the following proposition, to which it is related by the use of an anaphoric pronominal reference. For example, in the expression "the woman whom you gave to be with me, she gave me . . . " (Gen. 3:12), the initial phrase "the woman you gave to be with me" states quite clearly and explicitly the topic and what follows is the comment. Such constructions are not necessarily designed for emphasis, even though they may involve a certain amount of focus. For the most part they serve the purposes of clarity and ease of style (Joüon, 1947, 477).

Transitionals. Transitionals are primarily of two types: (1) those which relate sentences one to another and (2) those which mark transitions between larger units such as paragraphs and complete sections. Koine Greek possessed an abundance of transitional markers between sentences. In fact, good Greek style almost demanded a transitional particle or phrase for every clause and sentence. For example, of the eighteen sentences in 1 Corinthians 12:4–26 only three sentences do not have a transitional particle, and the three sentences which have no such particle begin with a conditional conjunction. Hebrew has many fewer such particles, even though it makes exceptionally frequent use of *vav*, "and." Many languages have even fewer transitional particles than Hebrew. In these paratactic structures there are important relationships between clauses, but they are simply not overtly marked by transitionals. Depending upon the grammatical patterning of a receptor language, it may be necessary to add certain transitionals for passages in the Old Testament and to delete some which occur in the Greek text of the New Testament.

The problems of transitional statements between paragraphs and sections are far more difficult to handle. For example, most translators begin 1 Corinthians 13 with the first verse. What is to be done, however, with the last part of 1 Corinthians 12:31, which really serves to introduce chapter 13 and may be very well rendered as "I want to show you a far superior way"? The focus seems to be upon what follows, not so much upon what precedes, and therefore many translators have chosen to combine 1 Corinthians 12:31b as an introductory statement to chapter 13.

Similarly, at the end of chapter 13 most translators simply finish the chapter with the statement, "The greatest of these is love." What immediately follows in 1 Corinthians 14:1a is actually a conclusion to chapter 13, since it is an admonition to "strive for love." It also serves as a transition to chapter 14 in that one is to strive for love and at the same time seek spiritual gifts, especially the gift of inspired utterance. The Greek text seems to suggest that one should "strive for love while one seeks spiritual gifts, especially the gift of inspired utterances."

Unspecified relations. In phrases such as *the resurrection of the dead* and *the goodness of the Lord,* there is no doubt about the meaningful relationship of the parts. In the phrase *the resurrection of the dead,* the dead are the ones who come back to life, and in the case of *the goodness of the Lord,* it is the Lord who is good. But in a phrase such as *Jesus of Nazareth,* there are a number of possible relationships: "Jesus who came from Nazareth," "Jesus whose hometown was Nazareth," "Jesus who grew up in Nazareth," or "Jesus who was a citizen of Nazareth." In some languages the typical way of indicating a person's relationship to a hometown is to say "so and so was born in such and such a place," but clearly this type of expression will not do in the case of the biblical phrase *Jesus of Nazareth.* The choice which a translator makes in this instance will depend upon the historical situation and the normal manner in which a receptor language would reflect this situation.

A far more complex relationship exists in a phrase such as *the God of Israel.* A strictly literal rendering of such a phrase may be misleading either in the sense that Israel must somehow or other possess a God or that Israel owns an idol. A more appropriate equivalent in some languages is "the God whom Israel worships," but it is also possible to employ a phrase such as "the God who protects Israel." The use of one or the other of these alternatives depends largely upon the context.

Unspecified participants. Though resolving the problems of unspecified relations may be complex, it is by no means as difficult as resolving the problems involved when the participants in events are not identified. In 1 John 4:18, the statement "perfect love casts out all fear" involves serious complications, for in some languages one cannot speak of one emotion doing something to another emotion. Some translators have rendered this expression in 1 John 4:18 as "if people perfectly love, then they will not fear at all." But clearly this type of love involves in one way or another the relationship between God and people. If one interprets this as the love which people have toward God, then one may translate "if people perfectly love God, then they will not fear at all" (Dodd, 1953, 120). But there is also a sense in which it is the love of God which eliminates any need for fear, and therefore one may translate "the fact that God loves us perfectly makes it impossible for us to fear" or " . . . means that there is no need for us to ever be afraid" (Haas, de Jonge, Swellengrebel, 1972, 113).

Purpose and intent. In some languages a syntactic marker indicates whether a statement implies specific purpose and intent (that is, an actor relationship) or whether there is no particular purpose or intent in an event and hence a so-called subject may really be an experiencer. For example, the English statement *he saw the man fall* generally implies that someone simply had a visual impression of an event and was not necessarily engaging in any effort to see what was happening. On the other hand, the statement *he looked at the man falling* does imply an activity and hence some type of purpose or intent. Similarly, the English verb *hear* suggests primarily an experiencer relationship, while *listen* implies some conscious activity on the part of an auditor. This distinction becomes important in the story of the woman who touched Jesus' cloak. In Mark 5:27 the woman was purposefully active in touching the cloak of Jesus, but in Mark 5:31 many people touched Jesus without intending to do so, without special design or purpose. The principal consideration is not whether such relationships are marked syntactically, as in some languages, or only by differences of vocabulary, as in English. It is important to recognize that such a distinction may be relevant in a receptor language and that every effort be made to reflect such a difference. One should note, however, that in this account of the woman with menstrual hemorrhaging there is a certain element of irony in the questions posed by the disciples to Jesus. One may actually prefer a double rhetorical question, for example, "Do you see the crowd pressing around you? Then how can you say, Who touched me?" (Bratcher and Nida, 1961, 175). In Mark 5:32 the mere use of the imperfect tense in *perieblepeto*, "he kept looking around," indicates an extended and penetrating look and therefore conscious purpose on the part of the agent.

Causative relations. Causative relations in grammar pose a number of problems. In some instances causation is morphologically marked by the forms of the words as, for example, in English, *to widen the road (wide* versus *widen)* and *to fell the tree (to fall* versus *to fell).* In Hebrew causation is generally marked morphologically by a prefixed *h-* in the so-called *hiphil* conjugation. From roots whose *qal* verbs are transitive, the causative *(hiphil)* may be doubly transitive as in "he caused the man to hear the words of the king" (Lambdin, 1973, 211).

Causative relationships may also be marked by the particular type of syntactic construction, that is, the nature of the verb and the participants in the event. Note, for example, such causative expressions as *he ran the horse* and *he ran the office.*

In Greek there is a very clear distinction in certain causative constructions between the causative agent and the immediate agent or actor. The preposition *hupo*, "by," may mark either an immediate or a causative agent, but *dia*, "through," always marks an immediate and not a causative agent. In the New Testament statements with regard to the creation of the world always indicate clearly that God is the causative agent while Christ is the immediate or effective agent. Some translators have failed to recognize this distinction and have rendered John 1:3 as "Christ created all things."

A number of causative expressions go largely undetected by translators. For example, the extremely rare Greek phrase "breaking my heart" in Acts 21:13 (an idiom borrowed from Hebrew) is essentially causative in meaning, namely "to cause me to suffer anguish." Such underlying causative expressions may sometimes be made explicitly causative even in an idiomatic form as, for example, "to make the heart heavy" or "to make one's stomach dry up."

In some languages even a verb such as *to persuade* is treated as a type of causative, and therefore *to persuade a person* must be rendered as "to cause a person to agree."

In a number of instances the relationship of a participant to a causative action can only be determined from the total context. In Mark 6:16 the Greek text reads literally "John, whom I beheaded." This refers to the action of Herod against John the Baptist. However, Herod did not himself actually behead John the Baptist, but as indicated later in the account, he sent an executioner to behead John the Baptist. Accordingly, it may be necessary to render Mark 6:16 as "John the Baptist, whose head I ordered cut off" or "whose head I told an executioner to cut off."

Joint participation. Coordinate series are often imprecise in indicating the relationship of participants to one another. For example, in English one may say *John and Bill climbed the peak,* and this will ordinarily imply that John and Bill did so together. However, one may add *separately* to indicate that the two persons performed the same action but at different times, for example, *John and Bill separately climbed the peak.*

In Acts 7:15 the Greek text says literally "and he and our fathers died," in which "our fathers" refers to the patriarchs of the twelve tribes. A literal rendering of this statement in some languages might very well imply that upon arrival in Egypt, Jacob and his sons all died together. Accordingly, it may be necessary in some languages to translate "he died and later his sons died, one after another" or "he died and later our tribal patriarchs died, one following the other."

Quantification. The quantification of events may be accomplished in two ways. For example, in English one may say *he spoke five times* and *he made five speeches,* but these two statements do not have the same meaning, for the term *speech* identifies something different from merely *to speak. Speech* designates an organized discourse, while *to speak* may simply designate an act of talking.

In order to treat an event as a structured unit and therefore be able to quantify it in terms of various episodes, a number of languages nominalize the corresponding verbs. Then to mention such events, it may be necessary to employ a lexically empty verb. In English, for example, one may say *he made a speech, he made a trip, he made a journey, he made an appearance,* or *he gave a performance, he gave a talk, he gave a speech, he gave a recital,* or *he did a job* and *he did a dance.* In English the verbs *make, give,* and *do* are largely semantically empty lexical units, but they perform a useful function in making it possible to speak of an event as a single unit and thus to quantify it in such statements as *he made five speeches, he gave two performances,* and *he did two jobs.*

In Revelation 1:1 the Greek verb *didōmi,* "to give," functions as a type of causative empty verb with *apokalupsis,* "revelation" (a nominalized form of the verb "to reveal"). In this context *apokalupsis* refers to a series of visions contained in the book known as the Apocalypse or the Revelation. By means of the noun form, each act of revealing is given a unitary character. In Revelation 13:14 *ta sēmeia,* "the signs" (events which have symbolic significance), occurs with the verb *poieō,* "to do," which functions very much like *didōmi* in Revelation 1:1 as a type of empty causative expression meaning "to cause to happen."

Time. Most of the translator's problems involving correspondences in temporal sequence are primarily lexical in nature. The problems involve different systems of reckoning time; for example, watches of the night, hours of the day, and months of the year. Some references to time, however, involve grammatical relationships. In the English statement *he came quickly* it may not be possible to determine whether the coming took place after a very brief period of time or whether the coming involved rapid motion, in which case the problem is not a matter of temporal sequence but of aspect of the action.

All references to time are obviously relative, either to the event of the discourse, as in the case of such adverbial expressions as "yesterday," "tomorrow," and "today," or relative to some other event, as in the case of "later," "then," and "next year." One type of reference to the time of a discourse is particularly confusing, namely the phrase "unto this day" as in Deuteronomy 2:22, Joshua 4:9 and 7:26, Judges 1:26 and 18:12. When such expressions occur within direct discourse, a reader is very likely to recognize the context of the meaning of "unto this day," but when such expressions are outside of direct discourse, many readers do not recognize the fact that such an expression refers to the time of the writing of the book itself and not to the present day of the reader. For example, in Deuteronomy 2:22 the reference to the Edomites taking over the territory of the Horites ends with a statement that the Edomites settled in the land and have remained there "to this day." This is clearly not a reference to the present time but to the time when the book of Deuteronomy was written, which raises a number of historical questions. Various attempts have been made to minimize the difficulty of such expressions. For example, Today's English Version reads "those stones are still there" in Joshua 4:9, and in Joshua 8:28 the phrase is rendered "which is still there today," and in Judges 18:12 the temporal element is incorporated into the larger context as "that is why the place is still called Camp of Dan." There seems to be no way to avoid difficulties of interpretation apart from some marginal note which draws attention to the fact that this reference to time relates to the period when the book was written.

Personal reference. In all languages there are ways of identifying three important classes of participants: the speaker (or speakers), the receptors (hearers or readers), and those spoken about, the so-called "third person." In a few languages there is also a "fourth person," that is to say, a second third person within a context.

A conspicuous feature of a number of languages is the distinction between inclusive and exclusive first person plural, that is, the meaning of *we* which includes those spoken to and the meaning of *we* which excludes those spoken to. Note, for example, the text of 1 Corinthians 9:10–12 in Today's English Version: "Didn't he really mean *us* when he said that? Of course that was written for *us*. The man who plows and the man who reaps should do their work in the hope of getting a share of the crop. *We* have sown spiritual seed among you. Is it too much if *we* reap material benefits from you? If others have the right to expect this from you, don't *we* have an even greater right?" The three references to the first person plural form *we* are clearly exclusive, for they do not include the believers in Corinth, but in the two references to the first person plural translated in English as *us*, one must raise the question as to whether Paul is speaking about himself and the other ministers or about all believers in general. The immediate context is clearly in favor of the interpretation which restricts the reference of *us* to Paul and his associates, but the larger context suggests something else to complicate the translator's work.

In 1 Corinthians 9:4–6 Paul speaks about his own position and his right to receive help from the churches. In verse 7 he argues that this is a general rule, which also is prescribed by the Law. The Law also contains the general rule, which is proven by the quotation from Deuteronomy 25:4. The implication of this quotation from Deuteronomy is to validate the rule of verse 7, which is referred to again in verse 10. Only in verse 11 does Paul apply the general rule to his own position. Accordingly, the references to *us* in verse 10 are best regarded as inclusive (Kijne, 1966, 174).

In some contexts there may be more than one so-called "audience." When the disciples asked Jesus to teach them how to pray, Jesus gave them a model prayer beginning "our Father in heaven." The disciples were in a sense the receptors, but the addressee in the prayer itself is God. In such a circumstance the form of "our" must be exclusive, not inclusive, for "our" does not refer to someone who is the father of both God and the persons speaking. In some passages, however, it is extremely difficult to determine whether a first person plural pronoun should be treated as inclusive or exclusive. For example, in John 8:33 the Pharisees answer Jesus by saying "we are the descendants of Abraham," and in doing so they make a clear distinction between themselves and Jesus. It would seem appropriate, therefore, for the Pharisees to use an exclusive first person plural. This would be indirectly denying that Jesus was a descendant of Abraham. In fact, it could be interpreted as a kind of sociological excommunication. If, however, one were to use the inclusive first person plural pronoun, much of the thrust of what is said in this dialogue would be lost, even though this is generally the solution followed by those translators who do not wish to suggest that even the Pharisees might dispute the lineage of Jesus.

In John 8:39 it is particularly important that the first person plural exclusive pronoun be used, for the Pharisees then claim "our father is Abraham," and in the very next statement Jesus claims that these Pharisees were not descendants of Abraham because they did not act as Abraham would have acted. The problem here becomes especially acute, since in Hebrew to be "the son of" or "the descendant of" a particular person implies behaving in accordance with what such a person would do. In such Old Testament contexts, being a descendant of someone has much more sociological than biological meaning. In some languages, accordingly, only a marginal note can help to clarify this type of figurative meaning.

Surface Forms and Underlying Meaning

The preceding review of various types of translational problems involving grammatical structures has consistently pointed to the basic problem of the discrepancy between surface forms and underlying meaning. For example, Romans 1:5, literally "we received grace and apostleship," contains the phrase *kharin kai apostolēn*, which is formally coordinate but semantically subordinate, since *apostolēn* is essentially the content of *kharis*, the gift of God, that is, Paul's apostleship was a gift from God. Furthermore, *elabomen*, with a first person plural subject, really refers to Paul himself. This use of the first person plural form to refer to a singular speaker or writer is common in both Classical and Koine Greek and is not restricted to epistolary contexts. To do justice to the underlying meaning of this expression in Romans 1:5, one can perhaps best translate this into English as "I received the privilege of being an apostle."

The very next phrase in Romans 1:5, *eis hupakoēn pisteōs*, literally "to the obedience of faith," contains an expression which on the surface level is formally subordinate, that is, *pisteōs* is grammatically subordinate to *hupakoēn*. However, in terms of the underlying semantic relationship, there is a coordinate structure which reflects a nominal transformation of a sequence that occurs commonly enough in its corresponding verb structure, namely, "believe and obey."

In Hebrew there are a number of formally coordinate clauses which are semantically subordinate. For example, a literal translation of Genesis 8:9 would be "and the dove found no place to set her foot, and she returned to him to the ark." The semantic relationship here is one of cause and effect, which has been reproduced by Moffatt as "as the dove could find no rest for the sole of her foot, she flew back to him in the barge."

In Genesis 44:34 the Hebrew text has coordinate clauses, literally, "for how can I go back to my father and the lad is not with me?" The clause "and the lad is not with me" is a circumstantial or conditional clause and should be rendered in English as "if the lad is not with me." The Septuagint translator used idiomatic Greek devices to express these subordinate relations. In the case of Genesis 8:9 the subordinate clause contains a dependent participial phrase, and in Genesis 44:34 the construction is a genitive absolute (Aejmelaeus, 1982, 100–10).

In a number of instances the problems involved in analyzing syntactic structure do not result from a mismatch between surface form and underlying meaning but from serious obscurity as to what the relationships may be. For example, in the phrase *to euaggelion tēs sōtērias humōn*, "the good news of your salvation" (Eph. 1:13), it is difficult to know precisely what the relationship is between "good news" and "salvation." Is it, for example, "the good news which tells how you can be saved" or is it "the good news that caused you to be saved" or is it "the good news that you are saved"? In view of the fact that *to euaggelion tēs sōtērias humōn* is in apposition with *ton logon tēs alētheias* (literally, "the word of truth"), it seems more likely that the phrase *to euaggelion tēs sōtērias humōn* means "the gospel whose subject matter is salvation," but other interpretations cannot be eliminated, and they have sometimes been preferred (Bratcher and Nida, 1982, 24). If, however, one chooses a translation such as "the good news that caused you to be saved," there may be serious problems in many languages since "the good news" as an inanimate object cannot "cause anything." As a result, it may be necessary to indicate an instrumental relationship, as in "the good news which God used in order to save you."

In Luke 2:14 *eudokias*, "good will" or "desire" or "being pleased with," is particularly ambiguous. In the first place, Luke 2:14 contains a serious textual problem in view of the presence of the variant reading *eudokia*. However, it is virtually certain that *eudokias* not only is the more difficult reading but also the original one (Metzger, 1971, 133). One may interpret

en anthrōpois eudokias (literally, "among people of good will") as referring
to people who possess a characteristic of good will, presumably toward
others. It is far more likely, however, that *eudokias* refers to God's good will
or pleasure toward people, and therefore one may translate "peace on
earth among people with whom he is pleased" or, in the active sense,
" . . . among people who please him." The likelihood of this latter interpretation is reinforced by the fact that an equivalent Hebrew expression
has been discovered in some of the hymns from Qumran which have the
phrase "the sons of his good pleasure," meaning "God's good pleasure"
(1QH 4:32).

As already noted, in some instances the rhetorical structure may provide significant insight as to the interpretation of a syntactic construction.
This is clearly true in the case of John 1:3b–4a, *kai khōris autou egeneto oude
hen ho gegonen en autō zōē ēn.* Traditionally, the phrase *ho gegonen* has been
combined with what precedes, and therefore the translation has been
"and without him was not anything made that was made. In him was
life." As mentioned previously, however, the rhetorical structure of John
1:1–5 involves picking up the last item in one clause and making a reference to this the first item in the next clause. This would mean, for example, placing the period immediately after *hen* and beginning the next
clause with *ho gegonen.* Accordingly, one may translate as "without him
not one thing came into existence. What did come into existence had its
life in him."

Isomorphisms in Syntax

It has been traditional with some linguists to speak as if grammatical
structures were essentially arbitrary, that is, without any isomorphic relations to nonlinguistic realities. On the contrary, however, there are a number of significant isomorphs, the most conspicuous being the relationship
between temporal events and clause order. Compare, for example, such
typical expressions as (1) *he remained there for a week in order to visit his
colleagues,* (2) *because it rained, they had to leave early,* and (3) *if he comes, we
will welcome him.* Such orders may be reversed in many languages, but in
general the order of propositions tends to follow or to be isomorphic with
temporal sequences.

One also generally encounters isomorphic relations in grammar between old and new information. In most propositions it is the old information which tends to precede the new information, and in everyday
experience it is new information which follows that which is old.

The fact that languages universally distinguish between speaker, those
spoken to, and those spoken about is certainly isomorphic with the basic
components in communication. Even more extensive isomorphic rela-

tions exist in the ways in which lexical and grammatical forms mirror various levels of status and rank within a society, as noted in the discussion of the interpersonal function of language (pp. 31–36).

Even the fact that syntactic structures are composed of paradigmatically and syntagmatically related sets is isomorphic with the fact that this is the fundamental way in which any linear series of repeated segments must be organized. In other words, the parts of such series must either precede or follow, or they must occur in a substituting relationship one to another. If we only knew more about the way in which the brain processes grammatical structures, we would no doubt be in a much better position to explain a number of other isomorphic relations between grammar and neurophysiological networks and processes.

8

Lexical Meaning

Lexical meaning can probably be best described as the meaning of parts of words, words, and combinations of words. The last category consists of so-called fixed phrases, idioms, and "sayings," the meaning of which cannot be determined merely by adding up the meaning of the constituent parts. The term "words" is to be understood essentially in its traditional sense and includes words of a single morpheme (a minimal unit of form having meaning) or of a combination of two or more morphemes which (1) occur generally in a relatively fixed order, (2) permit only a few, if any, intrusive morphemes or words, and (3) have a restricted internal distribution (relatively few classes of items which join to form words) but a very extensive external distribution, which means that words tend to combine with a great many different other words.

The morphemes which may be combined to form words are generally of three major classes. They may be (1) roots or stems as, for example, in *dance, run,* and *good;* or (2) derivatives, in which there is (a) a significant change of the word class, as in *dance/dancer,* or (b) a qualifying element as in *run/re-run;* or (3) inflected forms involving grammatical categories which are semantically separable from the stems or words to which they may be attached. For example, the inflectional suffix *-s* in the word *runs* indicates agreement with a third person singular subject, while at the same time it marks present or habitual time, as in the phrase *he runs.* Another identically-sounding inflectional suffix marks plurality, as in *boys.* In both Hebrew and Greek there are a number of these inflectional affixes marking person, aspect, number, and agreement, though in Greek the possibility of elaborate derivative and inflectional forms is much greater than in Hebrew. Note, for example, the Greek word *proeuaggelizomai,* consisting of *pro-* "before," *eu-* "good," *aggel-* "to announce," *-iz-* "to cause," *-o-,* a stem formation signaling indicative mode, and *-mai,* first person singular subject (middle or passive, but with so-called deponent verbs, active).

Idioms and adages (conventional sayings with figurative meanings) have their own internal meaning, with its literal significance, as well as their external meaning (the meaning of the unit as a whole) which cannot be derived simply from knowing the meaning of the parts. Accordingly such an expression is regarded as a lexical unit and treated in the same way as any single word.

For example, the idiom *heap coals of fire on someone's head* has an obvious literal internal meaning, but this is not the meaning of the expression as a whole. The actual source of the figurative meaning cannot be determined, but in certain passages it must refer to being so kind to a person as to cause that individual to be ashamed.

To become acquainted not only with some of the characteristics of lexical meaning but also to be able to employ certain techniques designed to discover the lexical meaning of words and phrases, it has seemed both wise and necessary to employ a good many illustrative examples coming from English, rather than concentrating exclusively on problems posed by Hebrew or Greek words and phrases. By using a language much better known to the average person involved in Bible translating, it may be possible to grasp more satisfactorily the methodology required for determining lexical meaning. Furthermore, there may be an additional advantage in this procedure because Bible translators who consult various English translations from time to time will be better prepared to understand why certain English expressions have been chosen as equivalents of the biblical terms.

Basic Factors Relevant to Lexical Meaning

1. Assumptions. There are a number of basic factors which significantly influence any approach to lexical meaning. These must be kept constantly in mind if one is to understand either how to determine the meaning of terms or how to use existing dictionaries with profit. The primary factors involve a series of fundamental assumptions about meaning. In the first place, one must assume that, in general, the correct meaning of a lexical unit in any context is that which fits the context best. In a sense, this also means that the correct interpretation is that which contributes least to the total context; in other words, the correct interpretation maximizes the relevance of the context rather than the relevance of any isolated word or phrase. The importance of this principle will become evident in studying lexical meaning on the basis of the range of usage, that is, the variety of contexts in which a particular lexical unit may occur. It is, for example, utterly hopeless to try to analyze the meaning of a Greek word such as *dikaiosunē*, typically rendered as "righteousness," without investigating all of the contexts in which this term occurs.

A second important assumption is that in any one context a lexical unit is likely to have only one meaning rather than several. Normally, the only exception to this principle is a context in which a lexical unit is marked (though sometimes subtly so) as having two or more meanings. This is often called "double entendre." As already noted, the phrase "living water" in John 4 must be understood as having a double meaning, namely, "water from a spring" and "water which makes life possible" or "water which gives life."

A third important assumption, which can also be recognized as a principle of interpretation, is that the literal or "unmarked" meaning of a lexical unit should be assumed correct unless the context points to some other meaning. For example, in Matthew 5:17 the Greek word *plēroō*, normally rendered as "to fulfill" or "to complete," has been interpreted by some persons as meaning "to give the true meaning to," but in the context of Matthew 5:17 ("do not think that I have come to destroy the law or the prophets; I have not come to destroy but to fulfill") it seems far better to assume that *plēroō* means what it usually means in such contexts, rather than assuming an unusual interpretation. This principal constitutes a warning for persons who are always looking for hidden meanings in a text, but who are more likely to be deceived by their own desires for novelty.

Another important assumption about lexical meaning is that there are no completely synonymous expressions. Two different words may be used to designate the same referent as, for example, in *keep off the grass* and *keep off the lawn*, but this does not mean that *grass* and *lawn* have identical meanings. Two different words may often be employed simply for the sake of stylistic variation, and even if two different words seem to designate the same referent, there is almost always some distinction in "associative meaning."

The final, and perhaps even the most important, assumption about lexical meaning is that, as already noted, signs are always defined by other signs. Such defining signs are of two quite different classes: verbal and non-verbal. The meaning of *chair* may be defined linguistically by signs which occur in the same semantic domain, for example, *bench, stool, throne,* and *pew*. But in a town meeting, the term *chair* in the statement *please address the chair* is marked by the practical non-verbal context as designating a person and not a piece of furniture.

One important reason for these assumptions is something already mentioned; namely, in all languages there are a strictly limited number of verbal signs to cover an infinite variety of objects, events, and abstracts. This means that, except for proper names, the meaning of a verbal sign cannot be a point but an area of meaning. For example, a word such as *chair* may designate not one particular piece of furniture but hundreds of different kinds of chairs and millions of different specific tokens. The central meaning of the word *chair* is relatively precise, but the margins of such an area may be indefinite and fuzzy. For example, there is no special problem in identifying a typical *shoe*, but how specifically does the meaning of *shoe* differ from the meaning of *boot*? There are many different types of construction and gradations of height, but how high and heavy does a shoe have to be before it is called a boot? The so-called core or central meanings of these terms are readily definable, but there are objects which seem to fit between the respective ranges. How small does a cup have to be before it becomes a demitasse, or how big before it becomes a mug? In the case of words such as *comprehend* and *understand*, the differences become even more subtle, for there is a conspicuous area of overlapping in the ranges of meaning. In addition, *comprehend* seems to be on a somewhat higher stylistic level (an aspect of associative meaning) than the more ordinary *understand*.

In view of the fact that there are a limited number of sounds in any one language, it is clear that there could never be a sufficient number of combinations of sounds to designate efficiently an infinite number of objects, events, and abstracts. As a result, the relation between verbal sounds and the meaning of linguistic units is largely conventional. Some words, of course, are onomatopoeic, that is, the sounds imitate, at least to some extent, the objects or events in question. For example, in the term *choochoo* there is a relationship of sound between the noise made by a railroad engine (at least of the old-fashioned steam type) and a train. Words such as *quack* and *hiss* are likewise onomatopoeic. Theoretically it would be possible for most languages to have a much higher percentage of onomatopoeic expressions than they do have. Some languages in Africa do employ numerous so-called ideophones. But it is both important and essential that the sounds of words not be tied strictly to the meaning, for this would radically reduce the flexibility of a language and make it exceedingly difficult to use words in extended meanings.

2. *Changes in meaning.* In attempting to analyze the meaning of lexical units, one must always face the fact that on all levels of structure, and especially in the meanings of words, languages are constantly in process of change. For example, the English verb *prevent* originally meant "to go ahead of," and it is precisely this meaning that occurs in Matthew 17:25 and 1 Thessalonians 4:15 of the King James Version. This meaning of "to go ahead of" is derived directly from the underlying Latin from which the English term *prevent* was borrowed, but at present the verb *prevent* means "to keep from occurring."

In some instances two words may actually change meanings in a reciprocal manner. In the seventeenth century the term *ghost* meant essentially what the term *spirit* means today, and what *spirit* meant in the seventeenth century is what *ghost* means at present. It is for this reason that most modern translations of the New Testament speak of "the Holy Spirit" rather than "the Holy Ghost."

In some instances a change of meaning in a term may occur very quickly. This has happened in the case of the English term *gay,* which has traditionally meant "happy" and "cheerful," but within the last twenty years or so *gay* in American English has come to designate homosexuals.

Even words which have been constructed for the sake of technical accuracy are not immune to change. For example, the word *gas* was invented by a Belgium chemist on the analogy of the Greek term *chaos* meaning "atmosphere." In its technical sense, *gas* designates a substance possessing perfect molecular mobility and the possibility of indefinite expansion, but this same word *gas* (as a reduction from *gasoline*) also identifies a flammable liquid.

The Christian community in New Testament times produced a significant change in the meaning of the Greek term *tapeinos,* which in secular Greek was used to characterize a base or vile person, but the Christians accepted this appellation *tapeinos* and transformed its meaning into "humble." This, however, is not significantly different from what has happened to the English word *awfully,* which historically occurred primarily in negative contexts but which is frequently used now in strong positive statements such as *awfully nice* or even *awfully good.*

3. *Types of names.* Verbal signs consist of three different types of names: proper names, class names, and names for relations within discourse. In the past some scholars have insisted that proper names do not have meaning but simply reference, since their function is presumably only to refer to unique objects rather than to apply to a class of items for which there may be important distinctive features. But if one adopts a broader definition of meaning based on semiotic relations, then any sign which designates anything has meaning even though that meaning may be strictly circumscribed. Such proper names certainly may have important associative meanings. For many people the English term *Jehovah* (a transliteration of Hebrew *Yahweh* by way of the vowels of Hebrew *Adonai* "Lord," as adapted through Latin by Galatinus in 1520) has very strong associative meanings in view of its occurrence in the King James Version. When some modern translators employed *Yahwe* or *Yahweh,* their translations were denounced by many as not only unfaithful to the text but heretical. The use of the term *Yahweh* was interpreted as a symbol of a modernistic attitude toward the Bible and about God. Some people, in fact, refuse even to read a translation which uses the form *Yahweh,* even though in other respects the translation may be exegetically quite conservative.

Titles appear to lie at the midpoint between proper names and class names, for they may designate unique objects, while at the same time identifying certain characteristics. The biblical expressions *The Almighty* and *The Most High* have become practically names for God, and the title *Christ* has become even in the Greek New Testament equivalent to a proper name. On the other hand, a proper name may acquire the role of a title, as in the case of the Latin term *Caesar*, which even in the New Testament has the extended meaning of "emperor."

There may, in fact, be a circular movement in the relation between proper names and titles. For example, a proper name may become a title and in turn acquire the function of a proper name. This is true, for example, of the Hebrew proper name *Shaddai*. In its original usage *Shaddai* should no doubt be distinguished from *Yahweh* (Eerdmans, 1947, 20). Evidently only at a later period, in which all divine powers were attributed to *Yahweh*, did *Shaddai* become another name for *Yahweh*. It is possible, therefore, for translators simply to transliterate the proper name *Shaddai* as has been done, for example, in the French text of the Jerusalem Bible. However, it also has become common practice to translate *Shaddai* as "The Almighty" or "Almighty God." To do so implies that the meaning of *Shaddai* is known. In reality, however, the meaning of *Shaddai* is very obscure. It is interesting that the Greek Septuagint translators arrived at a so-called "etymological meaning" by reading the Hebrew as *she-day,* and they interpreted this as "he who is sufficient," in Greek, *ho hikanos* (Tov, 1976, 540).

Class names designate the real world of objects, events, and abstracts and thus serve to designate multiple referents or tokens. These class names are by far the most common. The names of relations involve primarily reference, agreement, and linkage. For example, the pronouns *I, you, he, she, it,* and *they* refer to the participants in a discourse: speaker, hearer, and those spoken about. In English, one sentence may contain the expression *the man* and a following sentence may then employ *he* as a reference to *the man*.

There is a certain amount of grammatical agreement in English in expressions such as *this boy* and *these boys,* but in Greek the patterns of agreement are far more extensive. The relation of linkage (traditionally spoken of as government) occurs in all languages. Such links do not define relations, but they do mark the fact that there are significant relations between lexical items. For example, in the expression *love of God* the preposition *of* indicates a link between *love* and *God,* but it does not specify the relation. In fact, this phrase may mean either "God loves (people)" or "(people) love God."

The analysis of lexical meanings is extremely complex. An English term such as *beautician* may at first appear to be relatively simple in meaning, and yet a careful analysis indicates highly complex relationships which may be described as "one who causes others to become more attractive."

This term, therefore, identifies a person, a causal relation, a change of state, and a comparative grade of an abstract. The biblical term *redeemer* is likewise complex, for it designates "one who causes someone else to be delivered from or become free from some type of restrictive circumstances." Furthermore, the implication is that this process involves costly payment or considerable effort. As experienced translators know, words with complex meanings must often be translated by phrases and not by some single word in a receptor language.

As already mentioned in previous chapters, there are two basic types of meaning: designative and associative. The designative meaning of any word consists of those distinctive features which determine the range of applicability of such a term in signaling particular referents.

Designative Meaning

"What is the meaning of that word?" This question is usually asked about the meaning of any word. In many respects, it is a misleading question, for most words have more than one meaning. In a dictionary of the Greek New Testament vocabulary of some five thousand words, there are somewhat more than 25,000 meanings in all. Even a relatively simple word such as English *walk* has three principal and quite distinct meanings. The first designates movement in space by an animate being using limbs. The second meaning designates a construction on which people may walk, and a third meaning is employed in the game of baseball and designates a batter going to first base after having received four pitches which are outside of the strike zone. Accordingly, one does not attempt to define "the meaning of a word" but rather one or more particular meanings of a word.

A particular meaning of a verbal sign consists of that set of features which determine the range of applicability of such a sign; that is, it consists of certain features which indicate whether the sign in question may be used to refer to or to designate certain objects, events, or abstracts. To determine the distinctive features, one must of course examine the range of contexts in which such a sign actually occurs.

As already noted in the discussion of certain basic assumptions and principles of semantics, there are two types of ranges. The first type is relevant in what may be regarded as a "contrastive definition" by stating the range of the meaning of a sign in terms of the ranges of competing signs, that is, signs within the same semantic domain. If, for example, we wish to determine a negative definition of *whisper*[a], oral communication in its unmarked sense, we must compare the range of *whisper* with the ranges of *shout, mumble, sing, shriek,* and *hiss.* All of these terms share the features of oral communication, but there are certain important distinctive differences. For example, *whisper* and *hiss* are voiceless (that is, the vocal cords are not vibrating), while *shout, mumble, sing,* and *shriek* involve voicing. *Hiss* is normally nonverbal. *Sing* differs from the other terms in being musical, while *whisper* is not. *Shout* and *shriek* also involve high volume, while *whisper* is predominantly low volume.

On the basis of these contrasts, we may define *whisper*[a] as an utterance which is voiceless, verbal, nonmusical, and with low volume, but this is only part of a definition of *whisper*[a].

Whisper[a] may also be defined contextually by its range of occurrence, for example, (1) *whisper in class,* (2) *whisper during the concert,* (3) *whisper his love to her,* and (4) *whisper behind his back. Whisper*[a] clearly carries a supplementary feature of secrecy, and in contexts 1, 2, and 4 there is an added feature of social disapproval, but for most speakers there must also be a feature of importance or they would not risk social disapproval to communicate. In context 3 there is a feature of intimacy and of positive content, while in context 4 the content is negative.

In terms of the contextual range of *whisper*[a], there is a degree of ambivalence, for it suggests importance for the speaker but often an unwarranted interruption on the part of those who overhear. In context 3 intimacy combines with importance, secrecy, and social approval, while in context 4 there is negative content and social disapproval.

If we extend the range of *whisper* beyond that of *whisper*[a] (voiceless, low volume, nonmusical, verbal, oral communication), we encounter two quite distinct uses. Compare, for example, (5) *a whisper campaign,* (6) *she is always whispering about her neighbors,* and (7) *the wind was whispering in the trees.* In contexts 5 and 6 the features of verbal communication and negative content exist, but the actual utterances are normally not voiceless or of low volume. If, however, we are to define the meaning of *whisper*[b] (in contexts 5 and 6), we must look not only to such practical contexts but also to the relevant semantic domain which includes such terms as *gossip, tattle,* and *criticize.* When the meaning of *whisper*[b] is compared with the core or unmarked meanings of *gossip, tattle,* and *criticize,* a good deal of overlapping is evident.

Whisper[c], as in context 7, is no longer verbal, but there is a feature of low volume which can be described as "a soft sound," but to define more precisely *whisper*[c] we need to place this in a domain of contrasting terms such as *hiss, roar,* and *whistle.*

Any complete statement about the designative meaning of a term requires both contrastive and contextual evidence, in which so-called "negative data" is supplied by the ranges of competing terms in the same domain and "positive data" is supplied by the contexts in which a term is used. The negative aspects of the definition are generally regarded as linguistic evidence, while the positive aspects are spoken of as encyclopedic.

For the most part, dictionary definitions reflect only an analysis of the so-called practical contexts, and for many persons this is the kind of information which is probably most helpful. For a translator, however, it is particularly important to recognize some of the finer shades of difference which can only be determined by analyzing the relationships between the meaning of a term as it contrasts with the ranges of applicability of other terms in more or less the same semantic domain.

Associative Meaning

The associative meaning of a term consists of certain features derived primarily from the practical contexts in which such a term is used, including people who habitually use such expressions and the circumstances in which such words frequently occur. As noted briefly in the previous section, proper names may have very important associative meanings. For example, in West Africa many Christians readily accept *Yesua* as a transliteration of *Jesus*, but they reject strongly the Arabic adaptation of *Jesus* in the form of *Isa*, for the name *Isa* suggests a strong association with Islam. For many people English terms such as *sanctification, propitiation,* and *predestination* have strongly positive associations, while for other persons these same terms are viewed quite negatively.

It is often difficult and sometimes even impossible to make verifiable statements as to the associative meanings of words in dead languages, but it is often possible to suggest certain distinctions. For example, in comparing the Hebrew terms *ga'al* and *padah* one can certainly say that they do overlap considerably in respect to designative meaning. Therefore, in prose contexts in which both verbs occur as, for example, in Leviticus 27:27, there is no reason to introduce different English verbs in a translation, for example, "buy back" and "redeem." This does not mean, however, that these two lexical items in Hebrew are completely synonymous with regard to associative meaning. The verb *ga'al* clearly had very favorable associative meanings because of its relationship to the family, whereas the associative meanings of *padah* relate to commercial law and therefore probably were predominantly neutral or negative (Stamm, 1971, 387). It is because of the positive associative meanings of *ga'al* that this term is almost exclusively used in the latter part of Isaiah.

The associative meanings of some words may be so negative as to cause avoidance. For example, in the Old Testament an oath and curse formula simply has the form "may the Lord do so to me and more also" (Ruth 1:17; 1 Samuel 3:17, 14:44, 20:13, 25:22; 2 Samuel 3:9, 3:35, 19:13; 1 Kings 2:23; 2 Kings 6:31; and in the plural in 1 Kings 19:2 and 20:10). The expression rendered as "so" is actually a euphemistic substitute for a curse which would normally be pronounced to indicate the nature of the punishment, such as sickness, loss of wealth, or death (Pedersen, 1914).

Some persons have refused to pay much attention to associative meanings because they have regarded them as too subjective and therefore too unstable, implying by the word "unstable" that associative meanings vary widely from person to person and therefore provide no sound basis for judgment or evaluation. The work of Osgood and his colleagues (1963, 1964) has clearly shown that associative meanings are every bit as consistent within a community of speakers as are designative meanings. Certainly in view of the importance of associative meanings for the acceptance of any text, it is imperative that translators pay special attention to these crucial features of meaning.

To appreciate more fully the significance of associative meaning and to determine how one can most effectively analyze such meanings, it is important to note the sources of such associative meanings. Probably the most conspicuous source are the persons who customarily use such expressions. The so-called "four-letter words" in English are regarded as crude and vulgar, not because of the referents which they designate but because of the persons who employ such terms. The body parts and functions designated by such four-letter words may also be designated by terms which are perfectly acceptable in technical contexts, for example, *defecate, urinate, copulate, penis,* and *vulva.*

The associative meanings of slang also derive primarily from the types of persons who tend to use such expressions. Similarly, *my dear, dearie, oh my,* and *goodness gracious* acquire the associative meaning of women's language in American English because these expressions are characteristic of usage by women.

Associative meanings may also arise from various types of language contexts. Expressions such as *verily, verily, in the beginning, in Christ,* and *in the heavenlies* all carry biblical associative meanings, while *to be or not to be* and *out damned spot* have Shakespearean associative meanings. These meanings depend upon frequent quotation of specific texts, but general language usage may also provide associative meanings. For example, the term *green* may have negative associative meanings for many people because of its occurrence in such phrases as *green at the gills, green with envy,* and *green on the job.*

Even the arrangement of a discourse provides important associative meanings. This is especially true of the format of poetic arrangement into lines. Some persons, for example, object strongly to the poetic arrangement of the principal chapters in the book of Job, since they regard this as "making a poem" out of what they prefer to understand as a more or less literal transcript of an extended conversation. For many persons the use of capitalization of the pronouns referring to deity carries the associative meaning of piety and devotion. At the same time, some persons often attribute important associative meanings to the use of red ink in printing the words of Jesus in the Scriptures. This type of associative meaning seems particularly anomalous, since a red-letter New Testament would suggest that for at least some persons, some parts of the New Testament are more inspired than others.

The geographical location from which certain verbal usages are derived provides important associative meanings. Some geographical dialects have more prestige than others in view of the status of the persons involved, and thus words which reflect different geographical areas constitute a basis for different associative meanings.

The places in which certain lexical units are typically used may contribute significantly to the associative meaning. Church usage has given such terms as *grace, redemption,* and *salvation* a special ecclesiastical flavor. And in baseball such terms as *home run, strike, ball,* and *home* not only designate features of the game but acquire important associations of meaning, particularly for baseball enthusiasts.

The time at which certain words or phrases may have been fashionable can also affect later associative meanings. Biblical expressions such as *behold, it came to pass,* and *he answered and said* not only have biblical associative meanings but they also sound very old-fashioned.

The nature of the referent of a word may also significantly affect its associative meaning. Note, for example, the positive associative features of such terms as *mother, home, life,* and *health* in contrast with the negative associative meanings in *terrorist, jail, death,* and *cancer.* Different words which designate the same referent may also reflect degrees of diverse associative meanings. Compare, for example, the series *father, papa, daddy, pop, pah,* and *my old man,* where the associative meanings depend in considerable measure upon the interpersonal relations of the individuals involved.

For the various meanings of *whisper* we can readily state certain obvious associative meanings. For *whisper*[a] there are the positive associative features of importance and intimacy and the negative features of disruption and antisocial behavior. For *whisper*[b] associative meanings are primarily negative in the sense of being antisocial and injurious, while for *whisper*[c] the associative meaning is positive and involves a pleasant sound, probably because a breeze whispering in the trees is associated with a refreshing breeze. But the associative meanings of *whisper* are marked primarily by the contexts.

Determining Designative Meaning

To illustrate some of the methods which may be employed in determining designative meaning, it is useful to consider the meanings of *coat.* One must first analyze the range of usage. The following ten typical contexts in which *coat* may occur will serve to illustrate some of the problems:

1. put on his coat
2. threw the coat on the chair
3. the dog's lush coat of fur
4. the dog's coat is constantly shedding
5. eider ducks have a thick coat of feathers
6. a coat of paint
7. a thin coat of snow all over the ground
8. the coat of grease is too thick
9. coat the side of the house
10. he will coat it with varnish

In all of these occurrences of *coat* there is a shared feature of meaning, namely "covering," so that one can see how the various uses of *coat* are to some extent related to one another. In certain instances, however, some speakers of English may prefer the term *coating*, as in context 8, *the coating of grease is too thick*.

Even a rapid review of the various uses of *coat* in the ten illustrative contexts soon reveals quite distinct meanings of *coat*, since in its various uses *coat* designates objects or events which relate to quite different semantic domains. In contexts 1 and 2 *coat* designates a garment, and this would normally be regarded as the unmarked meaning of *coat*, since this is the meaning occurring in the least specified type of context.

In contexts 3, 4, and 5 *coat* designates a natural growth on an animate being, but in contexts in 6, 7, and 8 *coat* designates a coating which is applied or occurs as the result of natural physical events. Finally, in contexts 9 and 10 *coat* designates an action which causes a coating.

A contrastive approach to determining the meaning of *coat*[a] requires one to compare *coat* with other terms in the same general semantic domain of artifacts which in one way or another serve as garments to cover the body. Terms which form a domain cluster with *coat*[a] include *sweater*, *robe*, *overalls*, and *poncho*. None of these terms identifies objects which would be called a coat, and hence one may say that the meanings of the terms which contrast in this way with *coat* help to define the meaning of coat[a]. There are, however, other terms which are different from the typical object designated by *coat*[a] but which may also be called a coat. Such a set of terms may be regarded as "included" taxonomically within the domain of the more generic *coat*[a]. Such terms include *topcoat*, *overcoat*, *suitcoat*, *dinner jacket*, and *tuxedo*. For many speakers of English the term *blazer* would also be included as a kind of coat, but other speakers reject such a classification.

For most speakers of English the term *mantle* overlaps with the meaning of *coat*, though technically a mantle is an outer garment which has no sleeves but is open down the front, in contrast with a poncho which has no such opening.

In addition to the contrastive data derived from comparing such a statement about the respective ranges of designative meanings of terms in the same or related semantic domains, one must also take into consideration certain encyclopedic knowledge gained from acquaintance with typical contexts. As speakers of English we can combine what we would know to be the linguistic uses of a term and thus arrive at definitions based on contrasts, but we inevitably combine encyclopedic knowledge of the referents themselves. This is something which cannot be readily done when one is trying to analyze the meaning of terms in a so-called "dead language" or in a language about which one has relatively little information. In such instances one must carefully analyze all of the possible contexts as, for example, in studying the meanings of Greek and Hebrew terms by using exhaustive concordances. One must then combine with that linguistic evidence the knowledge which is derived from archaeological, historical, and cultural data and finally come to a definition based on both linguistic contexts and data about the presumed referents.

For *coat*[a], one can define the designative meaning as "an outer garment with sleeves, reaching from the shoulders to at least the waist and fastened in front." One may also indicate such optional features as having a hood and reaching as far down as the ankles, but normally not below the knees.

There are a number of additional features about coats which are not necessary for any definition but which may be culturally significant, particularly for certain kinds of coats. For example, coats are made of relatively heavy material, including cloth, leather, and plastic. They may have buttons, zippers, and/or a belt. Some coats are normally worn both inside and outside of a building, while others are only worn outside and in relatively inclement weather. Some objects included in the range of *coat*[a] may be worn outside of other garments included within the range of *coat*[a], for example, an overcoat on top of a suitcoat.

One may then employ this same approach to the other three meanings of *coat*, and in each case both linguistic and encyclopedic information can be combined so as to determine the specific semantic potential of the term *coat* in the distinct semantic domains.

Within the semantic domains which have been mentioned so far, the relationship of designative meanings involves included sets, contrastive sets, and overlapping sets, but there are other types of sets which are significant for semantic domains. In the case of events, for example, it may be useful to consider reverse processes as in *do/undo* and *tie/untie*. The prefix *un-* does not indicate negation but reversal. Another important relationship in certain events is the shifting of perspective, as in the series *buy/sell* and *borrow/loan*, and in the term *rent*, which has two quite distinct meanings depending upon the semantic perspective, for example, *he will rent the house from the owner* and *the owner will rent him the house*.

For abstracts the relationship of polar opposition between designative meanings is particularly important as in *good/bad, tall/short*, and *yes/no*. Various types of series which may also be significant include: (1) unlimited series, for example, *one, two, three, four, five*, etc.; (2) graded series, for example, *cold/cool/warm/hot* and *general/colonel/major/captain/lieutenant/ sergeant;* and (3) repeated series, for example, days of the week and months of the year.

Determining Associative Meaning

As already noted, Charles Osgood and his associates (1952, 1955, 1957, and 1964) have pioneered in analyzing associative meaning by the development of profiles based on a matrix marked off by polar contrasts of pairs of adjectives such as *good/bad, beautiful/ugly, strong/weak, light/dark, high/low,* and *warm/cold*. The ratings which people give to these affective contrasts are amazingly stable for any speech community, and they are highly indicative of people's reactions. However, employing the techniques which Osgood and others have developed implies a great deal of psychological research and experimentation. But certain approaches to these problems, employing Osgood's techniques, can be done in a simpler manner (Nida and Taber, 1969, 94–96).

One way of approaching the problem of associative meaning is to analyze the responses of people to certain terms on the basis of several scales, for example, appropriateness, value, formality, social class, ethical significance, and impact.

Appropriateness involves the reaction of persons as to whether a certain expression fits the context or is disruptive or out of place. Value involves not merely the cost of a referent but the usefulness and utility of either the referent or the verbal expression. The scale of formality depends upon the persons involved in a discourse and the setting in which it occurs. As already noted in the discussion of rhetorical meaning, formality may range from intimate to ritual.

Social class refers to the prestige and status of expressions, based on the prestige and status of persons who customarily use such expressions. The scale of ethical values, with such contrasts as *good/bad* and *helpful/ destructive*, involves both the nature of the referents and the ways in which certain words are considered by persons as inherently good or bad. Some persons, for example, object strongly to the use of so-called swear words, even though they are completely appropriate for the kinds of persons whose language is being represented.

The scale of impact is particularly important, since the associative meanings of certain words may range all the way from striking to boring. Words with highly generic meanings such as *matter, thing, object,* and *means* have very little associative impact, while terms such as *tornado, shark,* and *terrorist* have high associative impact.

Coat[a] has in general a more or less neutral associative meaning. Coats are used almost universally in the English-speaking world, and in view of the highly generic value of *coat*[a] (in contrast with *overcoat, topcoat,* and *suitcoat*), one would expect *coat*[a] to have very little positive or negative associative meaning. There are certain situations, however, in which *coat*[a] may carry associative meaning. In some offices certain types of employees are expected to wear a coat, while others may work in shirtsleeves. Certain restaurants are known for requiring a coat and tie, and in a number of emerging countries a coat is a very high prestige symbol which marks the wearer as having arrived socially and economically. One may therefore say that the associative meaning of *coat*[a] ranges from neutral to positive in evaluation.

Literal and Figurative Meanings

Most designative and associative meanings of lexical units are what are traditionally called "literal," but some meanings are "figurative" in view of a radical distinction in semantic domains between the literal and figurative usage. As already noted, there are a number of different types of expressions which may be regarded as figurative. These may range all the way from a single word such as *fox,* as in Luke 13:32 where King Herod is spoken of as a fox, to extended expressions, including adages such as *strain out a gnat and swallow a camel,* meaning to be overly particular about minor details while missing the significance of important matters.

In treating figurative meanings one must always be concerned with their corresponding literal significance, for in figurative meanings there is always a factor of psychological awareness of both the literal and the figurative meanings. There is no conventional use of *coat* in a figurative sense, but it does occur figuratively in the statement *he usually applies at least three coats of footnotes to cover up his cracked thinking.* This figurative meaning of *coat* in the sense of "an applied series" is based on the third meaning in the above analysis, and the relevance of this meaning of *coat* is heightened by the expression *cracked thinking,* since in painting one must often apply at least three coats of paint to cover up cracks. It is the context as a whole (the syntagmatic relations) which serves to mark, or point to, the figurative meaning. In this statement, however, *cracked* is also figurative, since it does not designate the feature of an entity, but of an event—namely, thinking. This figurative usage of *cracked* is somewhat more conventional, however, since one may speak of a person as *cracked up* if suffering from mental derangement.

It is important to note that the differences in literal and figurative meanings of lexical units (morphemes, words, and idioms) is a matter of lexical semantics, but the use of figurative meanings in a particular utterance as a means of creating impact and/or aesthetic appeal is a matter of rhetorical meaning, treated in Chapter 6.

The principal difficulties encountered by translators result from the diversities in the practices and beliefs of distinct cultures. It is not, therefore, strange that there are a number of problems in Bible translating since the world view and the behavioral patterns of the biblical world are in many respects very different from those of present-day cultures.

One very important feature of figurative meanings is that they tend to be "culture specific," that is, they usually reflect a particular cultural pattern of behavior or mode of understanding. The previous statement with regard to *three coats of footnotes* has a basis in fact, since many writers who are lacking in content tend to employ an abundance of footnotes (even ones which are irrelevant) to give the impression of scholarship.

Some scholars have argued for the meaning of *fox* in Luke 13:32 as "rapacity," which was certainly a characteristic of King Herod, but to translate the correct meaning of *fox* in this biblical context, it is important to determine how people of biblical times were most likely to employ the term for "fox" in a figurative sense. In the Talmud, for example, the fox is regarded as "the slyest of all beasts." In Greek, the term *alōpēks* "fox" is used in the same sense. Since this same figurative meaning occurs in a number of European cultures, it is probably a so-called "loan metaphor." One must not conclude, however, that this type of figurative meaning of *fox* is universal. In fact, in many African cultural settings this characteristic is assigned to a variety of other animals and even to insects, for example, tortoises, hares, and spiders (de Waard, 1974, 107–16).

Figurative meanings may range from the obvious to the obscure to the completely unknown. Consider, for example, the following six idioms in Tsonga (Ntsanwisi, 1968):

1. *to lack a head* "to be stupid"
2. *to tie the tongue* "to be silent"
3. *to have a long heart* "to be patient"
4. *to crush a bug* "to use foul language" (the crushing of a bug almost always causes a stink, even as foul language is offensive to people)
5. *to bite the ear* "to eat the firstfruits of the season" (an activity regarded as inappropriate unless preceded by proper ritual)
6. *the spring of an impala* "the fact that children act like their parents" (based on the belief that any embryo learns to behave like its mother while still in the womb)

Certain biblical figures of speech are misunderstood because of a failure to take into consideration the local cultural usage and because of a desire to impose upon such a figure a meaning associated at least in part with one's own culture. This has frequently happened with the Hebrew idiom, found in Psalms 60:8 and 108:9, which literally means "upon Edom I cast my shoe." This idiom developed out of what was originally a symbolic gesture described in part in the book of Ruth. This practice, however, no longer existed even when the book of Ruth was written and therefore it required explanation (Ruth 4:7). The idiom in the Psalms means "taking possession of something" and concretely in this context means "taking possession of the land of Edom." The average English-speaking person without a knowledge of the cultural background of Old Testament times would regard a statement such as "upon Edom I cast my shoe" as indicating utter contempt for Edom. This seems to fit well the overall historical context since the Edomites were the traditional enemies of the Jews, but this idiom really means that God regards Edom as his own possession and therefore something for which he has concern. In the *Français Courant* the idiomatic expression has been retained but explained in a translation meaning "I have rights over Edom and have thrown my sandal on it." In the German *Die Gute Nachricht* translation, the meaning has been expressed as "I have thrown my shoe on Edom in order to indicate my right of possession."

In these two renderings of this rather difficult idiom in Hebrew, there are subtle differences between the French and German texts. In French one can still see the idiom and presume its meaning, while in the German text the relation between the idiom and its meaning is stated overtly in terms of purpose. In some languages a significantly different type of expression has been employed. For example, in Bamoun, spoken in the Camerouns, the rendering means "I put my war spear into the soil of Edom," but a footnote is added to give the literal Hebrew idiom. In Bamoun, putting a spear into the soil of an area does not have anything to do with conquest but serves only as a symbol of possession. In a modern Dutch translation, cultural equivalence has been obtained by a rendering which means "I have set my feet on Edom."

Genesis 49 contains a number of figurative expressions used in the account of the blessings pronounced by Jacob on his various sons. Some of these figurative expressions require a good deal of cultural background if readers are really to understand. For example, "he ties his young donkey to a grapevine" in Genesis 49:11 is likely to be understood as meaning that Judah is indeed a fool, for no intelligent person would ever tie a young donkey to a grapevine, since the donkey would certainly eat it down. The significance of this expression is found in the fact that Judah is to be so rich and prosperous that he can well afford to do such a thing, even as the latter part of the same verse indicates that Judah is to "wash his clothes in blood-red wine," another reference to ostentatious wealth rather than to stupidity. A translator, however, may want to retain the literal statements in Genesis 49, but this will surely require a number of marginal notes as a means of providing a basis for understanding the correct significance of such figurative expressions.

As already noted in the discussion of rhetorical meaning, there is a tendency for some translators to avoid figurative meanings. It seems to be so much easier to employ literal equivalents rather than to search for possible parallel figurative correspondences. One should, however, avoid the tendency to delete or de-metaphorize figurative expressions, for figures of speech add insights, contribute impact, provide aesthetic enhancement, and can be very important in contributing in-group identification. When an idiom in a receptor language can be employed without introducing cultural distortion, it certainly should be utilized.

Degrees of conventionality in figurative meanings. In addition to different degrees of intelligibility of figurative expressions, there are also different degrees of conventional use. In the Bible the use of *heart* in the sense of "mind" is so conventional as to be no longer figurative, and the formula *son of . . .* is so frequent in occurrence as to have deceived some translators into translating this formula literally. The expressions "sons of the evil one" (Matt. 13:38) and "sons of those who murdered the prophets" (Matt. 23:31) might appear to be readily understood, but in reality the chances are that people will misunderstand the meaning. In Matthew 13:38 "sons of the evil one" does not refer to the actual sons of the devil but to people who act like the devil, and "the sons of those who murdered the prophets" are simply those who act like the persons who murdered the prophets.

Phrases such as "sons of disobedience" (Eph. 2:2) and "sons of this age" (Luke 16:8a) will amost inevitably be misunderstood, and the same certainly applies to "sons of the resurrection" (Luke 20:36) and "son of destruction" (John 17:12). In almost all such instances it is important to indicate clearly the relation between the persons involved and the event which they experience or participate in, so that "sons of disobedience" may be rendered as "those who habitually disobey" and "sons of this age" may be rendered as "people who act like most people living at this time." The phrase "sons of the resurrection" may be rendered as "those who will rise from death," while "son of destruction" may be rendered as "one who is bound to be destroyed."

The idiom "the sons of the bride chamber" or "the sons of the wedding hall" (Mark 2:19) almost always requires some semantic restructuring, for the Aramaic idiom refers either to the friends of the groom or to the wedding guests in general. A strictly literal translation of this figurative expression can lead readers to think of illegitimate children born before the marriage or of children conceived at the time of the consummation of the marriage.

The Old Testament expression "to lie with one's fathers" (occurring more than thirty times) is a standard euphemism employed to refer to the death of a king and not to the place of burial, but to translate this literally in some languages can lead to serious misunderstanding. On the other hand, a literal rendering of the phrase "circumcised of heart" may mean absolutely nothing.

As already noted in Chapter 3, figurative meanings are of two principal classes: metaphors and metonymies. Metaphors are based upon some type of similarity relation, while metonymies depend upon some kind of association. God may be spoken of as "Father," since he is presumed to have certain characteristics of a father, primarily authority and provision for offspring. The Scriptures speak of people as sheep, a meaning derived from the relation between the behavior of sheep and that of people. But the basis of comparison in a metaphor frequently remains implicit in biblical texts.

When Christ speaks of himself as "the door" (John 10:7, 9), this is likewise based upon a relation between the entrance to an area and the fact that Christ constitutes a means for people to enter into this new life. In translating this figure of the "door," it is essential to focus upon the entranceway and not upon the door as a barrier to entrance. For example, one may translate as "I am the door for the sheep" or "I am the gate for the sheep."

Metonymies are even more frequent in occurrence than metaphors, and they sometimes constitute even more difficult problems. Many persons, for example, understand the biblical phrase "to believe in his name" as requiring a believer to believe in a particular name of Jesus. In reality, however, the term *name* is simply a substitute for the person himself, and therefore "to believe in his name" means "to believe in him."

Determining figurative meaning. Determining the meaning of a figurative expression is not significantly different from the procedures employed in determining the designative or associative meaning of a term used literally. First, one must attempt to find the contextual range of a figurative expression. This may be much more difficult than first assumed, for figurative expressions are used frequently in highly specific contexts and tend to have highly restrictive meanings.

The next step in procedure is to search for other figurative expressions which may belong to the same general semantic domain. For example, if one is attempting to determine the designative meaning of *get the point,* it is well to compare this expression with such other figurative expressions as *see the light* and *catch on.* One may also compare *get the point* with non-figurative expressions such as *comprehend, understand,* and *grasp.*

In order to determine the meaning of a figurative expression on the basis of certain syntagmatic relations, often spoken of as "encyclopedic information," it is important to determine what may be certain similarities or connections between the literal and figurative meanings. This can often be done by examining a variety of contexts in which such an expression may be used as, for example, in *get the point of a story, get the point of the criticism,* and *get the point of the remark.* In these contexts the term *point* obviously does not refer to the acute angle of some projection, but rather to something which is crucial and particular about a statement or a concept. Accordingly, one can probably define the meaning of the figurative expression *get the point* as "to come to understand the principal and/or crucial element of a communication."

Special problems in translating figurative expressions. In some instances an expression may have both a literal and figurative meaning in the biblical text but be understood only in a literal sense in a receptor language. In Amos 4:6, for example, the phrase "cleanness of teeth" can refer to the fact of teeth being clean, but its primary reference is to a state of famine which results in people's teeth being clean. In some receptor languages, however, a literal rendering would refer only to the condition of the teeth and would immediately suggest the use of a toothbrush and toothpaste. Accordingly, many translators must render this reference in Amos 4:6 as "I will cause a famine."

Some translators are inclined to modify figurative expressions because they are "culturally disturbing" from the standpoint of their own cultural outlook. Translators generally do not hesitate to employ such anthropomorphisms as "the arm of God," "the hand of God," and "the eyes of God," but they often object strongly to such statements as "lift up your spear and ax against those who pursue me" (Ps. 35:2–3b), since this type of expression reflects a view of a warrior God. In reality, however, there is no way of or reason for escaping such concepts in the imprecatory psalms.

Some figurative expressions are extremely difficult to render satisfactorily. The phrase "dead to sin" (Rom. 6:2) is particularly complex. *Dead* can only be understood in the sense of "not responding to," and *sin* must be related to "the impulse to sin." Literal translations of "dead to sin" are usually quite meaningless. Accordingly, in most languages it is necessary to employ an expanded phrase such as "unresponsive to the temptations to sin" or even "to be just as though dead as far as being tempted to sin is concerned." Some translators have attempted to preserve a good deal of the figurative flavor of this expression by rendering it as "to sin no more than a dead man does."

Perhaps the greatest danger in literal translations of figurative expressions is that these literal renderings usually lead to distortions of meaning. The literal rendering "cover" in the biblical phrase "to cover sins" often results in people understanding "to cover up sins," namely, to hide one's wrongdoing. A literal translation of Psalm 85:3 "you have covered all their sin" is often understood to mean that Yahweh had purposely covered up the people's sins. In a high percentage of languages one cannot speak of "covering sin" in the sense of "forgiving sins"; rather, it is necessary to employ such expressions as "to wash away sins" (Timorese) or "to turn one's back to sins" (Kpelle).

The literal rendering of some figurative expressions may produce very negative associative meanings as, for example, in the case of an oath being solemnized by "putting the hand under the thigh" (Gen. 24:2). In biblical times to make an oath while touching the genital organs involved ratification on the basis of a person's most powerful symbol, namely, his capacity to reproduce. Such a procedure, however, seems to many persons in the Western world to be both vulgar and crude, and in certain other parts of the world such a statement suggests erotic stimulation. Traces of this type of ritual, however, have been found in various parts of the world (Jeremias, 1906, 395). Spurrell (1896, 218) quotes a striking Australian parallel in which one man may seat himself cross-legged upon the thighs of another, place his hands under the thighs of his friend, and make a solemn pledge to avenge a death. According to Abraham Ibn Ezra (1092–1167 A.D.), the ceremony of making a vow by touching the genitals was still a custom in India in his day.

In the two instances in Genesis (24:2 and 47:29) the ceremony takes place in the context of a deathbed scene. Later exegesis of this custom has seen an appeal to the covenant of circumcision (Targum Jonathan, Rabbi Shelomoh Yizhaki, and Jerome), a symbol of subjection (Ibn Ezra), or an invoking of posterity. Such attempts, however, are later rationalizations. In a number of languages it may be extremely difficult to find a functional equivalent for this gesture. The translation equivalent in a language like Bamoun is "to lick the forehead." Although with such an expression one remains in the same semantic domain of body parts, the culturally deviating translation makes a note obligatory (de Waard, 1971, 107–15).

Inadequacies in Traditional Approaches to Biblical Lexicography

Before undertaking a detailed analysis of an approach to determining the meanings of certain key biblical expressions, it may be useful to discuss briefly certain traditional approaches to biblical lexicography and in this way to highlight important differences between the methods outlined here and those which are typical of most bilingual dictionaries of biblical languages and books on word studies.

One of the most evident mistakes made by those who seek to explain the meanings of words is to depend upon the presumed history of a word, in other words, its "etymology." Since the term *etymology* means literally "true meaning" or "genuine meaning," people have often assumed that if they are following an etymological approach, they will arrive at the correct meaning of a word or phrase. One of the most commonly misunderstood terms is the Greek word *ekklēsia*, "church" or "gathering." Some persons have insisted that the true meaning of *ekklēsia* is "called out ones," meaning that the Christian is to be separated from the world. Though one might derive this meaning from the meaning of the constituent parts of this word, nevertheless in New Testament times *ekklēsia* simply meant a grouping of persons constituted by membership. Therefore, *ekklēsia* differs in meaning from *okhlos* "crowd," which could also be a gathering of people, but without membership. Similarly, *ekklēsia* contrasts with *plēthos* "multitude," indicating a somewhat larger group than would be designated by the normal meaning of *okhlos*.

On the basis of a Sanskrit cognate, one may show that *eukhomai*, normally translated "to pray" in the New Testament, originally meant "to brag" or "to be proud of." Since men often called upon the deities for help on the basis of what they had performed on behalf of the gods, it is easy to see how "to brag" acquired the additional meaning of "to pray." But this historical development does not determine the significant features of meaning of *eukhomai* in the New Testament.

The issue of language cognates is of particular importance in the case of Hebrew, in which a whole science of comparative philology has been developed. A typical case of overemphasis upon cognate meanings can be seen in the treatment of the Hebrew verb *niham*, to which such meanings as "comfort" and "repent" have been given. According to one treatment (Snaith), the verb actually means "to take a breath of relief." This sense is based upon the meaning of the Arabic cognate "to breathe hard as of a horse." On this basis scholars have concluded that a change of mind is involved in the meaning "repent," without any supplementary features of sorrow or regret. James Barr (1961, 117) has clearly demonstrated that the meaning of "breathing of a horse" in a cognate language cannot determine the meanings of Hebrew *niham* in a biblical text.

The verb *niham* involves not only being sorry for others and thus "to have compassion," but to be sorry about one's own behavior and therefore "to repent of one's own wrongdoing." An extended meaning of ''being sorry for oneself'' involves ''comforting oneself'' or ''being comforted,'' and may also extend to the sense of "relieving oneself" by taking vengeance. Such a series of extended meanings is not at all unusual, and there is certainly no need to go back to an Arabic cognate involving the hard breathing of a horse (Van Dyke Parunak, 1975, 527).

Another inadequacy of traditional approaches to the meaning of words is the failure to deal satisfactorily with associative meanings. In Colossians 2:8 Paul uses the term "philosophy" in a decidedly unfavorable sense, for it is immediately combined with a phrase meaning "empty deceit." This is actually the only occurrence of the word *philosophia* in the New Testament. It would be wrong to assume that this associative meaning of the Greek term was peculiar to the entire Christian community, for in Colossians 2:8 *philosophia* occurs in a very restrictive context and is specifically applicable to the view of the false teachers attacked by Paul. It is the very expression which these teachers probably used concerning themselves in order to assert more authority. Therefore, their own designation is quoted. Paul does not reject philosophy as such, even if it remains true that in contrast with Philo and Josephus, early Christianity wanted to be understood as a *sophia* "wisdom" and not as *philosophia* (Michel, 1970, 182). The direct borrowing of the term *philosophy* in an English translation of Colossians 2:8 would produce an intellectual jolt, since most persons are not familiar with any negative associative meaning attached to the English term *philosophy*. The translator should therefore avoid the term *philosophy* and use an expression such as "human wisdom."

One of the conspicuous inadequacies in traditional approaches to the meaning of terms in bilingual dictionaries is their almost total dependency on glosses. This means that a number of different words may appear to be completely synonymous, since there is no evident distinction based on the glosses which are employed.

For example, the Greek terms *homileō, sunomileō, dialogizomai, sumballō,* and *antiballō* are frequently given glosses such as "converse," "discuss," and "talk with." Actually, *homileō* means "to speak with someone, with the implication of a response from the one spoken to." The verb *sunomileō* is very similar in meaning to *homileō*, except for the fact that the prefix *sun-* emphasizes the reciprocal responses involved. The verb *dialogizomai* may also be translated "to converse" or "to discuss," but it really means to engage in a somewhat more detailed discussion of a matter. The verb *sumballō*, however, as in Acts 4:15, can also be translated "to converse" or "to discuss," but it may be more adequately defined as "to confer on a series of proposals," while *antiballō* involves "discussing conflicting opinions."

Dictionaries frequently mention figurative meanings, but rarely do they attempt to discuss different but related figurative meanings. Note, for example, the following Greek terms used figuratively: *oikia* (Luke 1:27) in a context referring to Joseph as being "of the house of David"; *sperma* (Rom. 1:3) in a context speaking of Jesus as "of the seed of David"; *haima* (Acts 17:26, Byzantine text) in a context in which all nations are described as being "of one blood"; and *sarks* (Rom. 11:14) in a context in which Paul speaks of the Jewish people as "my flesh." These four Greek terms are figurative designations for kinship. The word *oikia* designates direct descent and the same ethnic community, but *sperma* in Romans 1:3 focuses somewhat more specifically on the factor of biological lineage. The word *haima* specifies that the referents are of the same species, but there is no relationship to direct descent; it simply emphasizes that the people involved are somehow biologically related. Similarly, the term *sarks* does not focus upon descent or lineage but rather upon ethic belonging and association.

Another serious difficulty which translators face in attempting to deal realistically with lexical meaning is that dictionaries frequently treat meaning in very unsystematic ways. Bauer's *Lexicon of the Greek New Testament and Other Early Christian Literature*, as first translated and edited by Arndt and Gingrich and later by Gingrich and Danker, employs classifications of meanings based on very different kinds of criteria. In many instances the order is simply historical; at times, however, basic distinctions are made on the basis of syntactic differences, and frequently the order is presumably a logical one, based on derivation. In addition to actual issues of lexical meaning, there are frequently long digressions which are more theological than semantic. Note, for example, the classification of the Greek term *logos:*

> 1. *speaking,* a. general (meaning), α. *word,* β. The expression may take any one of many different forms, so that the exact translation of *logos* depends on the context: statement, question, prayer, prophecy, command, report, story, account, proverb, proclamation, instruction, teaching, message, speech; γ. of a statement of definite content: assertion, declaration, speech, statement; δ. plural *logoi* is used (1) either of words uttered on various occasions, of speeches made here and there or (2) of words and expressions that form a unity whether it be connected discourse, a conversation, or parts of one and the same teaching, or expositions on the same subject; ε. the subject under discussion: matter, thing, subject; ζ. of written words and speeches: of the separate books of a work: word, writings; b. of revelation by God, α. God's word, command, commission; promise, commandment, law; β. of the divine revelation through Christ and his messengers: the Christian message, the gospel, divine word. 2. computation, reckoning, a. account, accounts, reckoning, accounting; b. settlement, account; c. respect, regard (eis logon tinos *with regard to, for the sake of*); d. reason, motive; e. pros hon hēmin ho logos *with whom we have to do;* f. concern for. 3. *the Logos, Christ as the Word.*

In the first place, there is little attempt to actually define any meaning of *logos.* Rather, the dictionary simply groups together seemingly related glosses. In the case of 1.a. β., the remark, "The expression may take any one of many different forms," is not particularly helpful. It includes so much as to be relatively useless. Certainly 1.ε   ., in which *logos* is "the subject under discussion" and may be rendered as *matter* or *thing* is quite distinct from what precedes and follows.

The distinction between a and b under 1, namely, between general speaking and revelation by God, is primarily theological rather than semantic. Also, the distinction in this case between b. *α*. and b. *β*. is again theological. Clearly the meanings of "account" and "settlement" are distinct, but these can scarcely be grouped together with the meaning of "with respect to" or "with regard to." Furthermore, the meanings of "reason" and "motive" should be listed as quite distinct from the rest of the meanings in this second major category.

As already implied in the discussions of range, most dictionaries fail to provide sufficient information about differences of range and therefore possible differences of meaning. The issue of range becomes particularly acute in connection with the Greek terms *agapaō* and *phileō*. Many persons have assumed that *agapaō* relates only to love of God (whether people's love for God or God's love for people) and that *phileō* refers to human love. An examination of the various contexts in the New Testament, however, indicates quite clearly that this is not the case. Both types of love are expressed by both terms. Both *agapaō* and *phileō* are also used of loving unworthy objects. For example, *agapaō* occurs in relation to "unrighteous gain" (2 Pet. 2:15) and "the world" (1 John 2:15), while *phileō* occurs in connection with "a place of honor" (Matt. 23:6) and "to be greeted with respect in the marketplace" (Luke 20:46).

Phileō is also used as a symbol of personal affection, though in Matthew 26:48 it is hypocritical in the meaning of "to kiss." One very important distinction in range between *agapaō* and *phileō* is the fact that *agapaō* can be commanded, but *phileō* is never used in the imperative sense of commanding a person to love someone else. A careful investigation of the total ranges of these terms would seem to indicate that *agapaō* refers to a deep appreciation of the worth and the value of a person or an activity, while *phileō* indicates a measure of affection based upon association. This does not mean, however, that in each and every context these distinctions are to be maintained. For example, in John 21 the shift from one to another of these verbs appears to be primarily a matter of rhetorical variation rather than of significant contrast in designative meaning.

In some instances one senses that there may very well be a distinction in meaning between two semantically related words, but on the basis of existing contexts it may not be possible to determine what the distinction is. For example, in the New Testament Greek one may presume that there is some slight difference of meaning between *blepō* and *horaō*, both of which are normally translated as "to see" or "to notice," and also between *legō* and *laleō*, usually translated "to speak" or "to talk." In presuming that there may be certain differences of meaning, one is tempted to see the distinctions which do exist to a considerable extent in Classical Greek, but one must not assume that these distinctions necessarily carry over for differences in the Koine Greek of the New Testament. The basic problem is that we simply do not have in the New Testament a sufficiently wide range of contexts which can provide a basis for describing at least some of the differences in associative meaning.

Dictionaries often do not adequately cover the possible range of meanings of a term. For example, *'akzari* (based on the reconstructed verbal root *kazar*) is usually given the meanings of "cruel" or "fierce." For this term there is an important affective component based on the morphology and especially highlighted by the suffixal morpheme *-i*. *'akzari* may, however, have the additional meanings of "disgusting" and "uncouth," as well as such meanings of unacceptable social behavior as "zealot," "enemy," and "alien" (Rabin, 1967, 219–30). In Proverbs 17:11 the phrase *mal'ak 'akzari* is not "a cruel messenger" but really a messenger bringing "a death sentence."

Closer attention paid to the issue of range would provide lexicographers with greater insight as to matters of meaning and reference. The unmarked meaning of Hebrew *mawet* is certainly "death." However, in Jeremiah 15:2 this unmarked meaning is impossible. In such a context *mawet* must refer to the disease which causes death, and in this context, more specifically the bubonic plague. This meaning should be indicated in a dictionary (Fohrer, 1968, 103).

For a Bible translator, one of the rather confusing and discouraging aspects of some dictionaries consists of the listing of various meanings without attempting to point out relations between such meanings. For example, under the biblical Hebrew root *kbd*, dictionaries list a number of different "meanings" such as *heavy, much, many, slow, abundant, burdensome, difficult, grievous, sluggish, dull, riches, respect, honor,* and *great*. A study of the range of meaning exhibited by the Hebrew root *kbd* reveals four different classes of meaning based upon designative and associative features: (1) those which designate quantity (without any value judgment) in terms of mass and number: *heavy, much, many, abundant,* (2) those which describe certain aspects of inertia: *slow* (without evidence of value judgment) and *sluggish* and *dull* (with a value judgment of disapproval), (3) those which specify certain culturally valued features: *riches, respect, honor, great,* and (4) those which designate abundance as a source of features having only negative value: *burdensome, difficult, grievous.*

This division into four classes immediately suggests certain relationships. The first class is neutral or central to the poles of positive and negative values. The meaning of *slow* seems to fall somewhere between the neutral series and the culturally disfavored ones, but the meanings of *sluggish* and *dull* are distinctly disfavored. Certain of the underlying relationships are pictured diagrammatically in the illustration on page 164.

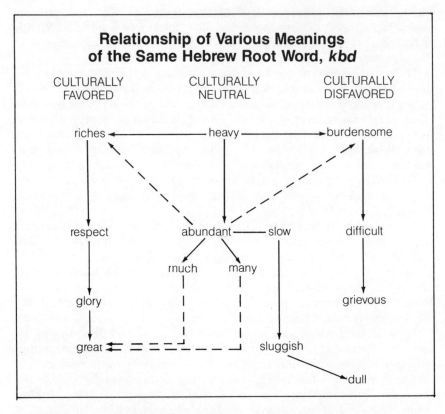

This chart is not intended to reflect the relation between the glosses as used in English but as they are employed to reflect biblical Hebrew, in which, no doubt, the nomadic or pastoral background of the people was an important factor in giving rise to a series of meanings in which a quantity of a substance could be either a base for wealth, if it had cultural value, or the cause of great inconvenience, if it were relatively valueless. The arrows are intended to show the presumed direction of derivation on the basis of what we know about such patterns of life and language usage, and the two types of arrows (solid and broken) designate two degrees of semantic relationship.

This type of diagram has the advantage of permitting an organization of diverse data into a relatively small compass, thus allowing for the study of otherwise overlooked relations. On the other hand, such a diagram includes a number of serious limitations: (1) the representation of the relationships between the meanings is overly simplified (several planes, plus a dimension of time, would be necessary if one were to diagram all the factors accurately), (2) the arrows imply a kind of etymological descent, which may or may not be true, and (3) instead of two degrees of inter-relationship, there are actually several, with a considerable reciprocal reinforcement which cannot be shown in such a diagram and could not even be fully ascertained from available evidence. In addition to all this, one must always be cautious about analyzing the meaning of a term in a foreign language through the use of glosses. It is almost inevitable that the language employed as a grid will tend to skew the data. Nevertheless, a statement about the various types of meaning of a term and their interrelationships can be helpful to a translator; otherwise, the long series of meanings given to the root *kbd* may seem only like a jumbled mess.

In dictionaries of biblical Hebrew there is a special problem, namely, the complications which occur in deciding whether a certain constellation of meaning should be related to one and the same root or to several homophonous roots. For example, are two distinct roots *halal* sufficient to explain such diverse meanings as "to flash forth light," "to praise," and "to act like a fool," or should one presuppose the existence of three homophonous roots? The Koehler-Baumgartner lexicon discusses the various meanings in terms of three homophonous roots. The dictionary by Brown, Driver, and Briggs sets up two homophonous roots, one meaning "to shine" and another "to be boastful, to praise, and to act like a fool." It would also be possible to have one root meaning "to praise" and another root which could combine "to shine" and "to act like a fool," if this could be related to some reconstructed meaning of "to appear" (as of a new moon). From this, one could derive the meaning of "to shine" and "to be a lunatic" and hence "to act foolishly," but in view of the data which is available for analyzing such problems, there is no sure way of resolving the issues.

Contrastive and Contextual Factors in Determining Meanings

Though it is possible to isolate contrastive and contextual factors involved in determining meanings, it is usually impracticable to do so. By studying the range of occurrence of a lexical item, we immediately sense certain different meanings on the basis of diverse semantic domains in which these meanings fit. At the same time, we instinctively compare the related meanings of different words which exist within a single domain, and we arrive at distinctions on the basis of competing ranges of such words. The most practical methodology, then, normally consists in (1) studying the range of occurrence of a lexical item, (2) setting up possible differences of meaning based upon different semantic domains in which certain clusters of uses seem to belong, (3) comparing the ranges of other words within such domains, and finally (4) arriving at a set of distinctive and supplementary features of meaning which may be crucial for determining designative and associative meanings. Only when this is done, can one study some of the implications of such an analysis for determining the closest natural equivalents in a receptor language.

A brief analysis of the Hebrew root *qdsh* may prove instructive. In the first place, there are a number of objects and events which may be spoken of as "being *qdsh*" (either in the adjectival or nominal constructions): arm, name, spirit, place, tabernacle, temple, ark, city, altar, sacrifice, vestments, vows, house, oil, incense, priests, people (of Israel), covenant, time of worship, God, throne of God, camp of Israel, heaven, angels, Sabbath. In other contexts the root *qdsh* may be translated as "to make holy," "to consecrate," "to dedicate," "to make taboo (positive)," "to observe as holy," "to honor as holy," "to regard as holy," "temple prostitute" (male or female), and "sanctuary."

The preceding list provides a kind of "telescoped resumé" of the typical range of *qdsh*, and from this range one may note the following meanings: (1) to be holy (in the sense of possessing certain features of positive taboo) either (a) as the result of inherent qualities (God, heaven, angels, arm of God, name of God, and Spirit of God), or (b) as the result of having been caused to become holy (place, tabernacle, temple, ark, city, altar, sacrifice, vestments, vows, house, oil, incense, priests, people (of Israel), covenant, time of worship, Sabbath); (2) to cause something to become holy and thus the object of special religious practice ("to make holy," "to consecrate," "to dedicate," "to make taboo"); (3) to behave or act on the basis of something being holy ("to observe as," "to honor as," "to regard as"); (4) a temple prostitute; and (5) the sanctuary.

To appreciate more specifically the designative and associative meanings of *qdsh*, it is essential to compare one of its crucial meanings, namely, "to cause to become holy," with related meanings of other roots, such as *ḥrm* and *ḥll*.

For the root *ḥrm* the closest corresponding meaning to the second meaning of *qdsh* (noted above) is "to devote or dedicate to destruction on the basis of divine sanction, either because God has commanded such or for the sake of honor to God." As the result of such an action, the objects in question acquire negative taboo. A further extended meaning of *ḥrm* involves the devoting of spoils to the temple treasury or sanctuary, and an additional meaning designates that which has been dedicated to destruction.

The closest related meaning of *ḥll* is "to cause something not to be sacred" in the sense of profaning that which is sacred and thus taking away its sacred character, as in the case of an altar, or belittling the sacred character of something, in the sense of "profaning the name of God." The root *ḥll* may also occur in the sense of "to pollute" in the meaning of "to cause negative taboo," for example, by contact with a dead body. Further meanings involve "causing dishonor to" and "that which has been profaned."

It is possible to compare the most closely related meanings of *qdsh*, *ḥrm*, and *ḥll* by employing the following matrix based on certain positive and negative features.

Comparison of the Shades Of Meaning of Three Different Hebrew Roots			
	qdsh	*ḥrm*	*ḥll*
	cause to become holy	cause to be destroyed	cause not to be sacred (profane)
1. as an expression of religous devotion	+	+	—
2. a feature of positive taboo	+	—	—
3. culturally approved	+	+	—

Matrices such as the one reproduced above have certain distinct advantages in that they focus upon certain significant contrasts, but such matrices may also be somewhat deceptive in that the contrasts are not always on the same level. Note, for example, that in the case of the second distinctive feature, there is a minus for both *ḥrm* and *ḥll*, but for *ḥrm* the minus indicates that there is negative taboo or even the absence of any taboo, while in the case of *ḥll*, the minus marks either the loss of a positive taboo, as in the case of profaning an altar, or the attribution of negative taboo, in that a profaned object must be avoided until it has been properly reconsecrated.

In the case of the third feature, namely, cultural approval, the plus feature is based upon the Old Testament biblical culture and not upon present-day attitudes in the Western World concerning so-called "holy wars."

To deal satisfactorily with all of the meanings of *qdsh*, *ḥrm*, and *ḥll*, it would be necessary to determine the distinctive differences in the case of each significantly different meaning, but the contrasts which already have been discussed provide at least a basis for dealing realistically with some of the translational problems in *qdsh* and also in large measure with the corresponding term *hagios* in New Testament Greek.

For the most part, the problems of translating Hebrew *qdsh* and Greek *hagios* involve three classes of contexts: (1) persons, vestments, altars, buildings; (2) temple prostitutes; and (3) inherently holy entities—Holy Spirit and God.

In most contexts where *qdsh* is used in connection with persons, vestments, altars, and buildings, one can speak of such objects as "being given to God" or "dedicated to God" or "consecrated for religious purpose." For example, in Deuteronomy 7:6 instead of translating "because you are a people holy to the Lord your God," it may be much more meaningful in many languages to employ a rendering such as "because you are a people dedicated to the Lord your God." Similarly, in Deuteronomy 33:3 the phrase "all his saints" may be better rendered as "all those who belong to him." In the New Testament the term *hagioi* is often best translated as "the people of God."

Some translators have insisted upon translating *qdsh* as "being separated," but frequently in receptor languages this means "being separated from" in the negative sense of "being rejected." Clearly, *qdsh* must be understood in the positive sense of "being separated to" or "dedicated to."

There is a special problem involved in Exodus 30:10 in which the altar of incense is spoken of as "holy of holy for the Lord." The semantic relationship is two-fold in that the altar is to be regarded as extremely sacred and at the same time dedicated to the Lord. Accordingly, it may be rendered as "it is to be an extremely sacred altar dedicated to the Lord" (as in Today's English Version).

When persons, vestments, altars, buildings, etc. are described as "being holy," it is often possible to employ a phrase based upon the process of becoming holy; that is, such objects may be described as "having been dedicated" or "having been consecrated."

In the case of the use of *qdsh* to designate temple prostitutes, it is essential to have some kind of marginal note indicating the role of such persons as symbols of fertility; otherwise, the distinctive role of such persons is completely obscured or distorted.

The most difficult problems involved in translating *qdsh* occur with those objects that are inherently holy, that is, objects which have not been made holy. In contexts involving such objects one certainly cannot use a term meaning merely "separated," for the Holy Spirit cannot be spoken of as "the separated Spirit of God" nor even as "the consecrated Spirit of God."

An even more serious mistake made by some translators has been to equate "holiness" with "cleanliness" or "whiteness," and they have therefore translated "Holy Spirit" as "the clean spirit of God" or "the white spirit of God." For a number of languages, especially in the South Pacific, there is no difficulty in using the local term *tabu*, but in some circumstances an indigenous expression for positive taboo has been so closely associated with local religious practices as to make it unacceptable to Christians. As a result, in a number of cases the Holy Spirit is simply spoken of as "the Spirit of God."

In many Chadic languages the Holy Spirit has been called "the shadow of God." At first glance this appears to be rather appropriate, but "the shadow" of a person is considered to be the double of such an individual. When someone dies, his shadow leaves him and continues to have an independent existence; also, during sleep a shadow can leave a human being and act independently. Since in many biblical contexts the Holy Spirit appears as an independently acting agent, the local speakers of Chadic languages quite understandably asked, "Was God asleep or was he dead every time his shadow acted?" Such negative factors in meaning have frequently led to borrowing from Arabic, as in the case of *ruuḫu* in Fulani (Kassühlke, 1982, 151–63).

In some languages one of the most crucial problems involving either *qdsh* or *hagios* occurs in contexts in which God is spoken of as "holy." Where there is no term involving positive taboo combined with ethical acceptability, some translators have simply used an expression meaning "the awesome one." This is often satisfactory provided it does not imply "causing fright." Accordingly, in some instances an equivalent of *qdsh* has been "the totally wonderful one" or even "the high one," while others have used "the pure one." The acceptability of such expressions depends upon the distinctive designative and associative features of such expressions within the local indigenous culture. One cannot judge the acceptability of expressions apart from their total range.

Another set of Hebrew terms presents quite a different range of difficulties in translation, but at the same time these terms also illustrate some of the typical complications which occur in lexicographical practice.

The noun *ḥeṣed* designates a relation of solidarity and reciprocal loyalty between relatives, friends, masters and servants, rulers and slaves, and God and his people. A second meaning based on this relationship of solidarity and loyalty designates those kind, merciful deeds which manifest such a relation. Typical English equivalents are *goodness, kindness, mercy,* and *piety*.

Traditionally, *ḥeṣed* has also been regarded as having the meaning of "lovely appearance" as in Isaiah 40:6, but rather than meaning "lovely appearance," it is more likely to mean "power, strength," since this seems to fit much better the context of Isaiah 40:6. This latter meaning is only recognized in the Targum, but there are other passages with this same meaning, for example, Psalms 44:27, 59:17, 94:18 and Job 10:12 (Whitley, 1981, 519–26). Although such a meaning has not been pointed out in any existing Hebrew dictionary, rejecting the existence of such a meaning results in violating the linguistic evidence (Sakenfeld, 1978).

A further derivative of the root *ḥsd* designates "one who is loyal and proves such by his actions."

A closely related Hebrew term, *ahabah,* designates the love which people may have for parents, wife, women, children, neighbor, and God, as well as God's love of people. A second meaning of *ahabah* refers to the love for and delight in such events as eating, drinking, sleeping, possessing wisdom, acquiring knowledge, and even engaging in folly and evil.

Derivatives of the stem *hb* designate "one who loves," "one who is loved," and "friend."

The third Hebrew word in this set, namely *ḥen,* designates "favor" and "acceptance" between people or from God to people. This meaning includes the unmerited kindness which may be shown by one of higher position to one in a lower position.

A second meaning of *ḥen* designates "elegance of form" and may apply typically to women, ornaments, words, and gazelles. The related verb stem *ḥnn* designates either "to show favor or pity" or "to seek such favor."

Some of the distinctive elements in the related meanings of the three terms *ḥeṣed, ahabah,* and *ḥen* may be highlighted by the chart below.

Related Meaning of Three Hebrew Terms

	ḥeṣed	*ahabah*	*hen*
1. reciprocity	+/—	+/—	—
2. sexual	—	—/+	—
3. covenant relation	+/—	—/+	—

Rather than use the conventional designation for plus and minus, namely ±, the positive and negative features involved in the range of usage of the respective terms indicate quite clearly that certain aspects of meaning occur far more frequently than others. For example, in *ḥeṣed* reciprocity and a covenant relation are dominant, but there are situations in which the context does not suggest either reciprocity or a covenant relation. In *ahabah* it is also true that reciprocity is more common than nonreciprocity, but the sexual feature is less frequent in the range than is the nonsexual, and the same is true for the covenant relation in *ahabah.*

There has been a tendency in the past to translate *ḥeṣed* almost exclusively by terms meaning "mercy," "goodness," and "kindness," though the King James Version often employs "loving-kindness." These are all possible meanings in certain contexts, but the two distinctive features of *ḥeṣed* are the covenant relationship and reciprocity. It is for precisely this reason that more modern translations focus upon the central meanings of *ḥeṣed*, namely "loyalty," "solidarity," and "love." The Revised Standard Version has rather consistently rendered *ḥeṣed* as "steadfast love." Other possible renderings are "constant love" and "loyal love."

Despite the fact that the term *love* in English has such a wide range of meaning, it is still probably the best equivalent of *ahabah* in most contexts, but in a number of languages quite different terms must be employed depending on the type of object involved in loving. For example, in some languages a special term is used for the love between those related by kinship, while quite a different term is used for persons who love members of the opposite sex in an amorous manner. The love of certain activities often requires still a third term.

Traditional translations in English often render *ḥen* as "grace," but the results may seem not only strange but even misleading. For example, in Genesis 6:8 the King James Version reads "but Noah found grace in the eyes of the Lord." In reality, of course, it was the Lord who was pleased with Noah, and accordingly Today's English Version translates "but the Lord was pleased with Noah." Similarly, in Numbers 11:11 the Revised Standard Version reads "and why have I not found favor in thy sight?" Since the focus is primarily upon the relationship of the superior to the inferior, Today's English Version has translated this expression as "why are you displeased with me?"

The Greek New Testament term *kharis* occurs with a number of different designative meanings which illustrate some of the complex problems of semantic focus. In general, *kharis* is translated "grace," but there are six significantly different meanings of *kharis* in the New Testament:

(1) attractiveness or pleasant quality (of words) as in Luke 4:22 and Colossians 4:6; (2) a favorable attitude as in Luke 2:52, "he gained favor with God and people" or "God and people were pleased with him"; (3) the event of showing favor or kindness to someone (for a discussion of this meaning, see the following paragraphs); (4) an objective token of favor and kindness, namely, a gift as in 1 Corinthians 16:3, "I shall . . . send them to take your gift to Jerusalem"; (5) an attitude of thankfulness, implying the expression of such, as in Colossians 3:16, "singing to God with thankfulness in your hearts"; and (6) the verbal expression of thanks as in 2 Corinthians 9:15, "thanks to God for his inscrutable gift."

The third meaning of *kharis* involves essentially three distinctive features: (a) a beneficent attitude on the part of the one bestowing favor, (b) the event of the bestowal, and (c) the resulting experience of the one who receives such favor or kindness. In a particular context, however, the focus may be upon one or more of these features, and the other features may be presuppositional, implied, or inferred. In Acts 14:26 ("they were commended to the grace of God"), for example, the focus may be upon God's beneficent attitude, but the implication is that God would express that attitude in the kindness and favor which the people would experience. In Romans 3:24 ("freely made righteous by his grace through the redemption in Christ Jesus") the focus likewise is upon God's beneficent attitude, but certainly this is expressed in what God did and implies a resulting experience. In Romans 12:6, however, in the phrase "according to the grace that has been given to us" the focus seems to shift to the particular event of showing kindness and favor.

In the phrase "as those who share in the grace of life" or ". . . the gift of life" in 1 Peter 3:7, the focus is either upon the event of giving a particular favor to people or upon the fact of their experiencing such a favor. In 2 Corinthians 1:15 the focus seems definitely to be upon the third distinctive feature in this meaning of *kharis*, since the final phrase of this verse may be translated as "in order that you might experience a second blessing" or "in order that you might be blessed twice." In Romans 5:2 the feature of experience seems to be definitely in focus, "through whom we had access by faith to this experience of grace in which we now live" or literally " . . . to this grace in which we stand."

But even in contexts in which the focus seems to be upon the experience of God's grace, both the beneficent attitude and the associated event are clearly presuppositional. It is possible to argue that instead of one meaning with three different distinctive features, any one of which may be in special focus, there are actually three different meanings, and this is the position taken by some scholars. However, whether the focus is upon one or more of these distinctive features of meaning depends very largely upon the context as a whole, and it is extremely difficult to assign to the word *kharis* three quite distinctive meanings based upon differences of focus, presupposition, or implication.

It is also important to recognize that *kharis* is only part of a somewhat larger cluster including *kharizomai, kharitoō,* and *kharisma.* One meaning of *kharizomai* parallels the third meaning of *kharis* in that it specifically designates the act of bestowing favor or kindness, and one may frequently render *kharizomai* in terms of the bestowal of a particular favor, for example, "to give sight to many blind people" (Luke 7:21) and "for you have been given the privilege of serving Christ" (Phil. 1:29). Note a parallel derivative in *kharitoō,* "for the gift which he gave us in his beloved Son" (Eph. 1:6).

In several contexts *kharizomai* has an extended and more restricted meaning of "to forgive," for example, "God forgave us all our sins" (Col.

2:13) and "to whomever you forgive anything, I shall forgive" (2 Cor. 2:10).

The Greek term *kharisma* also parallels the third meaning of *kharis* with focus upon the end result of the action of bestowing favor or kindness, for example, "the blessings of God are unchangeable" (Rom. 11:29) and "God's gift is eternal life" (Rom. 6:23).

For the most part the relationship between the various meanings of *kharis* suggests a logical development. A favorable attitude (meaning 2) is likely to result in action which reflects this attitude in some specific manner (meaning 3). Such action may take the form of some particular object, namely, a gift of money as in 1 Corinthians 16:3 (meaning 4), and the response of persons who receive such an expression of kindness would logically result in an attitude of thankfulness (meaning 5), and this thankfulness may in turn be expressed in a particular verbal form (meaning 6).

What seems somewhat illogical is the relationship between the first and second meanings. If, however, one takes into consideration a frequent meaning of *kharis* in nonbiblical texts, one encounters the meaning of *kharis* as "beauty of form" and concretely in the personified expression of this in "the Graces." The meaning of "beauty of form" is also related to the meaning of "beauty of action and behavior," to which the New Testament meaning of attractiveness or pleasantness of words is related.

Because the various meanings of *kharis* seem to form a logical linear series, it does not follow that this is necessarily the actual historical order in which the meanings developed. Some extensions of meaning no doubt do reflect historical processes, but a set of meanings of a particular word is more likely to form a kind of constellation in which there are a number of interacting relationships.

Evidence for the Meaning of Lexical Units

A translator dealing with contemporary texts has a great advantage over a Bible translator in that frequently he can consult an author as to precisely what was intended, and even if the author is not available, at least there are a number of native speakers of the language of the text, and one can therefore obtain valuable information which is often not included in dictionaries.

For the Bible translator, however, the situation is far more complex, because the availability of relevant information is often quite restricted. There are, however, three principal sources of information which are particularly relevant for a Bible translator. These include (1) biblical texts, (2) biblical languages (including especially data in lexicons and grammars), and (3) historical and cultural information with regard to the setting of the communication.

The biblical texts themselves undoubtedly constitute the most important basis for determining the meaning of lexical units. Within the text it is the immediate context of a paragraph or section which has the highest priority. One may, however, look to the document as a whole, and as a further step, one may examine the total corpus of any one writer. This movement from the immediate to the larger context and in turn from the larger to the more immediate context is extremely important, as may be noted, for example, in determining the meaning of *hoi Ioudaioi* "the Jews" in the Gospel of John. In most of the contexts the reference is not to all Jews as a nation but specifically to the Jewish authorities. In some contexts one can even define more precisely which authorities are being referred to. A precise identification of the participants involved in any text is often crucial, not only to the designative but also to the associative meaning.

If there is still significant doubt as to the meaning of a term, one can also look to other books of Holy Scripture. For passages in the New Testament one can examine not only other books of the New Testament but Old Testament usage as well. In view of the fact that so many lexical usages in the New Testament reflect the more or less literal translation of the Hebrew in the Septuagint Greek version, one can often only appreciate certain distinct meanings of the New Testament Greek terminology by noting the manner in which distinctive Hebrew meanings have come into the Greek New Testament by way of the Septuagint.

One may also expand the range of so-called textual evidence by examining texts of either religious or secular content written at approximately the same time as the biblical texts. This is not difficult in the case of the New Testament, but it is extremely difficult in the case of the Old Testament, for there are almost no important confirming documents in Hebrew except for those which shed light indirectly through early commentaries. The only important exceptions are a limited number of Hebrew epigraphs (Diringer, 1934; Moscati, 1951); nevertheless, even this limited evidence is important. For example, the Lachish ostracon number 4 mentions in lines 10 and 11 the word *mase't* (literally, "going up") as an abbreviation of *mase't 'ashan* (literally "going up of smoke"). This is a technical expression for a smoke or fire signal: "And my lord may know that we wait for the signals from Lachish" (Donner and Röllig, 1968, nr. 194). The same practice of communicating a message through fire or smoke signals occurs in the narrative of Judges 20:38 and 40 and in Jeremiah 6:1. This type of interpretation of the text from Judges is indirectly confirmed by the inscription. Unfortunately, even some recent translations into English have missed this comparative evidence.

For the New Testament there is a great deal of material written by the early Christian Fathers, and such texts can be extremely helpful. Also, for the New Testament there is an abundance of evidence for the nature of Koiné Greek. No longer is it necessary to think of New Testament Greek as a kind of "Holy Ghost language," simply because it is not like Classical Greek.

For the New Testament there is further insight to be gained from early translations, which in a sense act as succinct commentaries but which in view of the selection of corresponding terms provide a good deal of light on the way in which early translators understood the meanings of the Greek terms.

For the Hebrew Old Testament some valuable evidence is supplied by the Greek versions, the Latin Vulgate, and the Syriac Peshitta. Some scholars also make considerable use of cognate languages in understanding Hebrew, and they look to more or less contemporary Ugaritic or to developments in Arabic for clues as to the meaning. This, however, can be overdone, even as Barr and others have pointed out.

Working with cognate languages is usually extremely complex. For example, the meaning of the Hebrew verbal form *yahush* in Ecclesiastes 2:25 is uncertain. As a result, a number of different renderings have been employed, for example, "hasten" (King James Version), "drink" (New American Bible), "enjoy" (Revised Standard Version), and "be anxious" (New English Bible). As in so many cases, the problem is partly a text critical one and partly a semantic one. On relatively objective grounds a B rating has been given to the Hebrew reading in the *Preliminary Report on the Poetical Books* prepared by the Committee for the Hebrew Old Testament Text Project. Evidence from comparative philology is therefore relevant. Scholars have actually suggested as many as eight different possibilities based on the vocabulary of different Semitic languages. As a result, a translator is really overwhelmed by the variety of choices, but who can actually say what the historical relevance of certain meanings of related roots is for the language of Ecclesiastes (Braun, 1973, 111)? Who is going to provide explicit bases for evaluating the comparative materials?

From the Hebrew context it becomes clear that the meaning of the verb should be either in the same physiological domain as "eat" or in an emotive domain, in which case it should show a contiguous relation with "eat." These considerations would seem to eliminate the proposals that the verb should mean "to worry" on the basis of Accadian (Ellermeier, 1968) or "to reflect" on the basis of Mishnaic Hebrew. Of the remaining proposals, two amount to more or less the same result, namely, "to enjoy oneself," though one is based upon Mishnaic Hebrew, Aramaic, and Syriac (Levy, 1912) and the other on Ugaritic (Dahood, 1958, 302–18). But it is the evidence supplied by Dahood which turns out to be decisive.

The historical and cultural setting is also extremely important for understanding the meaning of words. This is particularly true for figurative language, which is based so often upon practices and beliefs peculiar to the culture. For example, in some contexts reference to "feet" is generally interpreted as being a euphemistic reference to the genitals, as in Exodus 4:25–26 (Hyatt, 1980).

Another example of the relevance of the cultural background can be found in Deuteronomy 11:10, which may be translated more or less literally as "Egypt . . . where you sowed your seed and watered it with your feet, like a garden of vegetables." There are two explanations possible with regard to this practice. Either it reflects the custom of marking the ground with foot-dug channels through which irrigation water would flow, or it refers to a water wheel which could be operated by foot or by the use of cattle. The choice depends largely upon dating procedures. If the reference is to the water wheel, we have an item almost completely unknown in most cultures today; hence the incomprehensibility of a literal translation. On the other hand, the context makes clear that hard work is involved. Therefore, in languages in which a cultural equivalent is lacking, one may render the passage as "you had to work hard to irrigate the fields."

The Translator's Exegetical Perspective

If one is to translate the Scriptures both correctly and without bias, it is essential to employ a valid exegetical perspective. In interpreting the Psalms, for example, mention has already been made as to the importance of looking to the meaning which such Psalms must have had in temple worship rather than attempting to go behind the Psalms on the basis of what a similar passage in Ugaritic may have meant. Studies of Ugaritic usage can be helpful and revealing, but they are only occasionally determinative. For example, in Psalm 73:23–24 the Hebrew term 'aḥar is usually rendered "afterward," and the relevant phrase is translated as "and afterward you will receive me with honor." This is done in spite of the fact that a preposition before the Hebrew word for "honor" is lacking. A comparison with the Ugaritic pair 'mn / aḥr allows one to render the Hebrew 'aḥar by "with," a meaning which has rightly been introduced into the most recent dictionaries. The text can therefore be rendered as "with honor you will receive me." This interpretation is reinforced by the chiastic structure of these verses, in which 'imak corresponds with we'aḥar and the preposition be in Psalm 73:23b corresponds with the same preposition in verse 24a (Fisher, 1972, 297).

For the Old Testament the most satisfactory exegetical perspective is perhaps best defined as that period of time in which the text was recognized as authoritative for both belief and practice, in other words, the time at which the text became recognized as "Holy Scripture." For the New Testament, a similar problem exists. Some scholars, for example, wish to go behind the existing text in order to determine what Jesus must have said and meant, even though the existing texts are significantly different. By means of literary criticism, one can make interesting speculations as to the original literary sources, but for the translator the most important issue is what the writer must have meant in the text as given. Not only must one avoid going behind the text, but it is also important not to read into the New Testament doctrinal positions which developed in later times. Reading back into a text a particular mode of baptism, a special theory of atonement, or a historical view of the letters to the seven churches in the book of Revelation can lead to distortion. It is important to let the books of Scripture speak for themselves. Writings which have endured for some two to three thousand years are not likely to need amplifications which are strictly marginal to the mainstream of scholarly insight.

The primary exegetical perspective of a translator is "what did the text mean to people who were the original receptors?" It is clearly the task of a preacher to take this biblical text and indicate to people what it should mean to Christians and others today. The whole concept of "holy war" is largely repugnant to most present-day readers, but this does not warrant a translator "toning down" statements about such conflicts or making them out to be merely struggles for national survival.

Assumptions About the Purposes of Biblical Texts

To fully appreciate the sources of evidence for the meaning of lexical units, it may be important to note certain assumptions which are particularly relative to the Scriptures. These are assumptions in addition to those which are relevant for ascertaining the meaning of any and all types of lexical units.

In the first place, one should assume that the biblical writers were not motivated by any desire to deceive readers. In other words, they were not attempting to perpetrate a hoax. A second assumption is that the writers were not trying to be obscure. They may not have always made their meaning perfectly clear, and we are not always in a position to understand the meaning in view of the fact that we do not possess all the background knowledge and information which they possessed. But except for apocalyptic writing (which was designed to be clear to a restricted audience), there certainly is no attempt to be obscure for the sake of mystical, esoteric communication.

A third assumption which is particularly relevant for the biblical texts is that the writers regarded what they were saying as both meaningful and significant. Furthermore, there is every indication that the writers brought to their task a degree of personal commitment and involvement.

A fourth assumption is that the biblical writers employed the literary genres and rhetorical devices which were familiar to the people of that day and which were and should be judged in accordance with their usage in that language-culture context.

Semantic Domains

As has already been noted, the relation between a lexical meaning and its set of references is never exclusively one to one, or even one to many, but actually many to many. The relevance of this observation is never more clearly illustrated than in a brief study of certain semantic domains. Not only within a language do meanings overlap, have indefinite peripheries, and occur in several layers, but between languages there are no exact correspondences. What is a central meaning for a term in one language may be a peripheral meaning for a corresponding term in another language, and there are constant instances of under- and overdifferentiation. This becomes evident in a brief glance at four closely related domains: *Know, Learn, Think,* and *Understand.* Note the following Old Testament and New Testament terms, each with a series of typical glosses which in one way or another fit within the four domains of Intellectual Activity.

Old Testament
1. *YDᶜ:* know, learn, find out, discern, distinguish, think, think about, consider, be acquainted with
2. *ḤKM:* knowledge, wisdom, skill, shrewdness, learned, prudent, wise
3. *LB:* mind, attitude, will, moral character
4. *BYN:* perceive, consider, distinguish, understanding, to understand, insight
5. *ZMM:* consider, plan
6. *SHPHT:* judge, judgment

New Testament
1. *Ginōskō:* learn, find out, understand, notice (perceive), know (a person), acknowledge
2. *Oida:* know (a person or thing), understand
3. *Epistamai:* know, acquainted with (persons or things), understand
4. *Logizomai:* consider, ponder, calculate
5. *Noeō:* perceive, think about, understand
6. *Nomizō:* think, consider, assume
7. *Noēma:* thought, mind
8. *Nous:* mind, way of thinking, attitude, thought, opinion
9. *Krinō:* distinguish, consider, evaluate, judge, decide
10. *Sunesis:* intelligence, insight, understanding
11. *Suniēmi:* understand, show insight
12. *Kardia:* mind, way of thinking
13. *Sophia:* wisdom, skill
14. *Sophos:* skilled, wise, learned

Note that not all of the possible glosses for the corresponding Hebrew and Greek terms are given but only those which relate to the four domains.

As a way of showing certain correspondences between the Greek and Hebrew terms and the sets of English lexical units, note the following four domains set up on the basis of the English terms *know, learn, think,* and *understand.* Broad definitions for the respective domains are given in the first line of each set.

1. *Know:* awareness of stored information (of all types and by whatever channel)
   a. be acquainted with (less evident awareness)
   b. knowledge (content)
   c. recognize (match new information with old)
   d. acknowledge (recognize and/or communicate the fact that two sets of information agree)

2. *Learn:* to acquire and store information
   a. find out, discover (looked for or unexpected)
   b. discern (by careful scrutiny, perception)
   c. distinguish (perceive differences)
   d. perceive, notice (awareness of relevant information)
   e. learned (having acquired much information)

3. *Think:* to process and manipulate information
   a. think about, consider (to process information in preparation for decision)
   b. mind (faculty or capacity for processing information)
   c. attitude (value presuppositions relating to information)
   d. will (faculty to decide and act)
   e. plan (about future activity)
   f. way of thinking (habitual mode of processing and deciding)
   g. thought (content of)
   h. opinion (content of tentative judgment)
   i. decide (to conclude a process of thinking by making a selection)
   j. judge (to decide after careful thought about alternatives)
   k. judgment (faculty or capacity to judge)
   l. judgment (content of decision)
   m. evaluate (to consider comparative values)

4. *Understand:* to process diverse information and arrive at some conclusion
   a. understanding (faculty or capacity)
   b. insight (unusual, valued understanding)
   c. intelligence (knowledge and effective capacity for understanding)
   d. wisdom (capacity for insight about valued modes of behavior)
   e. wise (characteristic of a person possessing wisdom)
   f. prudent (to employ wisdom about future implications of behavior)
   g. skill (capacity for valued activity of a technical or practical nature)
   h. shrewdness (capacity for effective decisions and behavior of possible doubtful moral validity)

Still further insight with regard to the nature of domains and the range of New Testament meanings may be obtained from simply reviewing a list of the ninety-three principal domains in the Greek New Testament Dictionary published by the Bible Societies:

1. Geographical Objects and Features
2. Natural Substances
3. Plants
4. Animals
5. Foods and Condiments
6. Artifacts
7. Constructions
8. Body, Body Parts, and Body Products
9. People
10. Kinship Terms
11. Groups and Classes of Persons and Members of Such Groups and Classes
12. Supernatural Beings and Powers
13. Be, Become, Exist, Happen
14. Physical Events and States
15. Linear Movement
16. Non-Linear Movement
17. Stances and Events Related to Stances
18. Attachment
19. Physical Impact
20. Violence, Harm, Destroy, Kill
21. Danger, Risk, Safe, Save
22. Trouble, Hardship, Relief, Favorable Circumstances
23. Physiological Processes and States
24. Sensory Events and States
25. Attitudes and Emotions
26. Psychological Faculties
27. Learn
28. Know
29. Memory, Recall
30. Think
31. Hold a View, Believe, Trust
32. Understand
33. Communication
34. Association
35. Help, Care For
36. Guide, Discipline, Follow
37. Control, Rule
38. Punish, Reward
39. Hostility, Strife
40. Reconciliation, Forgiveness
41. Behavior and Related States
42. Perform, Do
43. Agriculture
44. Animal Husbandry, Fishing
45. Building, Constructing
46. Household Activities
47. Activities Involving Liquids or Masses
48. Activities Involving Cloth
49. Activities Involving Clothing and Adorning
50. Contests and Play
51. Festivals
52. Funerals, Burials
53. Religious Activities
54. Maritime Activities
55. Military Activities
56. Courts and Legal Procedures
57. Possess, Transfer, Exchange
58. Nature, Class, Example
59. Quantity
60. Number
61. Sequence
62. Arrange, Organize
63. Whole, Unite, Part, Divide
64. Comparison
65. Value
66. Proper, Improper
67. Time
68. Aspect
69. Affirmation, Negation
70. Real, Unreal
71. Mode
72. True, False
73. Genuine, Phony
74. Able, Capable

75. Adequate, Qualified
76. Power, Force
77. Ready, Prepared
78. Degree
79. Features of Objects
80. Space
81. Spacial Dimensions
82. Spacial Orientations
83. Spacial Positions
84. Spacial Extensions
85. Existence in Space
86. Weight
87. Status
88. Moral and Ethical Qualities and Related Behavior
89. Relations
90. Case
91. Discourse Markers
92. Discourse Referentials
93. Proper Names

The study of lexical meaning in terms of domain structures is crucial to the process of translating, because translators' primary semantic problems do not result from the different meanings of the same word (as listed in traditional dictionaries) but from the related meanings of different words, that is, from a cluster of meanings which constitute the semantic domain or field. By the use of a lexicon based on such domains of meaning, the semantic contrasts in lexical units become more evident, since the range of meaning of any term is defined primarily by the meanings of related terms. The meaning of a verbal symbol can never be defined in isolation, but only by comparison and contrast with other terms in the same or contiguous domains. The listing of so-called synonyms and antonyms in standard dictionaries is of some help, but it is rarely enough. A translator needs to consider the entire constellation of related meanings if the closest natural equivalent is to be correctly chosen.

Translating has often been described as the most complex intellectual activity in which any person can engage. It may not be the most complex, but in many respects it is one of the most challenging in view of the complexity of language structures and the infinite variety of cultural entities, practices, and beliefs. Words only have meanings in terms of the cultures which they reflect and of which they are a part. Accordingly a translator needs to be not only a linguist but also in certain respects an anthropologist. Anyone undertaking to translate the Bible also needs to be a biblical scholar or at least one who is familiar with the findings of specialists in the field. But what makes Bible translating so particularly challenging is its claim of divine origin and universal relevance.

APPENDIX A

Diverse Theories of Translation

Though some persons insist that they neither have nor need a theory of translation—they just "do it"—nevertheless they approach the task of translating with at least some underlying rationale. This may be only a set of basic rules, but it represents what one may regard as either an incipient theory or a partially systematic approach to translating. In general, there are four basic theories of translating which have been dominant at various times and which actually serve in a complementary fashion. These are philological, linguistic, communicative (communication theory), and sociosemiotic.

The philological approach to the problems of translation focuses on the literary character of the source text (Brower, 1959; Cary, 1963; and Steiner, 1975). Special interest is displayed in the thematic structure and style of the discourse, but there is usually greater focus upon the source (the writer and the setting of the document) than upon the receptors. The basic issue in the philological approach has been either to bring the message to the people or to bring the people to the message. In other words, one must decide whether to adjust the form of the message to the capabilities of the receptors or to encourage the receptors to gain sufficient background knowledge so as to appreciate fully some of the intricacies of the source text.

To state the dilemma in the now classical words of Schleiermacher, "The translator can either leave the writer in peace as much as possible and bring the reader to him, or he can leave the reader in peace as much as possible and bring the writer to him" (Störig, 1969, 39; Wills, 1982, 33). For Schleiermacher the translator can only prove his stylistic competence by blending his own language with the foreign one (and not in the opposite direction) in such a way that the source language is preserved in his translation.

The philological approach played a particularly important role in classical times, a period in which the conflict between the literalists and the nonliteralists was often intense. Most of the translators of the Septuagint, made in the second century before Christ, were literalists (Jellicoe, 1968, 47–52). These translators were by no means as literal as Aquila, whose text has served textual critics so well because it introduces the Hebrew in such awkward Greek. Some Latin translations of the Greek classics were likewise very literal, but Roman authors such as Horace and Cicero opposed literal translating; and Jerome, taking his cue from the more enlightened attitudes of his day, produced the Vulgate translation in a form of Latin which was regarded by some as so free as to be even heretical (Schwarz, 1963). Jerome's basic principle of translating is recorded in his letter 106 to Sunnia and Fretella, "For the same rule that we have often laid down is to be followed in translation: where there is no damage to the sense, the euphony and the properties of the language into which we are translating are to be observed" (Kelly, 1976, v–vi).

For his day, Luther's approach to translation was certainly a communication breakthrough, thus setting the stage for important departures from a tradition dominated by ecclesiastical Latin. Such a breakthrough can best be illustrated from Luther's own words, "man mus die mutter jhm hause / die kinder auff der gassen / den gemeinen mann auff dem marckt drumb fragen / und den selbigen auff das maul sehen / wie sie reden / und darnach dolmetzschen / so verstehen sie es den / und merken / das man Deutsch mit jn redet" (Arndt, 1968, 32). This may be translated into English as, "One must inquire of mothers in their homes, of children in the street, and of the average man in the market, in order to determine exactly how they speak. One must then translate on the basis of this, so that people will understand and realize that someone is speaking with them in German."

More recently the problems of a philological approach to translation have been much more effectively defined and meaningfully discussed, especially by Hilare Belloc (1931), Ortega y Gasset (1937), James S. Holmes (1970), Roger Fowler (1972), and Richard Bjornson (1980).

A linguistic approach to translation is perhaps best illustrated in the work of Catford (1965), in which the focus of translation principles revolves about the differences in linguistic structure between the source and receptor languages, but see also Andreyev (1964), Darbelnet (1977), and Enkvist (1978). Basically the linguistic approach to translation involves a series of rules of correspondence, which prove to be particularly important in developing machine translation, but rules of correspondence based on contrastive linguistics are too dependent upon surface structures and do not deal adequately with the underlying semantic relationships. It is one thing to make up certain rules about changes from passive to active verbs, from singular nouns to plurals, from gender distinctions in one language to nongender forms in another, and for shifts of rhetorical questions into emphatic statements, but unless the functions of such formal differences are clearly understood and reckoned with, a resulting translation can be a kind of mechanical retranscription. Furthermore, a strictly linguistic approach to translation frequently overlooks the communicative aspect of discourse.

In view of the limitations of a linguistic approach to translation, one based on communication theory has served to provide translators with a somewhat broader approach to their problems. As a part of communication the difficulties of translating are considered primarily in terms of source, message, receptor, feedback, noise, channel, medium, with a good deal of attention paid to impact and redundancy, as aspects of information theory. This is the approach to translation problems reflected primarily in the work of Nida (1964) and Nida and Taber (1969), as well as of a number of other persons, for example, Kade (1968), Neubert (1968), Wilss (1982), Vázquez-Ayora (1977), and Reiss (1971). In this communicative approach to translation issues, the focus is on the extent to which the meaning of the source text is transmitted to receptors in a form that they can understand and appreciate. In other words, the role of the receptors is highlighted by being made the target of the process of communication.

To a certain extent the approach to translating based primarily on communication theory lacks adequate breadth, in that it has not provided a sufficient basis for understanding the nature of linguistic signs on all levels of discourse, nor does communication theory provide adequate insight into the relationship of language to culture. It is precisely for this reason that an approach to translation based on a sociosemiotic orientation seems to be so important (Nida and others, 1983; Nida, 1984a; and de Beaugrande, 1978). Closely related to this socio-semiotic approach to translating are the sociolinguistic insights which emphasize the close relationship between social behavior and language use (Pergnier, 1978).

A proper understanding of the sociosemiotic orientation to interlingual communication helps one understand better not only the meanings of words, sentences, and discourse structures, but the symbolic nature of the events and objects which are mentioned in discourses. It is not enough, for example, to translate Matthew 5:1 as "he sat down to teach," unless a reader will realize that this had the symbolic significance of Jesus assuming the role of a rabbi. The sociosemiotic approach to translating will also alert a translator in the Orient that though a dragon is a symbol of danger and violence in the Western World, it is a symbol of prosperity and good luck in many parts of the Orient.

This sociosemiotic approach to translating is particularly important in distinguishing between designative and associative meanings. Furthermore, this approach emphasizes the fact that everything about a message carries meaning. Even the wrong typeface and format can seriously undermine or distort the meaning of a discourse.

All of the various approaches to the process of translating are valid, though the sociosemiotic orientation appears to have certain advantages because it is more all-embracing. This attitude toward the contribution of various theories to translating is not a matter of being opportunistically eclectic but of taking seriously Turbayne's insights in his book *The Myth of Metaphor* (1962). Various theories have validity for various aspects of physical and behavioral phenomena, and no one theory can explain everything. Like metaphors, scientific theories are perspectives which provide important insights on certain aspects of complex relations. Accordingly, a translator should take full advantage of the significant contributions which have been made by scholars employing quite different theories about interlingual communication.

Frequently the question is raised as to whether translation is a science, an art, or a skill. In reality, of course, it is all three. It is a skill because to a certain extent the procedures can be taught, and persons' capacities for doing a satisfactory piece of work can be significantly improved. It is an art in the same sense that a literary production is an art. If the production of an artistic literary discourse in one language requires a measure of aesthetic sensitivity and artistic skill, then the reproduction of such a literary discourse in another language involves a somewhat commensurate artistic ability. Translation is also a science in the broad sense of the term, for it is an activity which may be systematically described and related meaningfully to various disciplines. In the strict sense of the word, however, translating is not a science but a technology, for it is built upon a number of scientific disciplines, including psychology, linguistics, communication theory, anthropology, and semiotics.

Special Problems Involved in Bible Translating

The same general principles of translating apply to the Scriptures as they do to any secular document, but there are special problems with regard to Bible translating. In the first place, there are difficulties posed by the cultural and temporal distance between the source texts and the present day. This distance serves to increase the obscurities and ambiguities usually resulting from our ignorance of the setting of the various discourses.

In the second place, the translation of the Scriptures differs from the translation of present-day documents because one cannot consult an author of any biblical book, and there are no informants who can provide insight on linguistic usage based on their own native use of such languages. There are, of course, persons who speak present-day Greek and Hebrew, but these languages differ significantly from what is to be found in the biblical texts.

In the third place, for any one writer in the Old Testament or New Testament there is a very limited corpus, so it is difficult to test for most stylistic patterns. Even the total corpuses of the Old Testament and New Testament are relatively restricted, and though the Old Testament is somewhat larger than the New Testament (approximately three times), it was produced by a number of different persons over a period of at least a thousand years. Furthermore, there is relatively little in Hebrew or even in closely related languages which comes from the same period. For the New Testament there is much more background data from the period of Koine Greek, but we still have only a tiny proportion of what once must have existed in the great library of Alexandria.

In the case of the Old Testament we are faced with a large number of rare words in the Hebrew text. There are also a significant number of so-called *hapax legomena,* words which occur only once in Hebrew literature. Scholars have often tried to solve the problems of meaning by comparing these words with cognate words in other languages (the so-called comparative philological approach), but this often creates further linguistic confusion.

In the fourth place, a translator of Greek and Hebrew texts is limited by the absence of adequate paralinguistic features. There are serious problems of word division, with very little evidence for intonational junctures, and most of what we might call "feedback" for the New Testament comes a century or more later in the writings of the Christian fathers. Feedback for the Old Testament is largely in the form of translations into Greek, Syriac, and Latin, or in the comments made by rabbinic scholars at a considerably later period.

In the fifth place, translators of the Bible are faced with the enormous problem of dealing with a wide range of literary genres. It may seem almost incredible that a collection of writings the size of the Bible should contain such diverse genres as history, personal narrative, legend, laws, proverbs, poetry, prophecy, apocalyptic, wisdom literature, dramatic history, letters (both personal and general), parables, and allegories, to mention some of the more important types of discourse.

As already noted, another significant problem faced by translators of the biblical texts is the crucial importance of history, which is always at the service of its theological import. But it is this aspect of the biblical text which provides the basis for claims of universal relevance. This is clearly reflected in the fact that books which have been traditionally regarded as historical books (Joshua through 2 Kings) are grouped with the prophets in the Jewish classification of the law, the prophets, and the writings.

Perhaps one of the really serious elements in Bible translating is the emotional involvement of both the translators and the receptors. For some translators it is apparently too much to let the original source speak for himself, for in the views of some people the book of James is not Pauline enough, and at times Paul is not Calvinistic enough. Emotional involvement, however, may be even more intense among receptors. Even the forms of proper names may constitute "theological issues." For some persons the Arabized name *Isa* seems degrading as a name for Jesus, and even the form *Ibrahim* seems unfit to designate Abraham. Some people object strongly if they do not find such technical terms as *propitiation, expiation,* and *sanctification;* they insist that in some way or other the Scriptures have been robbed of meaning, even though many persons find it difficult to explain the meanings of such derivatives from Latin. Even the use of paragraphing in contrast with printing each verse as a separate unit has been condemned as an attempt to rob the Scriptures of their sacred form. It is little wonder, therefore, that Bible translating has sometimes engendered far more heat than light. One can only hope, however, that a broader and more insightful approach to the problems of Bible translating, studied in terms of functional equivalence, will lead to a better appreciation of the issues and a more informed way of resolving some of the problems.

APPENDIX B

Procedures in Publishing Bible Translations

Procedures in Bible translating are both numerous and varied. To understand and appreciate the relevance of various procedures, it is important to treat them under several different but related topics: (1) typical inadequate procedures, (2) preliminary procedures, (3) team structures, (4) review structures, (5) supplementary personnel, (6) steps in the translation process, both general as well as specific for different types of translation teams, (7) testing, (8) proofreading, (9) administrative procedures, and (10) postpublication efforts. All ten topics will not apply to each potential translator of the biblical text, but the stages involved in translation are covered, whether the translation is for a single chapter, an entire book, or a complete text of the Bible.

Typical Inadequate Procedures

It may be useful to mention three typically inadequate procedures, which may be easily identified in terms of three different kinds of translators: (1) "the naive translator," (2) "the rule translator," and (3) "the adaptor translator."

The typical naive translator rendering the Scriptures into his own mother tongue probably has little or no knowledge of the original languages, Greek and Hebrew. If his knowledge of these languages is minimal, he will probably want to use simple dictionaries and will not want to bother with something as complex as the various editions of Bauer in English. Such a person is likely to use translations in other languages, or he may take an existing translation in his own language and decide to "improve" on it. He may want to use some commentaries, usually however, not those based on Greek and Hebrew, for most naive translators avoid commentaries which do not settle for "the one and only valid meaning."

Fortunately, there are relatively few such naive translators, who, with only minimal background knowledge and the most elementary helps, plunge into translating, often word by word or verse by verse. They usually do not realize that it may be essential to study the entire text before beginning to translate any one sentence.

There are even a few naive translators who undertake to translate into a language which is not their mother tongue. There have even been some mission boards which have encouraged new missionaries to spend their second six months of language study in a program for translating the Bible. This practice is justified as an advantageous way to learn the foreign language. The results of such a process are lamentable, both for the language learner and for the resulting translation.

Some missionaries have recognized their inadequacy in translating and therefore have simply turned a Bible text over to an informant with limited or no training in translation matters. The missionary then attempts to review the translation more or less on a word-for-word basis to see if everything is included, but it is the rare missionary who can evaluate or correct matters of style.

The number of "rule translators" is considerably larger than the number of strictly naive translators. These "rule translators" try to make their translations follow very strict rules of lexical and grammatical concordance. They may actually have some limited introduction to linguistics, and as a result they often attempt to analyze the grammatical structures of the receptor language so as to determine the percentage of various types of expressions, for example, active versus passive verb phrases, the average number of clauses in a sentence, the order of dependent clauses with respect to a main clause, the number of attributives that are likely to precede or follow a noun, the preponderance of similes over metaphors, and the statistical probability of expressions of setting coming first in a sentence. When such persons discover that perhaps eighty percent of occurrences of a particular grammatical construction have a specific form, they feel that it is both safe and prudent to adjust their own translation to this dominant eighty percent pattern. Unfortunately, however, they do not always realize that it may very well be the additional twenty percent which provides impact, focus, and emphasis. Not only does a strictly rule-dominated translation tend to sacrifice meaning for form, but it generally ends up being stylistically monotonous and flat.

"Adaptor translators," however, seem rarely to be concerned with rules and percentages or translation principles. They are usually more interested in getting "the big idea" across and are happy to rework the forms of the text so as to make them as congenial as possible to receptors. If an idea seems too complex, such translators often feel justified in omitting it, particularly if a substitution seems to fit the context better and is more understandable to receptors. To make sure that people fully understand the text, such translators often put in rather extensive explanations, and as a result what they produce is a type of targum, a combination of translation and commentary.

Preliminary Procedures

Certain aspects of preliminary procedures have already been treated in Chapter 3, dealing with the theme of "Basic Issues," where considerable emphasis has been placed on a careful study of what is both needed by and acceptable to a constituency. This inevitably means wide discussions with church leaders and the general laity, but valid judgments with regard to what is both needed and acceptable can rarely be obtained from people unless there are sample materials of various types which provide alternatives for judgment. Questionnaires without materials which can be compared and evaluated are often a waste of time and energy.

If a revision is being contemplated, it is essential that people have an opportunity to indicate the kinds of changes which they think a revision should include.

One of the most important preliminary procedures involves setting up basic principles to be followed in the preparation of a translation or a revision. These principles (often numbering between twenty-five to forty) must cover the entire range of features, including the underlying Greek and Hebrew text, the types of commentaries to be consulted, the level of vocabulary, the degree of syntactic complexity, the ways in which figurative language may be adapted, the format for poetic and liturgical material, the extent of syntactic embedding of clauses within one another, the treatment of direct and indirect quotations (particularly when they occur in a number of layers), the handling of rhetorical questions, punctuation and paragraphing, types of marginal notes, section headings, and such additional supplementary features as introductions, a glossary, an index, and maps.

A number of principles can be derived from a careful study of what is needed by and acceptable to the constituency for whom the translation is being prepared, but the actual formulation of principles must be worked out by the team of translators in close cooperation with consultants and representatives of the sponsoring organization.

By preliminary work on a number of typical passages for the Old Testament and New Testament, a team of translators can prepare a careful statement of such principles for the approval of the sponsoring organization. Agreement on such principles can serve to greatly facilitate later acceptance of the text by those responsible for publication. Furthermore, these principles are very important in the work of the translation team so as to insure both coherence and consistency in rendering the text. In addition, the existence of such well-defined principles has great psychological value in team discussions, for members of the translation team can direct their discussions to the principles rather than against one another. The principles may need to be modified from time to time in the translation process, but when a change in the principles is introduced, then the team must determine to what extent previously translated materials can be adjusted so as to make them conform to the modified or added principles.

Team Structures

Bible translating can no longer be regarded as a one-person job. To translate the Scriptures satisfactorily requires a great deal of highly specialized knowledge of biblical languages and cultural backgrounds. In addition, there are a very wide range of literary genres in the Scriptures, so that in one way or another Bible translating is essentially a cooperative undertaking.

This cooperation, however, may take any one of five different principal forms: (1) a translation team of three to five persons, (2) a drafter with two to four close collaborators, (3) a team of joint drafters (usually only two), (4) stylist-scholar teams, and (5) a translation team with a resource person.

A typical translation team should consist of from three to five persons. It is rare that more than this number should undertake such a task, for the addition of personnel does not necessarily speed up the undertaking. What is important is that the team consist of the very best persons possible, and if such can be arranged, they should work on a full-time basis.

Members of the team translate various portions of the text of the Scriptures and at the same time review carefully the work of other members of the team. Each member of the team is assigned a particular portion of the Scriptures to translate; his work is then shared with other members of the team who make suggestions for improvements. Those which are fully in accordance with the accepted principles are automatically incorporated, and the team then discusses those issues on which there is not complete agreement.

All the members of such a team must have the capacity to do translating work and must be emotionally capable of providing constructive criticism and receiving such criticism. Their competence must be such as to gain mutual respect.

Often one member of the translation team is appointed as chairman. This can be useful if such an individual can lead without dominating. In some teams, however, the chairmanship rotates on a daily basis, or the function of chairmanship rests with the person whose translation is being discussed at the time.

A translation team consisting of one drafter and several close collaborators has often proved to be extremely effective, provided the drafter is himself not only highly competent but also emotionally capable of receiving extensive criticism. The collaborators in such instances must review materials carefully, make all suggestions which seem relevant, and then be prepared to discuss the translation with complete openness and objectivity.

In some instances a text is prepared by joint drafters (rarely more than two), who uniquely combine stylistic gifts and biblical backgrounds, are fully congenial, and may be said to operate "on the same wave length." Such persons actually prepare the text together. In this way they have the advantage of immediate feedback and of maximal use of their complementary abilities. In such a circumstance no one person can be a prima donna.

In the case of stylist-scholar teams, the usual process of translating should be reversed. Rather than having a scholar prepare a somewhat literal translation which is then revised by a stylist, it is the stylist who should prepare the first draft, but only on the basis of extensive preliminary discussions with the biblical scholar. Only later is the text gone over carefully by the scholar and various options discussed. For certain projects there may be several different stylist-scholar teams working together.

A team consisting of a group of translators together with a resource person is typical of a number of evolving situations in the "missionary world." In the past, it has been the practice for missionaries to undertake the task of translating by the use of so-called "native informants." This procedure, however, has not proven fully satisfactory, and gradually this practice is changing. Native speakers of the receptor language are now usually given sufficient training so that they themselves can produce the basic drafts. Then the text is reviewed by a resource person, often a missionary or local scholar who has background knowledge of the original languages and a good deal of understanding of textual and exegetical problems.

The specific ways in which these various team structures proceed to do their work is considered in much greater detail under the heading of *General Procedures in Translating* and in the immediately following sections.

The selection of persons to participate in the various translation teams as either drafters or collaborators is often a complex process. In the first place, anyone responsible for organizing such a program (for example, a Translations Consultant of the United Bible Societies) tries to obtain as much information as possible about varoius persons who might serve either as stylists or as biblical scholars.

In many instances it is useful to bring together such persons (often fifteen to twenty) to discuss the need of a new translation or revision and some of the basic principles which might be adopted. Time is then given for the participants to prepare sample drafts of various passages of Scripture. In this process it soon becomes evident that some individuals have not only unusual abilities in translating but also the kind of personality which makes it possible for them to cooperate meaningfully on a team. In many cases it may also be advantageous to invite the more competent persons to a second session in which further, more effective evaluation can be undertaken.

Review Structures

Regardless of how well qualified a team of translators may be, it is essential to have two types of persons who will review the text. The first set of reviewers should consist of a relatively small group of persons (usually eight to ten) who are especially competent either as biblical scholars or as stylists. These persons do not meet as a committee to review all that the translators have done, but they are sent the texts and are asked to submit their comments in writing. They may be called together for a discussion of particularly difficult issues and for a fixed agenda. Such a review committee may include members of the Translations Committee of the sponsoring organization, but such a review committee should not consist entirely of members of such a Translations Committee.

It is particularly important that this relatively small group of reviewers know precisely what they are to do. This means that they must become acquainted with the basic principles and procedures in the project, must be informed from time to time as to the relevance and importance of their comments and suggestions, and be remunerated in one way or another as a means of insuring their continuing participation.

A considerably larger group (often between twenty and fifty persons) acts as consultants. These persons do not meet together as a committee but send in their comments in writing. They consist of church leaders who may be strategic for ultimate acceptance of the text, persons who may not be particularly competent but who regard themselves as authorities, and a number of individuals of ordinary backgrounds who may be extremely helpful in reflecting the attitudes and views of the general constituency. It may be that some of the persons in this consultative group prove so useful and valuable to the project that they may be asked to become a part of the smaller review panel.

Supplementary Personnel

In addition to the persons serving on translation teams and as reviewers and consultants, there are several other persons who may have important roles to perform in certain projects. These include a translations consultant, a local coordinator, a secretary, an editor, and a copy editor.

The United Bible Societies' Translations Consultant, for example, is particularly important in the preliminary procedures, which involve a careful study of what is needed by and acceptable to the constituency, the selection of the members of the translation teams, the training of such translators, and periodic consultations with such teams.

A local coordinator may be extremely useful, particularly in larger projects, to deal with logistics of meetings, payments to translators and reviewers, purchase of supplies, and for monitoring the flow of manuscripts between consultants. He may also be important in arranging for and supervising secretarial help.

Stylists are often called in to help on projects, often after basic drafts have been prepared; it is far better, however, if they can work directly with the team of drafters. If that is not possible, it is usually important for the consultant to act as a type of mediator between the biblical scholars and the stylists. In many instances biblical scholars are not particularly sensitive to stylistic matters, since most of what they are in the habit of writing is more or less technical prose, and they need the help of the translations consultant to interpret the role and importance of stylistic features of the text.

One or more secretaries may be crucial for the efficient operation of a committee. Insofar as possible, word processors should be used to speed up the task, but when word processors are used, it is extremely important to have backup copies on tape or disk.

An editor of a text is a particularly crucial person. Such a person may actually be a member of the translation team, but he or she is essential for matters of consistency in spelling, punctuation, and format, for checking the reference system, and particularly for guaranteeing balance and consistency in marginal helps.

A copy editor (or production editor) has the responsibility of preparing a text for the publishers. This often consists of marking a manuscript for contrast in type face, format, runover lines (especially in poetry), and spacing for major and minor divisions. In some instances the editor may also serve as copy editor, but the function of the copy editor is so specialized that ordinarily this responsibility is assigned to a person with particular experience and background.

General Procedures in Translating

In the translation process, there are two basic types of procedures: (1) those that are generally applicable to all types of teams and (2) those which are specifically related to the manner in which a team is structured.

The general procedures include: (1) background study, (2) amount of time and circumstances for the drafting process, (3) the phases of analysis, transfer, and restructuring, (4) translation units, (5) the mechanics of formulation of the text, (6) successive drafts, (7) order in which various books are to be translated or revised, and (8) the preparation of supplementary material.

Background study. Before undertaking to translate any book of the Bible, it is essential that one master the material available in scholarly commentaries based on the original languages. This is particularly important to obtain an adequate understanding of the cultural and historical setting and to appreciate the distinctive themes and emphases. In addition, one should in advance of translating carefully read any handbooks or guides prepared by the United Bible Societies for the assistance of translation teams.

Amount of time and circumstances for the translation task. Insofar as possible, one should be able to work without a series of constant interruptions, since for most persons interruptions are the most effective devices for killing creativity. Furthermore, interruptions tend to produce inconsistencies in the translation process.

In addition to avoiding circumstances in which there are numerous interruptions, it is also important to be able to work continuously on a particular project. One should be able to give a minimum of a week at a time for the translation activity in order to "get into the swing of it." At the same time, it may be important not to translate for more than six hours a day. Very few people can maintain the mental alertness required of verbal creativity for more than six hours. Effective translation work requires extreme concentration, and this is particularly true when one attempts to combine accuracy of content with a pleasing style.

Basic phases in the translation process. The three basic phases in the translation process are analysis, transfer, and restructuring, as described in considerable detail in *Theory and Practice of Translation* (Nida and Taber, 1969). The basic components of analysis have been dealt with in detail in the three chapters treating rhetorical, grammatical, and lexical meaning in this volume.

Analysis is the most basic and crucial aspect of the translator's task, since the phases of transfer and restructuring are dependent upon it. Analysis consists in looking beneath the formal level of rhetorical, grammatical, and lexical structures to the underlying semantic relations. This normally implies amplifying the text so that all of the semantic features are explicitly recognized or stated and the relations between the parts made clear. How explicit or detailed the analysis should be depends upon the degree of semantic and formal complexity of the source text.

Some translators have assumed that the analytical process amounts

simply to reducing the meaning of any statement to its barebones propositional form, but this is too reductionist in methodology. For example, such
statements as *he killed him, he stabbed him to death,* and *he slashed him to
death with a butcher knife* could all be regarded as propositionally equivalent to *he caused him to no longer live.* But the lowest common denominator
of propositional equivalence too often overlooks the details of the event in
question and seriously disregards the difference in impact in the three
statements.

In any analysis of a text, one anticipates what one knows will be involved in the second phase, namely, transfer. If one realizes that in a receptor language it is not possible to say literally "he praised him," then
the analysis will anticipate this fact by suggesting possible semantic redistribution of components in a statement such as "he said, That one is
great."

Most of the problems arising in the process of transfer involve the following differences between source and receptor languages: (1) overdifferentiation and underdifferentiation of the lexicon, (2) obscurity as to the
specific aspect of events, (3) direct and indirect forms of information, (4)
diversities in status systems, (5) ecological specialties, (6) cultural specialties, and (7) lack of correspondence in form and meaning of rhetorical
patterns between source and receptor languages. All of these problem
areas have already been treated in considerable detail, especially in Chapters 5–8, but perhaps some additional discussion concerning the issue of
obscurity will reveal the close connection between analysis and transfer.
For example, there is a good deal of obscurity in a phrase such as *the fear of
death.* In a number of languages one simply cannot be so obscure, since
the fear of death may mean "being afraid of what causes death" or "being
afraid of the process of dying" or "being afraid of being dead." The problems of transfer may actually force one to give more careful consideration
to the phase of analysis.

It would be quite wrong to think that one first engages in a comprehen-
sive analysis of a text before ever beginning to consider transfer from
source to receptor language. Likewise, it is equally wrong to consider
problems of transfer without at the same time recognizing the level of
restructuring in which one must be engaged in preparing a text for a particular constituency. In fact, all three phases of translation go on almost
simultaneously for a translator, and in many instances, almost subcon-
sciously.

In the process of transfer there are three basic types of adjustment: redistribution, deletion, and addition. In these three processes certain
modifications are obligatory and others are optional. In the redistribution
of semantic elements, whether on a lexical, syntactical, or rhetorical level,
there should be no actual increase in information, but the same informa-

tion is simply given in a somewhat different form. For example, in Matthew 21:38 the Greek term *klēronomos* "heir" must be translated in some languages as "one who some day will own the property." The use of eight words instead of a single word in Greek does not increase the amount of information; it is only that the distinctive features of meaning of *klēronomos* are distributed among several words.

A somewhat more complex problem in redistribution of information occurs in the use of *logos* "Word" in John 1:1. In a number of languages it is impossible to use an expression meaning "Word" and have it directly or indirectly apply to a person, unless there is some indication that the term is used as a title. Therefore, in some languages translators have employed "the one called the Word." In the Greek text the use of the term *logos* points clearly to its significance as a title.

Syntactic redistributions are some of the most common. In the Greek text of the New Testament there are a number of long, involved sentences, and translators have often found it necessary or expedient to break up such long sentences. For example, Romans 1:1–7, which is technically one sentence in Greek, is rendered as five sentences in Today's English Version, as four sentences in the New International Version, as six sentences in the Spanish *Version Popular,* and as eight sentences in the German translation *Die Gute Nachricht*. More significantly even, the whole chapter of Proverbs 2 can be analyzed syntactically as one sentence, with a protasis stating the condition (1–4) and a long apodosis (5–22) expressing a double result. Modern translations, however, normally end up with approximately twenty sentences.

Deletion would appear to be a matter of loss of information; on the contrary, it is simply a device for shifting information from an explicit to an implicit level. Repeatedly in Greek, and to a somewhat lesser extent in Hebrew, the distinction between singular and plural is marked overtly in a text. But in Chinese, as well as in a number of other languages in the Orient, the category of number may be left entirely to the context, and thus in the translation process of transfer, what is overtly marked in the source language may become covertly marked in the receptor language. One should always avoid any kind of superfluous information or illegitimate paraphrase (Margot, 1979, chapter 4). The art of translating is the art of leaving implicit what can be left implicit.

In the case of additions there are a number of problems relating to possible increase of information. Certain obligatory categories in a receptor language may require the addition of information when no such specific data exists in the biblical text. For example, in some languages one cannot speak of Jesus and his disciples going to Cana (John 2:1–2) without indicating whether the persons involved had been to such a place before, that is to say, were they going for the first time or were they returning to a place where they had been. There is nothing specific in the text which would indicate whether or not Jesus had been in Cana before, but one could presume in view of the total context that Jesus probably had been in Cana before. This is very likely when Cana can be identified with the traditional Kefr Kenna, which is only a few miles from Nazareth. Even other suggested places like Ain Kana or Khirbet Kana remain within a few hours' walking distance from Nazareth.

In a number of instances obligatory categories required by the receptor language may be filled out on the basis of indirect information as, for example, in the case of older and younger brothers normally marked by the order of names. In Cambodian there are two distinct words for "brother," one designating the elder brother and one designating the younger (Clavaud, 1973, 419–22). Greek, on the other hand, does not make such a distinction. The translator in such languages cannot avoid making a choice when rendering "Simon and Andrew the brother of Simon" (Mark 1:16) or "James the son of Zebedee and John his brother" (Mark 1:19). If one understands the brothers of Jesus in a literal sense, then the use of a term for "younger brothers" may deny the tradition of the perpetual virginity of Mary. In Ruth 1:2 and 5, the order of the names of the sons of Elimelech is Mahlon and Chilion, but in Ruth 4:9 the order is reversed: Chilion and Mahlon. The storyteller's use of chiasm may provide the right explanation here (Campbell, 1975, 151), but the translator should not become a victim of this rhetorical device. The order of the names of the sons and their wives in chapter one would suggest that Ruth was Chilion's wife and that Orpah was the wife of Mahlon. Only in chapter 4, verse 10, do we learn that this is wrong and that in reality Ruth is Mahlon's widow.

When additions are optional rather than obligatory, it is usually better to indicate such data in marginal notes. For example, readers may be astonished by the statement in John 4:27 that the disciples were "amazed that Jesus was speaking with a woman." The reason for such amazement may very well be explained in a footnote indicating that according to the customs of the day, rabbis would normally not speak to a woman under such circumstances. In certain instances, however, it may be useful to indicate in the text the meaning of some symbolic action which might otherwise be misinterpreted. For example, in Acts 7:54 the statement "they gnashed on him with their teeth" may be interpreted simply as an idiom and then translated as "they were very angry with him," or the expression may refer to an actual gesture involving the literal grinding of the teeth. Such a gesture in some languages, however, implies either intense anxiety or fear rather than anger. Accordingly, it may be useful to translate this expression in Acts 7:54 as "they ground their teeth in anger against him." Again, however, the use of the phrase "in anger" only makes explicit what is implicit in the original text.

Restructuring means modifying the results of the phases of analysis and transfer so as to produce the closest natural equivalent on the level most intelligible and acceptable to the constituency for whom the translation has been prepared. This process of restructuring often involves restructuring for particular formats. Some of what is printed as poetry according to the editors of our Hebrew Bibles may be much closer in content to what is prose in a receptor language and thus should be printed as prose. On the other hand, a number of passages printed in the Greek New Testament as prose involve essentially liturgical poetry and can very well be restructured as poetry in a receptor language text.

Translation units. There has been a tendency for many translators to translate word by word, phrase by phrase, or even sentence by sentence, without realizing that probably the most useful unit in translating is the paragraph, but not necessarily the paragraphs which occur in traditional texts of Greek and Hebrew or even the paragraph units of some translations into modern languages. Increasingly, present-day approaches to literary analysis and discourse structure recognize the importance of the short paragraph as being the fundamental thought unit. It is this type of unit which constitutes for the translator the best basic unit in which to deal with individual sentences and the best unit to consider in paying attention to groups of related paragraphs. For example, parallelism of wording and the marking of such units by section headings is particularly important in Matthew 5:21–48.

The mechanics of formulating the text. Some translators find it emotionally and intellectually necessary to write out a text by longhand. They have become so used to "thinking with their fingers" that any other process seems mentally confusing and frustrating. Other translators, however, much prefer to type out translations, and when they can use word processors this becomes especially strategic in saving time and energy, since corrections can be introduced readily and it is not necessary to retype complete texts. A major translation recently done before word processors were available required five complete retypings of the biblical text.

For some translators, however, there are distinct advantages in dictating at least the first draft of a translation. This often provides greater freedom of expression, greater opportunity for concentration, and the escape from the enslavement of the eyes to word order. One translator in an American Indian language, who was also an accomplished interpreter, proved to be an excellent translator as long as he was interpreting the text on the basis of having heard it read, but when he himself was reading the text, he almost inevitably followed the original too literally and even awkwardly.

Bible translators are increasingly concerned with the hearers of the text, since in general far more people hear the Scriptures read than read them for themselves. One of the important ways in which the text can be better prepared for the hearers is to introduce hearing into the translation process. For example, it is valuable for a draft translator to translate orally, either as he types or writes down a text. Even after translating, it is useful to record the text immediately and then listen to it, first without following the typed manuscript and then while following it. In this way a number of stylistic mistakes can be readily noted, for our ears are usually more tuned to matters of style than are our eyes.

Some translation teams of two (sometimes three) persons have found it useful to do basic drafts together so as to formulate the translation in a setting which provides the means for immediate feedback and opportunities to hear the text formulated and reformulated by different members of the team. When a formulation seems satisfactory, it can then be immediately put into a word processor and later read into a recorder, so that it can be heard two or three times. In this way translators can spot additional expressions which might be misunderstood by hearers or which might strike hearers as awkward.

Successive drafts by individual translators. For the original draft of a translation one should aim to produce the text rapidly and with a kind of creative freedom which will lead to good style. Such a draft should then be set aside for at least a period of a week, until one has forgotten the precise formulation of the text. Then this preliminary draft should be reviewed carefully for content, with special attention paid to accuracy and consistency. This conspicuously marked-up text should again be set aside for a week or so, and even recopied if necessary, so that it can again be reviewed, but in the second review the focus should be upon style. After modifications have been introduced into the text, it is then ready to be shared with others, including one's colleagues on the same translation team or possibly with various revisers and consultants.

In the past there has been a tendency to translate a first draft in a painstaking manner aimed at producing the highest possible degree of formal correspondence. At a later stage the text has been reviewed for style. This, however, has proven to be the wrong approach. It is almost impossible to take a stylistically wooden and awkward text and introduce proper stylistic features. On the other hand one can take a stylistically good translation and "tighten it up" in terms of accuracy of content. No doubt the first requirement for a translator is to be an excellent stylist. In many instances, however, there is a need to have a stylist on a committee who should not be first of all a philologian, but an expert in effective communication. Such a stylist, admittedly a rare jewel, should have a final say about features of form. Experience has shown that the proposals of a good stylist silence all discussions.

Order in which biblical books are to be translated or revised. The order in which biblical books should be translated or revised by a team depends upon two major factors: the needs of the constituency and the competence of the translators. If translators are highly qualified for the task, there is really no basic difference in the order of selection of books, but for any new team working on the New Testament, it is often advisable to follow the order of Mark, Acts, John, and Romans, after which one can proceed to translate almost any book. For the Old Testament, translation teams have often discovered that it is well to follow the order of Ruth, 1 and 2 Samuel, 1 and 2 Kings, Esther, Genesis, Proverbs, and then Psalms, as a way of moving from simpler prose material to more complex liturgical and poetic passages. If, however, there is an existing New Testament and translators are asked to produce an Old Testament, there is often strong pressure for the Psalms to be translated before any other books of the Old Testament are produced. In general, however, this is unwise, since any translation team needs to "cut their teeth" on something far simpler.

Supplementary material. The addition of some supplementary materials can be delayed until after at least a major portion of the biblical text has been completed in draft form and reviewed by translation teams. The materials which can be introduced at a later stage include a reference system, a glossary, an index, maps, illustrations, a table of contents, and introductions. But as the translation process proceeds, it is essential that certain supplementary materials be introduced during the process of drafting the basic text to be reviewed. This involves the introduction of section headings, marginal notes covering plays on the meanings of words, alternative readings, alternative renderings, and essential information of a historical and cultural nature. In addition, one must also make a list of terms to be included in a glossary or Bible dictionary to be published with the text. Section headings are probably better chosen immediately after the rendering of a particular section, since it is very useful to employ as section headings expressions which come from the following text.

The introduction of marginal notes at an early stage is also essential, since the form of the translation is often dependent upon what type of information will be put in marginal notes. Similarly, marginal notes can best be formulated at the time when issues of text and interpretation are being carefully considered.

Special Procedures in Translating

All of the above steps in the translation process apply to all of the different types of teams which may be engaged in Bible translating, but for each type of team there are certain aspects of procedures which need to be incorporated. For example, in the case of the team of three to five persons, in which each member of the team translates and reviews the work of other members of the team, the assignment of books to be translated by the various members of the team is normally made by the translations consultant or possibly by a local coordinator, but a decision as to who should undertake a particular book must depend upon both interest in and ability for the particular type of literary genre and content. As already indicated, each member of the team prepares a text which is then sent to other members of the team. They in turn are supposed to review such drafts carefully and make suggestions for improvement. These suggestions are then returned to the original drafter, who automatically incorporates all of the suggestions which seem to be in accord with the basic principles adopted by the team and approved by the sponsoring organization. At the same time, however, a list should be made of all those points on which there may be significant differences of opinion, so that these matters can be discussed in a joint meeting of the translation team.

Many translation teams prefer to read over the entire text orally in a joint meeting of the team. Some groups even read the entire text two or three times, but this procedure is highly questionable. In the first place, suggestions made during the reading of the text are often made without due consideration of various factors, something which is eliminated if people are required to put into writing the results of their careful study of a text. Furthermore, members of a team may not engage in a sufficiently thorough review of the text, since they assume that any special problems will arise during the reading of the text. If a text has been carefully reviewed by the members of a team, practically all crucial problems can surface by this process, but any member of a team may bring up at a later time matters which do not seem to have been satisfactorily treated by the original drafter.

If an unusually long discussion occurs during a meeting of the team, it may be useful to ask two members of the team to study the matter between sessions and come back with a suggested improvement. This procedure is usually better than attempting to arrive at a satisfactory verbal formulation by the entire group.

If in the discussions of a team there are special problems which result in more heat than light on the subject, it is better to make a list of such matters, which can then be referred to a consultant or reviewed again by the team after a time, during which the original emotional setting of the discussion has been largely forgotten or at least is no longer a matter of serious concern.

Insofar as possible, decisions as to the appropriate text to be submitted to reviewers and consultants should be arrived at by consensus. When it is necessary to vote on a matter and when the vote is closely divided, it is important to refer alternative suggestions to reviewers and consultants.

In general, material should be sent to reviewers and consultants book by book, and the comments made by such persons should be returned to the local coordinator or editor for careful review and classification. This generally results in far speedier and more consistent decisions to be made by the translation team. Before these suggestions are reviewed by the team as a whole, however, the individual drafters of various books should look over the material, accept evident improvements, and then highlight for the team a list of matters for discussion. At the same time, it is very important for the translations consultant to review these suggestions in order to be able to advise the team in a more effective way as to what can and should be done with these recommendations.

On the basis of agreement with the sponsoring organization, it is very useful to put out preliminary drafts of certain selected books or portions as a test of the translation. Almost inevitably such preliminary drafts will undergo revision before the completion of an entire New Testament or Bible.

In general it is unwise to submit to printers the text of a Bible book by book as translators proceed. Inevitably, there are important issues which arise at later stages in the translation process, and these will require alterations in what has been done at an earlier stage. Printers should receive a text for which there will be strictly minimal later changes.

In the case of a team consisting of a single drafter and several close collaborators, the same general procedures should be followed. The drafter's collaborators should receive the typed text and should make careful written comments on it. All of the comments which are within the range of adjustments prescribed by the principles should be incorporated into the text by the original drafter. When there are significant differences of opinion expressed by collaborators, these should be listed by the drafter and put on an agenda for discussion by the whole team. The text should then be revised on the basis of the discussions and submitted to the reviewers and consultants. Further procedures are essentially similar to those in which all the members of the team participate in the drafting process.

When two or possibly three translators work out the text in joint consultation, it means that one or more persons must either write or type the text. In some instances a secretary may be available to put the text immediately onto a word processor. After the text has been prepared in first draft, each member of the team should review the text personally and note possible problems. Then, the drafters meet together and discuss all of the possibilities for significant modification. Once these translators are satisfied with the text, it should then be submitted to the various review procedures.

For many secular translation projects, and in some instances for Bible translating, the drafting of the translation is done by a stylist in very close cooperation with a scholar. In fact, for some projects it may be useful to have several teams of such stylist-scholar pairs. A stylist should not, how-ever, undertake a translation without first reading for background infor-mation and having an opportunity to discuss the text carefully with a scholar. Furthermore, the stylist should be able to consult with such a scholar at any time, normally by telephone, concerning any special prob-lems in interpretation which might arise.

The stylist produces a first draft, which is reviewed carefully by the scholar in order to "tighten up the text" and to make it agree with valid interpretations of the text in the original languages. Then the stylist and the scholar should discuss together the various alterations proposed by the scholar. It is often useful to have this done together with the transla-tions consultant of the sponsoring organization. This role as a mediator is extremely important for successfully interpreting the scholar's views to the stylist and the significance of the stylist's contribution to the scholar. On the basis of these discussions a revised text is then prepared and is ready for the various review procedures.

In those instances in which a team of translators works very closely with a resource person, the procedures are quite similar to those cases in which a stylist and a scholar work closely together. In the first place, the resource person should have an opportunity to discuss in advance a num-ber of the basic problems of the text, including both textual difficulties and problems of interpretation. He should also be in a position to provide general background information. Those who are preparing the actual drafts should then be assigned responsibilities for various sections of a text, but the resource person should be available at any time. It is ex-tremely frustrating for a translator who does not have adequate back-ground to be confronted with problems which cannot be readily resolved. This is often so frustrating as to cause a translator to want to give up the job.

Testing

The testing of a translation has often been one of the least understood processes, since some persons have seriously confused readability, intelli-gibility, and acceptability of a translation. Readability is simply a measure of the ease with which people can read a text. Intelligibility is a measure of the capacity of people to understand the text correctly, and acceptability is a measure of the readiness with which people are happy to receive such a text and read it. A translation of the Gospel of John is often quite readable because of the relatively simple syntax and vocabulary, but the Gospel of John is not easily understood, for the vocabulary is often abstract rather than concrete and generic instead of specific. The text also includes a number of events with highly symbolic meanings.

Acceptability of a text depends very largely upon the style, but for certain constituencies some texts of the Scriptures may be more acceptable than others. For example, in the Muslim world the Gospel of Matthew is generally more acceptable than the other Gospels. For one thing, it begins with a genealogy starting with Abraham, and it contains a number of references to fulfilled prophecy cited from the Old Testament. But for the Gospel of Mark, Muslim anathema is waiting at the first verse when the variant reading "Jesus, the Son of God" is put into the text. Since many scholars believe that there are strong reasons for not considering this text as original, such a stumbling block should not be introduced in the very first verse (Slomp, 1977, 143–50), especially if the translation is being prepared primarily for an Islamic constituency.

Most popular systems for testing readability have been based on such superficial features as the number of syllables in words, the number of words in a clause, the number of clauses in a sentence, and the frequency of particular words in general usage. Recent extensive analyses of such systems for measuring readability have shown that all of these parameters are basically poor indicators of the ease or difficulty in reading. The situation becomes even more confusing when persons writing about readability almost inevitably confuse this with intelligibility.

A far more scientific approach to the problems of readability involves tests for what is known in communication theory as "transitional probabilities," that is, the degree of probability that the next word in a phrase or sentence is likely to occur. The so-called "cloze technique" consists of omitting every fifth word in a written document of at least 250 words. People are then given the document and asked to fill in the word which seems to be most appropriate for the context. The higher the number of correct entries, the greater the readability. The same type of test may be performed by dropping every tenth word in an oral presentation to a group of persons, and then counting how many wrong guesses there are, before someone in the group suggests the right term. With the cloze technique, however, there is no set standard for determining the measurement of readability. One can only do this on the basis of comparing a particular text with one of the same literary genre which has been produced on more or less the same literary level and read by persons with comparable background experience.

Another method for testing a translation is to have a native speaker of the language read the text to other native speakers. Those who are testing the readability of the text then follow the written text and mark carefully all instances in which a reader may stumble, hesitate, produce wrong forms, or seem confused. If two or more readers have difficulty at the same point in the text, then clearly there must be some difficulty in the translation. Such a test does not reveal what the problem is, but it points out those places where some stylistic modification in the text is no doubt desirable.

One can also test for the validity of a translation by questions and answers as to content, but a questioner should never ask people directly to explain a passage to the questioner. It is important that people be asked to explain the meaning of a text to other persons who have not themselves read the text or heard it read.

The real test of any translation is to be found in at least some sample publications. The reactions of reviewers and consultants who are themselves usually specialists in the subject matter are rarely adequate, for these persons are not close enough to the average receptor for which such a translation is being prepared. Specialists are frequently too knowledgeable to be able to identify with the possible reactions of the general public.

Proofreading

Proofreading is an extremely important process, though it is often regarded as a completely thankless task. People assume that anyone can be a proofreader if only he or she is careful enough, and so mistakes in proofreading are condemned without sympathy for those undertaking the task.

For any major publication it is essential that several persons proofread the galleys or page proofs. At least one or more of the persons constituting various kinds of teams of translators should read the text. In many instances it is useful to employ a professional proofreader, who may not have had any earlier connection with the project. One of these persons, or perhaps the copy editor, must have final responsibility for collating the various corrections coming from the proofreaders, for only one master list of corrections should be returned to the printer.

In proofreading it is essential to make a distinction between reading for content and reading for form (including spelling, punctuation, and format). For content, it is important to have at least two persons, one reading the original manuscript and another person following the galleys or page proofs. For details of spelling, punctuation, and format, one person who is meticulous about such matters can read the text without at the same time listening to a reading of content.

The use of word processors in the preparation of manuscripts and the direct incorporation of such material into the process of composition eliminates a number of mistakes. When, however, computers make mistakes, they can be horrendous. Accordingly, one cannot take for granted that what is satisfactory in a word processor printout will be equally satisfactory in galley or page proofs.

Administrative Procedures

Whether one is engaged in the preparation of a text in a language which has had nothing of the Bible before, or whether this is simply a revision of an existing text or a new translation in a language which may have had the Scriptures for several centuries, there are certain administrative procedures which are particularly relevant. In a sense, they tend to overlap with certain procedures relating to the direct translation task, but there are certain aspects of these administrative procedures which need to be carefully coordinated with the translation process.

Administrative procedures are involved primarily in recognizing the need for a translation or revision, selecting the translation team, arranging for financing, and finally giving approval to the text.

In general it is unwise for a sponsoring organization to promote the idea of new translations and revisions. When one goes around offering money to anyone who will translate the Scriptures into some new language, there is normally no lack of enthusiastic response, but this does not mean that there is a legitimate linguistic and religious need for such a translation, nor is there any guarantee that the potential receptors will really be interested in having such a translation. Of course, there may be some neglected situations which very much need to be remedied, and translations consultants should always be alert to such circumstances, but especially in the case of revisions, it is very important that there be some expression of recognized need on the part of the constituency which uses a text. Once it becomes evident that there is a need for some new translation or revision, then the sponsoring organization must investigate all the relevant factors as thoroughly as possible, not only with clerical and lay leadership in the churches, but with school teachers, linguists, editors, and writers.

In areas in which there are several closely related dialects, it is particularly important to determine which dialect is linguistically central and at the same time ethnically acceptable. In some instances the speakers of closely related dialects have completely refused to accept the Scriptures in a dialect other than their own because of a long history of intertribal discord and enmity. On the other hand, in a number of cases speakers of quite distinct dialects have been able to overcome linguistic barriers. Determining the dialects or languages into which the Scriptures should be translated and published is much more of an ethnological than a linguistic problem.

Translators should be specifically invited by the sponsors, such as the Bible Societies, to undertake their work. It is generally not wise to have translators appointed by their own constituencies, since this tends to make the translation task a political undertaking. Translators should be selected on the basis of their scholarly and stylistic competence, not on the basis of church affiliation, though it is certainly useful to have the widest possible representation on such teams.

Since the lead time in investigating the need for a translation or a revision and the setting up of such a process normally takes at least a year or so, it is usually not too difficult to anticipate the financial factors involved and thus be able to incorporate requests in time for budget approval. It is important to recognize that for the most part at least fifty percent of the costs of Bible Society translation projects is being carried by local constituencies, that is, by the local churches. This is extremely advantageous, as a means of encouraging local participation and thus guaranteeing that the translation, once it is published, will be used.

Postpublication Efforts

One would assume that submission of the manuscript would end the translators' responsibilities and work, but that is rarely the case. Even before the translation is actually published, it is important for those who have participated in the project to prepare articles and/or a book explaining and illustrating the principles and procedures employed in the preparation of the text. It is important that the distinctive features of the publication be highlighted, so that at the time of publication necessary background information can be made available.

In general, it is not wise to produce a great deal of advance publicity, since this often unduly alarms people, and the text is frequently criticized before people have an opportunity to see the actual translation.

Even after a translation is published, there is a considerable amount of correspondence. People want to know why a verse reads one way rather than another. Some readers point out obvious typographical errors, and other persons raise objections to the underlying text which has been followed by the translators.

Regardless of how uninformed some objections may be, it is essential that letters be answered in a sympathetic and appreciative way. Unless one takes seriously the objections which people raise, it is impossible to really help people understand what has been done and why.

It is best that the correspondence be handled by the staff of the sponsoring organization rather than by the translators themselves, since in many instances translators tend to be unduly defensive of what they have done. Those who do handle such correspondence must be fully acquainted with both the principles and the procedures employed in the development of the text.

In addition to adequate publicity and competent handling of correspondence, it is essential for someone to prepare a list of corrections to be introduced into the text within a period of at least one year. These corrections involve typographical errors, omissions and additions, and even such problems as page order.

Revisions of actual content, interpretation, and style, however, should wait for probably two to three years, so that one can have carefully studied all the problems relating to the text. Most texts should never be regarded as in any sense definitive or final. In fact, all texts should be subject to review every three to five years so as to keep texts abreast of research in manuscript evidence, insights with regard to exegesis, and crucial developments in the meaning of terms. At the same time it is important to keep such changes to a minimum, since nothing is quite so frustrating to the users of a biblical text than to have constant changes being introduced.

Of all the procedures employed in the translation process, the most important is ultimately the constant alertness to the spiritual implications of the message of the Scriptures as expressed in the lives of those involved in the task. It simply is not enough to translate the message of life into words; it must also be translated into life by those engaged in the process of translating. This becomes the best guarantee of intellectual humility and inspired creativity in making the message of life come to life.

BIBLIOGRAPHY

From One Language to Another

Abbreviations

CBQ	Catholic Biblical Quarterly
JBL	Journal of Biblical Literature
NTS	New Testament Studies
RHPR	Revue d'Histoire et de Philosophie Religieuses
TBT	The Bible Translator
VT	Vetus Testamentum
VT Suppl.	Supplements to Vetus Testamentum
ZAW	Zeitschrift für die alttestamentliche Wissenschaft

Aejmelaeus, Anneli. 1982. *Parataxis in the Septuagint.* Helsinki: Suomalainen Tiedeakatemia.

Aland, Barbara. 1982. "Monophysitismus und Schriftauslegung." In Peter Hauptman, ed., *Unser ganzes Leben Christus unserm Gott überantworten.* Göttingen: Vandenhoeck & Ruprecht, pp. 142–67.

Andreyev, N. D. 1964. "Linguistic Aspects of Translation." In E. Delaveney, ed., *Traduction Automatique et Linguistique Appliquée.* Paris: P. U. F., pp. 121–41.

Arndt, E. (ed.). 1968, (M. Luther) Ein Sendbrief von Dolmetschen. Halle/Saale.

Bailey, K. E. 1975. "Recovering the Poetic Structure of 1 Cor. 1:17–22." *Novum Testamentum* 17:265–96.

Barr, James. 1961. The Semantics of Biblical Language. Oxford: Oxford University Press.

Beentjes, P. C. 1982. "Inverted Quotations in the Bible: A Neglected Stylistic Pattern." *Biblica* 63:506–23.

Belloc, Hilaire. 1931. *On Translation.* Oxford: University Press.

Bjornson, Richard. 1980. "Translation and Literary Theory." *Translation Review* 6:13–16.

Black, Matthew. 1971. An Aramaic Approach to the Gospels and Acts. Oxford: Clarendon Press.

Blass, F. and A. Debrunner. 1961. *Grammatik des neutestamentlichen Griechisch.* Göttingen: Vandenhoeck & Ruprecht.

Boadt, Lawrence. 1975. "The A:B:B:A Chiasm of Identical Roots in Ezekiel." *VT* 25:693–99.

———1983. "Intentional Alliteration in Second Isaiah." *CBQ* 45:353–63.

Bratcher, R. G. and E. A. Nida. 1961. *A Translator's Handbook on the Gospel of Mark.* Leiden: E. J. Brill.

———1982. *A Translator's Handbook on Paul's Letter to the Ephesians.* New York: United Bible Societies.

Braun, R. 1973. *Kohelet und die frühhellenistische Popularphilosophie.* Beihefte ZAW 130.

Brower, Reuben A. ed. 1959. *On Translation.* Cambridge: Harvard University Press.

Brown F., S. R. Driver, and C. A. Briggs. 1968. *Hebrew and English Lexicon of the Old Testament.* Oxford: Clarendon Press.

Bultmann, R. 1953. *Das Evangelium des Johannes.* Göttingen: Vandenhoeck & Ruprecht.

Campbell, Edward. 1975. *Ruth.* New York: Doubleday.

Cary, Edmond. 1963. *Les grands traducteurs français.* Geneva: Librairie de l'Université.

Catford, J. C. 1965. *A Linguistic Theory of Translation.* London: Oxford University Press.

Ceresko, Anthony R. 1982. "The Function of Antanaclasis in Hebrew Poetry." *CBQ* 44:551–70.

Charles, R. H. 1971. *The Revelation of St. John.* Edinburgh: T. & T. Clark.

Clark, D. J. and J. de Waard. 1982. *Discourse Structure in Matthew's Gospel.* Scriptura. Special Issue I.

Clavaud, Jean. 1973. "Problems Encountered in Translating the New Testament into Modern Cambodian." *TBT* 24:419–22.

Clements, R. E. 1980. *Isaiah 1–39.* London: Marshall, Morgan & Scott.

Clifford, R. J. 1979. "Style and Purpose in Psalm 105." *Biblica* 60:420–27.

Conzelmann, H. 1963. *Die Apostelgeschichte.* Tübingen: J. C. B. Mohr.

Cunchillos, J. L. 1976. *Estudio del Salmo 29.* Valencia: Institución San Jerónimo.

Dahood, M. 1958. "Qoheleth and Recent Discoveries." *Biblica* 39:302–18.

———1967. "Congruity of Metaphors." In *Hebräische Wortforschung.* Leiden: E. J. Brill, pp. 40–49.

Dalman, G. 1898. *Die Worte Jesu.* Leipzig: J. C. Hinrichs.

Darbelnet, Jean. 1977. "Niveaux de la Traduction." *Babel* 23:6–17.

de Beaugrande, Robert. 1978. *Factors in a Theory of Poetic Translation.* Assen, The Netherlands: Van Gorcum.

de Waard, Jan. 1968. "Un manuel de traduction orale pour le pays Bamiléké." *TBT* 19:131–43.

———1971. "Do You Use 'Clean Language'?" *TBT* 22.107–15.

———1974. "Biblical Metaphors and Their Translation." *TBT* 25:107–16.

———1977. "The Chiastic Structure of Amos v 1–17." *VT* 27.170–77.

———1979a. "The Translator and Textual Criticism." *Biblica* 60:509–29.

———1979b. "Vers une identification des participants dans le livre de Michée." *RHPR* 59:509–16.

———1981. "'Homophony' in the Septuagint." *Biblica* 62:551–61.

————1982. "The Structure of Qoheleth." In *Proceedings of the Eighth World Congress of Jewish Studies*. Jerusalem, pp. 57–64.

Diringer, D. 1934. *Le iscrizioni antico-ebraiche palestinesi*. Firenze.

Dodd, C. H. 1953. *The Johannine Epistles*. London: Hodder and Stoughton.

————1976. "New Testament Translation Problems I." *TBT* 27:301–11.

Doke, C. M. 1958. "Some Difficulties in Bible Translation into a Bantu Language." *TBT* 9:57–62.

Donner, H. and Röllig, W. 1968. *Kanaanäische und Aramäische Inschriften*. Wiesbaden: Otto Harrassowitz.

Dufour, Jean-Paul. 1983. *Tradition et innovation*. Thése de doctorat de III° cycle Université de St. Etienne.

Edwards, Richard A. 1976. *A Theology of Q*. Philadelphia: Fortress Press.

Eerdmans, B. D. 1947. *The Religion of Israel*. Leiden: E. J. Brill.

Ellermeier, F. 1968. *Qohelet I* Abschnitt Z, Einzelfrage Nr F Herzberg.

Ellis, E. Earle. 1978. *Prophecy and Hermeneutic in Early Christianity*. Grand Rapids: Eerdmans.

Enkvist, Nils Erik. 1978. "Contrastive Text Linguistics and Translation." In Lillebill Grähs, Gustav Korlen, Bertil Malmberg, eds., *Theory and Practice of Translation*. Bern: Peter Lang, pp. 169–87.

Fiebig, P. 1912. *Die Gleichnisreden Jesu im Lichte der rabbinischen Gleichnisse des neutestamentlichen Zeitalters*. Tübingen: J. C. B. Mohr.

Fisher, Loren R. 1972. *Ras Shamra Parallels I*. Rome: Pontifical Biblical Institute.

Fohrer, Georg. 1968. "Twofold Aspects of Hebrew Words." In P. R. Ackroyd and B. Lindars, eds., *Words and Meanings*. Cambridge: University Press, pp. 95–105.

Fokkelman, J. P. 1975. *Narrative Art in Genesis*. Assen: Van Gorcum.

Fowler, Roger. 1972. "Style and the Concept of Deep Structure." *Journal of Literary Semantics* 1:5–24.

Freedman, D. N. 1980. *Pottery, Poetry, and Prophecy*. Winona Lake: Eisenbrauns.

Frendo, A. 1981. "The 'Broken Construct Chain' in Qoh 10.10b." *Biblica* 62:544–45.

Fueter, P. D. and J. Voorhoeve. 1963. "Communiquer l'Evangile au pays Bamiléké." *Le Monde non-chrétien* 68:242–52.

Güttinger, Fritz. 1963. *Zielsprache*. Zürich: Manesse Verlag.

Haas, C., M. de Jonge, and J. L. Swellengrebel. 1972. *A Translator's Handbook on the Letters of John*. London: United Bible Societies.

Haenchen, E. 1957. *Die Apostelgeschichte*. Göttingen: Vandenhoeck & Ruprecht.

Hofstadter, Douglas R. 1980. *Goedel, Escher, Bach: An Eternal Golden Braid*. New York: Vintage Books.

Holmes, James S., ed. 1970. *The Nature of Translation: Essays on the Theory and Practice of Literary Translation*. The Hague: Mouton.

Hyatt, J. P. 1980. *Exodus*. London: Marshall, Morgan, and Scott.

Hymes, Dell. 1974. *Foundations in Sociolinguistics: An Ethnographic Approach*. Philadelphia: University of Pennsylvania Press.

Jellicoe, Sidney. 1968. *The Septuagint and Modern Study*. Oxford: Clarendon Press.

Jeremias, A. 1906. *Das Alte Testament im Lichte des Alten Orients*. Leipzig: J. C. Hinrichs.

Jeremias, J. 1950. Article *thura*. In *Theologisches Wörterbuch zum Neuen Testament*, III. Stuttgart: Kohlhammer, pp. 173–80.

Joüon, Paul. 1947. *Grammaire de l'hébreu biblique*. Rome: Pontifical Biblical Institute.

Kade, Otto. 1968. "Kommunikationswissenschaftliche Probleme der Übersetzung" in *Grundfragen der Übersetzungswissenschaft*. Beihefte zur Zeitschrift Fremdsprachen 2:3–20.

Kapelrud, A. S. 1954. "Genesis 49:12." *VT* 4:426–48.

Kassühlke, R. 1982. "Bibelübersetzen trotz kultureller Distanz." In H. Reinitzer, ed., *Was Dolmetschen für Kunst und Arbeit sei*. Vestigia Bibliae. Hamburg: Friedrich Wittig Verlag, pp. 151–63.

Kelly, Louis G. 1976. *Working Papers on Translatology I*. Ottawa: University of Ottawa.

Kijne, J. J. 1966. "We, Us, and Our in I and II Corinthians." In *Placita Pleiadia*. Leiden: E. J. Brill, pp. 171–79.

Kissane, E. J. 1964. *The Book of Psalms*. Westminister, MD: Newman Press.

Koehler, L. and W. Baumgartner. 1967–83. *Hebräisches und Aramäisches Lexikon zum Alten Testament*, I–III. Leiden: E. J. Brill.

König, E. 1900. *Stilistik, Rhetorik, Poetik*.

Kselman, John S. 1977. Semantic-Sonant Chiasmus in Biblical Poetry. *Biblica* 58:219–23.

Ladmiral, J. R. 1979. *Traduite: théorèmes pour la traduction*. Paris: Payot.

Lambdin, Thomas O. 1971. *Introduction to Biblical Hebrew*. New York: Charles Scribner's Sons.

Langer, Suzanne K. 1951. *Philosophy in a New Key*. New York: New American Library.

Lettinga, Jan P. 1980. *Grammaire de l'hébreu biblique*. Leiden: E. J. Brill.

Levy, L. 1912. *Das Buch Qoheleth*. Leipzig: J. C. S. Hinrichs.

Lidzbarski, M. 1900–15. *Ephemeris für semitische Epigraphik*. Giessen: Töpelmann.

Louw, Johannes P. 1973. "Discourse Analysis and the Greek New Testament." *TBT* 24:101–17.

Lund, N. W. 1942. *Chiasmus in the New Testament*. Chapel Hill: University of North Carolina.

Magonet, Jonathan. 1976. *Form and Meaning. Studies in the Literary Techniques in the Book of Jonah*. Bern and Frankfurt: Lang.

Margot, Jean-Claude. 1979. *Traduire sans trahir*. Lausanne: L'Age d'homme.

Martin, Raymond A. 1974. *Syntactical Evidence of Semitic Sources in Greek Documents*. Cambridge, MA: Society of Biblical Literature.

Massyngberde-Ford, J. 1975. *Revelation*. Garden City: Doubleday.

McKane, William. 1970. *Proverbs*. London: SCM Press.

Metzger, Bruce M. 1971. *A Textual Commentary on the Greek New Testament*. London and New York: United Bible Societies.

———1977. *The Early Versions of the New Testament*. Oxford: Clarendon Press.

Michel, O. 1970. Article *philosophia*. In *Theologisches Wörterbuch zum Neuen Testament*, IX. Stuttgart: Kohlhammer, pp. 169–85.

Miner, E. 1961. *Japanese Court Poetry*. Stanford: Stanford University.

Moscati, S. 1951. *L'epigrafia ebraica antica*. Rome.

———1969. *An Introduction to the Comparative Grammar of the Semitic Languages* Wiesbaden: Otto Harrassowitz.

Mounin, Georges. 1957. "La traduction devient-elle un problème de premier plan?" *Critique* 127:1052-71.

───────1976. *Linguistique et traduction*. Bruxelles: Dessart et Mardaga.

Mussies, Gerard. 1983. "Greek as the Vehicle of Early Christianity." *NTS* 29:364.

Neubert, Albrecht. 1968. "Pragmatische Aspekte der Übersetzung." In A. Neubert, ed., *Grundfragen der Übersetzungswissenschaft*. Beihefte zur Zeitschrift Fremdsprachen, 2:21-33.

Nida, Eugene A. 1964. *Toward a Science of Translating*. Leiden: E. J. Brill.

───────1975. *Componential Analysis of Meaning*. The Hague: Mouton.

───────1984a. *Signs, Sense, and Translation*. Cape Town: Bible Society of South Africa.

───────1984b. "Rhetoric and Style: A Taxonomy of Structures and Functions." *Linguistic Sciences* 6:287-305.

Nida, Eugene A. and Charles R. Taber. 1969. *Theory and Practice of Translation*. Leiden: E. J. Brill.

Nida, Eugene A. and William D. Reyburn. 1981. *Meaning Across Cultures*. Maryknoll, N. Y.: Orbis Books.

Nida, Eugene A., Johannes P. Louw, Andres H. Snyman, and J. v W. Cronje. 1983. *Style and Discourse*. Cape Town: Bible Society of South Africa.

Ntsanwisi, H. W. E. 1968. *Tsonga Idioms*. Braamfontein, South Africa: Sasavona Publishers.

O'Connor, M. 1980. *Hebrew Verse Structure*. Winona Lake: Eisenbrauns.

Orlinsky, Harry M. 1974. *Essays in Biblical Culture and Bible Translation*. New York: Ktav Publishing House.

Ortega y Gasset, José. 1937. "Miseria y esplendor de la traducción." *La Nación*, May-June, Buenos Aires.

Osgood, Charles E. 1952. "The Nature and Measurement of Meaning." *Psychology Bulletin* 49:197-237.

───────1963. "Language universals and psycholinguistics." In J. H. Greenberg, ed., *Universals of Language*. Cambridge: M. I. T. Press, pp. 236-54.

───────1964. "Semantic Differential Technique in the Comparative Study of Cultures." In A. K. Romney and R. G. d'Andrade, eds., *Transcultural Studies in Cognition*. Special Publication of *American Anthropologist*, 66, No. 3, pp. 171-200.

Osgood, Charles E. and P. H. Tannenbaum. 1955. "The Principles of Congruity in the Prediction of Attitude Change." *Psychology Review* 62:42-55.

Osgood, Charles E., George J. Suci, and P. H. Tannenbaum. 1957. *The Measurement of Meaning*. Urbana: University of Illinois Press.

Pederson, J. 1914. *Der Eid bei den Semiten*.

Pergnier, Maurice. 1978. "Language Meaning and Message Meaning: Towards a Sociolinguistic Approach to Translation." In David Gerver and H. Wallace Sinaiko, eds., *Language Interpretation and Communication*. New York: Plenum Press, pp. 199-204.

Plöger, O. 1983. *Sprüche Salomos*. Neukirchen: Neukirchener Verlag.

Rabin, C. 1967. "Three Hebrew Terms for the Realm of Social Psychology." In *Hebräische Wortforschung*. Leiden: E. J. Brill, pp. 219-230.

Rad, Gerhard von. 1968. *La Geneva*: Labor et Fides.

Radday, Y. I. 1981. "Chiasmus in Hebrew Biblical Narrative." In John W. Welch, ed., *Chiasmus in Antiquity*. Hildesheim: Gerstenberg Verlag, pp. 50–117.

Reiss, Katharina. 1971. *Möglichkeiten und Grenzen der Übersetzungskritik*. München: Max Hueber Verlag.

———1976. *Texttyp und Übersetzungsmethode*. Kronberg: Scriptor Verlag.

Roth, W. M. W. 1962. "The Numerical Sequence x / x + 1 in the Old Testament." *VT* 12:300–11.

———1965. *Numerical Sayings in the Old Testament*. VT Suppl. 13. Leiden: E. J. Brill.

Sakenfeld, K. D. 1978. *The Meaning of HESED in the Hebrew Bible*. Missoula: Scholars Press.

Sasson, Jack M. 1979. *Ruth*. Baltimore-London: Johns Hopkins University Press.

Schleiermacher, F. 1969. "Über die verschiedenen Methoden des Übersetzens." In H. J. Störig, ed., *Das Problem des Übersetzens*. Stuttgart, pp. 38–70.

Schwarz, W. 1963. "The History of the Principles of Bible Translations." *Babel* 9:5–22

Slomp, Jan. 1977. "Are the Words 'Son of God' in Mark 1:1 Original?" *TBT* 28:143–50.

Smit-Sibinga, J. 1963. *The Old Testament Text of Justin Martyr: I, The Pentateuch*. Leiden: E. J. Brill.

Snaith, N. H. "The Language of the Old Testament." In *The Interpreter's Bible*, I, pp. 225ff.

Spurrell, G. J. 1887. *Notes on the Hebrew Text of the Book of Genesis*. Oxford: Clarendon Press.

Stamm, J. J. 1971. Article *g'l*. In E. Jenni and C. Westermann, eds., *Theologisches Handwörterbuch zum Alten Testament*, I. München: Chr. Kaiser Verlag, pp. 383–94.

Steiner, George. 1975. *After Babel: Aspects of Language and Translation*. Oxford: University Press.

Stendahl, Krister. 1954. *The School of St. Matthew*. Lund: Gleerup.

Störig, H. J. (ed). 1969. *Das Problem des Übersetzens*. Stuttgart.

Stuart, Douglas K. 1976. *Studies in Early Hebrew Meter*. Missoula: Scholars Press.

Taylor, Charles. 1970. *Sayings of the Jewish Fathers*. Amsterdam: Philo Press.

Torrey, Ch. C. 1933. *The Four Gospels: A New Translation*. New York: Harpers.

Tov, E. 1976. "Three Dimensions of LXX Words." *Revue Biblique* 83:529–44.

Toy, C. H. 1970. *The Book of Proverbs*. Edinburgh: T. & T. Clark.

Tsumura, D. T. 1983a. "Literary Insertion in Biblical Hebrew." *VT* 33:468–83.

———1983b. "Janus Parallelism in Nah 1:8." *JBL* 102:109–11.

Turbayne, Colin Murray. 1962. *The Myth of Metaphor*. New Haven: Yale University Press.

Turner, Nigel. 1976. *A Grammar of New Testament Greek: Vol. IV, Style*. Edinburgh: T. & T. Clark.

Van Dyke Parunak, H. 1975. "A Semantic Survey of NHM." *Biblica* 56:527.

Vassiliadis, P. 1985. "Martyria Iésou in Revelation." *TBT* 36:129–33.

Vázquez-Ayora, Gerardo. 1977. *Introducción a la Traductología*. Washington, D. C.: Georgetown University Press.

Weiss, J. 1897. "Paulinische Rhetorik." *Theologische Studien* 191.

Westermann, Claus. 1981. *Genesis*. Neukirchen: Neukirchener Verlag.
Whitley, C. F. 1981. "The Semantic Range of Ḥesed." *Biblica* 62:519–26.
Wildberger, Hans. 1965. *Jesaja*. Neukirchen: Neukirchener Verlag.
Wilss, Wolfram. 1982. *The Science of Translation*. Tübingen: Gunter Narr Verlag.
Ziegler, J. 1967. *Duodecim prophetae*. Göttingen: Vandenhoeck & Ruprecht.

SUBJECT INDEX

SCRIPTURE INDEX

OLD TESTAMENT

DEUTEROCANON

NEW TESTAMENT